The Necessity of Artspeak

The Necessity of Artspeak

The language of the arts in the Western tradition

ROY HARRIS

continuum
LONDON • NEW YORK

Continuum
The Tower Building, 11 York Road, London, SE1 7NX
370 Lexington Avenue, New York, NY 10017-6503

First published 2003 by Continuum

British Library Cataloguing-in-Publication Data
A catalogue record for this book is available from the British Library.

ISBN 0-8264-6068-2 (hardback)
   0-8264-6079-8 (paperback)

Library of Congress Cataloging-in-Publication Data
Harris, Roy, 1931–
   The necessity of artspeak : the language of the arts in the western tradition / Roy Harris.
      p. cm.
   Includes bibliographical references and index.
   ISBN 0-8264-6068-2 (hb) -- ISBN 0-8264-6079-8 (pb)
   1. Semiotics and the arts. I. Title.

NX180.S46 H37 2002
701'.4--dc21

2002071590

Typeset by Kenneth Burnley, Wirral, Cheshire
Printed and bound in Great Britain by Biddles Ltd, Guildford and King's Lynn

Contents

Bloss aus allgemeinen Begriffen über die Kunst vernünsteln, kann zu Grillen verführen, die man über lang oder kurz, zu seiner Beschämung, in den Werken der Kunst widerlegt findet.

Lessing

When I see a writer, a word-man, among a number of painters, I shake my head. For I know that he would not be there unless he was up to something.

Wyndham Lewis

Preface

'The trouble with art,' wrote a critic recently, 'is that it fits any theory' (Winterson 2001). This presumably betokens the critic's exasperation either with the Protean concept 'art' or with the endless ingenuity of theorists. A rather different question is whether all kinds of theories fit all kinds of arts. And a different question again is whether there are any theories that an art has to fit in order to maintain recognition of its status as an art. These further questions inevitably bring us to the interface between the arts and the language in which they are discussed.

The critic quoted above goes on to remark:

> While science polices its objectivity, art has none. Art is a dialogue, sometimes a shouting match, always an exchange. (Winterson 2001)

It does not take a linguist to point out that this kind of artspeak belongs to a discourse that would have been inconceivable either in Plato's day or in Diderot's. 'Dialogue' and 'shouting match' are notions that are more applicable to what may be said about works of art than to the works themselves. This is a measure of the extent to which, nowadays, it is often difficult to divorce the work from the verbal fanfares or denunciations that accompany it.

It has become one of the platitudes of postmodernism to claim that 'works of art exist in environments that have been saturated in language' (Scobie 1997: 7) and, more generally, to insist on the linguistic embeddedness of all aspects of culture. But the frequency with which such platitudes are reiterated reflects the pervasive tendency of the postmodernists to project the deep linguistic muddles in their own thinking about 'texts' on to everything they write about. Deploying the modish jargon of deconstruction is not, in my view, the way to throw any light on the role of language in our understanding – or misunderstanding – of the arts. I shall therefore avoid it here.

Nor would I wish my subject to be confused with that ancient chestnut concerning the validity of treating the various arts as 'languages'. This hoary topos continues to be debated by academics in a half-hearted way (e.g. Hagberg 1995; Clarke and Crossley 2000), but any genuine interest in the outcome has long since drained away. For my purposes it is best in any case to steer clear of question-begging metaphors. A simpler approach is needed.

The idea that the arts and works of art need to be explained verbally to the public is part and parcel of a long-running debate, with a history that goes back to Graeco-Roman antiquity. Among the contributors to this debate were some of the most eminent artists, philosophers and critics of their day. It is this debate which sets the framework for the present book, which examines the development of Western artspeak from a linguistic point of view. Although scholars have undertaken studies of particular arts at particular periods (e.g. J. J. Pollitt's study of the terminology of painting, sculpture and architecture in ancient Greece: Pollitt 1974), and compiled glossaries devoted to the terminology of individual arts, or devoted essays to particular areas of the subject (e.g. Baxandall 1991 on the language of art criticism; Hausman 1991 on the use of figurative language in art history), such publications do not envisage the evolution of Western artspeak as a continuous multi-lingual development. Nor do they attempt to examine this discourse from the viewpoint of linguistic theory. Here I shall try to do both.

This falls far short of attempting a 'history' of artspeak. Desirable as such a history might be, it would require many volumes and many collaborators. This book does not provide anything of the kind, even in outline. How Vasari uses the term *grazia* or T. S. Eliot the term *classic* are topics that do not fall within its purview. Nor does it examine particular passages of artspeak and show how skilfully or otherwise the message is verbally presented. Instead it focuses on those developments of artspeak which are central to defining what an art is. It also proposes an analysis of artspeak, of the linguistic phenomenon itself. But that is a different kind of enterprise from the historian's or the stylistician's.

For a linguist, the most direct approach to artspeak is by way of its basic vocabulary. If we were restricting our attention initially to English, that vocabulary would have to include the word *art* and its cognates and their derivatives (*artist, artistic, artifact*, etc.) as key terms. It would also include words semantically related to these key terms, such as the designations of particular art forms (*film, dance, lithography*, etc.), of their practitioners, and of their art products (*symphony, play, portrait*, etc.). It would also include expressions identifying various subcategories of art (*fine art, abstract art, verbal art*, etc.). And it would include critical terms used in appraisal of the arts and their products (*beautiful, ugly, original, inspired, tasteless, well-made*, etc.). For languages other than English similar lists could be compiled. Such lists would presumably be open-ended, but in principle they could be drawn up, along the same lines as a linguist might seek to compile any other specialized lexicon of terms relating to a particular field, from nuclear physics to climatology.

However, considering a discourse in terms of the lexical network linking its constituent vocabulary can take us only so far. That may be adequate in order to distinguish in practice between one form of discourse and another discourse from a different field, which uses a quite different vocabulary. Distinctions of this order may suffice to distinguish, let us say, the sports page of the daily newspaper from the financial page. But vocabulary alone cannot tell us what assumptions were made or what values were held by its users. It can at most tell us what distinctions they drew, but not how these distinctions were regarded, nor why other distinctions were not drawn instead. What dictionaries alone cannot explain is what role a discourse plays in – and how it is shaped, maintained and modified by – the life of the society that brought it into existence. We cannot, in short, characterize any discourse adequately until we move from the level of lexical items to the level of assertions. And here the case of artspeak begins immediately to present problems, which may seem on first inspection intractable.

For most of its long history in the Western tradition, artspeak has been a locus of controversy. According to sceptics, its main function has always been to create a mystique surrounding the work of certain artists – poets, painters and musicians in particular. For the less sceptical, the very existence of artspeak bears witness to the heights human civilization has reached; for artspeak is seen as a language forged in order to express lofty truths about human creativity and spiritual goals, truths which it would be impossible to express adequately in any less rarified discourse, truths to which less privileged cultures have yet to graduate.

My point of departure is the recent comment of the artist who complained about the current situation in the arts: 'What bugs the general public is often not the work itself, but what the experts say about it.' In a similar vein, the French art critic Jean-Philippe Domecq argued (Domecq 1999: 48) that 'essentially it is discourse that makes fashions' ('*c'est essentiellement du discours qui fait les modes*'). He was referring specifically to the art market of the late twentieth century. But both observations could stand as comments on a whole tradition of discussion in the arts. The concern these comments express can be readily appreciated by anyone who looks through the list of artspeak aphorisms appended to this Preface. Individually and taken in isolation, each pronouncement might be defended. Collectively, they give the impression of self-appointed authorities pontificating in a language which they themselves have not fully mastered.

There is a well-known anecdote about a debate in St Petersburg between Diderot and Euler in which Euler produced an algebraic equation which he claimed proved the existence of God. He then challenged the nonplussed

Diderot to give a mathematical refutation (Struik 1948: 182). Although the story may be apocryphal, it captures an interesting psychological point: the more opaque a formula is, the more difficult is the task of providing any easy demonstration of its invalidity. Even those who have not understood the original formula may be reluctant to claim that there is no truth in it. Artspeak, like the algebra of Euler's stratagem, can be a language sufficiently obscure to impress the audience, even while baffling them.

That may be why linguists have preferred to keep out of the fray and leave it to aestheticians. But that is a mistake. For the language of aesthetics is only a relatively recent dialect of artspeak and does not go back earlier than the eighteenth century. Artspeak did not suddenly spring into existence when German philosophers recognized and baptized a new branch of philosophical inquiry. Western artspeak has been many more centuries in the making and drawn upon linguistic tools supplied by many languages. It has developed its own specialized genres, ranging from the biography of the artist (a genre inaugurated in the Renaissance) to the modern exhibition catalogue. Nor can the matter safely be left to art historians. For what is nowadays called 'art history' (another eighteenth-century invention) is itself a manifestation of artspeak, not vice versa: in order to understand the former we have first to make sense of the latter.

What a linguist is sure to point out is that a number of important terms in Western artspeak have changed in meaning over the centuries. So too have prevailing fashions in the rhetoric of artspeak, even though certain themes and clichés are recurrent. When Hans Georg Nägeli claimed that Bach's B minor Mass was the greatest work of art of all time and all peoples he was speaking a universalist artspeak that seemed acceptable to his contemporaries, but now sounds archaic at best. The hyperbole itself has to be distinguished from the discourse that makes the hyperbole possible in the first place. Today even the most enthusiastic of Bach's devotees would think twice about making such a claim. Not because hyperbole has gone out of fashion, but because that register of artspeak is no longer viable. It is not that Bach's work has been surpassed or fallen from favour. But it now seems doubtful whether sweeping panchronic claims of this order are meaningful.

All forms of language 'date' with the passing of time, and artspeak is no exception. What complicates matters in the case of artspeak is that the very basis of comparison on which such diverse enterprises as music, painting, poetry, architecture, dance – and many more – are all reckoned as arts has never at any stage in the development of Western culture been satisfactorily elucidated. In other words, a historical question-mark hangs over the generalization itself.

It would be idle for anyone nowadays to suppose that a serious examination of artspeak can proceed on the assumption that we have before us a *tabula rasa* on which we are free to inscribe our own definitions of the words *art, artist, artistic,* etc. That would not only be naive but suggest historical ignorance into the bargain. Discussion of art and the arts can proceed only by means of socially, politically and educationally 'loaded' terms, because there is no 'unloaded' (i.e. neutral) vocabulary available. And – as we now realize – there never has been. That, in a nutshell, is the trouble with artspeak. Artspeak has always been propaganda.

But to leave it at that would conceal the full complexity of the problem. It is evident to everyone that the artspeak of the present day is not the artspeak of Bach's day, and even less the artspeak of the middle ages. Where the arts are concerned, every age has had its own language, based on cultural assumptions which usually go far beyond the immediate practical concerns of the arts in question. If we do not examine those underlying assumptions, we shall never come to terms with the inner rationale of different forms of artspeak. And to that extent we shall tend either to dismiss or to be taken in by a discourse we do not understand, even though we may think we do. The history of artspeak is important if only because we need to be aware of how systematically or erratically its later forms retrospectively impose reinterpretations upon the arts of earlier periods.

Today the whole question of artistic value-judgments appears in a perspective that would have been scarcely imaginable before the Enlightenment. This is not merely a matter of changing standards or tastes. Nor is it simply that new technologies have created new art forms, or that the boundaries of old art forms have altered in consequence. Something much more fundamental has taken place. It is this more fundamental shift that will be one of my main concerns, and in order to deal with it there is no alternative but to focus on the changing role of artspeak.

These changes, I shall argue, have been mainly articulated and established not through the production of revolutionary works (although there have been plenty) but through the medium of words. The works themselves might well have languished in obscurity, had they not been suitably described and presented verbally by their makers or by the influential commentators of the day. But that is not in itself a novelty. Throughout the centuries, artspeak has taken propositions about art that would have been regarded as nonsense by previous generations and made what used to be nonsense sound rational or even, in the fullness of time, self-evident.

The chapters that follow are grouped into an Introduction and three sections. The Introduction ('Artspeak and Necessity') explains what the book as a whole is attempting to do and why. The first section ('Part I: Traditional Artspeak') presents a historical survey of some important themes in the development of artspeak from Graeco-Roman antiquity down to the Enlightenment. Here such notions as the 'liberal' arts, 'the beautiful' and 'the sublime' are examined. The second section ('Part II: Artspeak Modern') deals with the renewal of artspeak after the Industrial Revolution and more recent examples. The third ('Part III: Artspeak and Communication') considers the whole gamut of Western artspeak from the point of view of three different theories of language. It offers a hypothesis which endeavours to explain both the traditional forms of artspeak and also the many apparent contradictions and anomalies that are so characteristic of artspeak at the present day.

*   *   *

My debts in writing this book are many. The first is to the art historian Robert Atkins who popularized the term *artspeak* (Atkins 1990). It will already be obvious from what I have said above that I shall be using this term in a broader sense than Atkins originally envisaged, i.e. not simply to include the current buzzwords used by critics in certain sectors of the art world, but to cover the whole range of discourse about works of art and their appreciation (or disparagement). For this the English language lacks any appropriate general word, and *artspeak* seems so well equipped to fill that gap that it would be a waste of verbal resources to squander it on anything less catholic. I therefore have no hesitation in thrusting that role upon it here. *Artspeak*, as I shall be using the term, thus includes but goes considerably beyond what David Carrier calls *artwriting*, which he restricts to 'texts by both art critics and art historians' (Carrier 1987: 141).

Some of my chapters began life as lectures given at the Ruskin School in Oxford and I would like to thank Stephen Farthing, formerly Ruskin Master of Drawing, for the opportunity of giving them. I would also like to express my thanks for what I have learned about artspeak from the following: Anna Tietze, of the Department of Historical Studies in the University of Cape Town; R. E. Alton, of St Edmund Hall, Oxford, *connoisseur extraordinaire*; Robert Richardson, of De Montfort University; and especially to Professor Ernst Gombrich who was kind enough to lend me a typescript of his (unpublished) Inaugural Lecture as Slade Professor of Fine Art at Oxford. For my understanding of one non-Western tradition I am indebted in particular to Philip A. Clarke (South Australian Museum) and Margaret F. Nobbs, both of whom tolerated my intrusions into their time and patience with great generosity. None of them should be suspected of complicity in the ideas here proposed.

Wherever possible, I have tried to illustrate points by direct quotation in preference to paraphrase or summary. Since most of the works in question are in languages other than English, I have used the translations of others, rather than providing my own, in order to avoid any suspicion that textual evidence is being slanted in order to suit my case. Occasionally I have supplemented translations by supplying the relevant words from the original text, either because I thought the translator might have strayed or because the original wording seemed to me to be of particular interest.

*   *   *

Is the enterprise, whether successful or not, worth attempting? I think so, because although I would not wish to claim that artspeak is more important than many other competing discourses that clamour for attention in the twenty-first century, I believe that there is something seriously wrong with the education system of a society that does not understand, cannot be bothered to understand, its own artspeak. That failure would betoken a failure to understand something more fundamental – the role that words play in articulating the social structures of culture. This role is profoundly underestimated today, both by experts on the arts and by experts on society, who cannot see that a theory of language engages both.

R. H.
Oxford, 2002

The artspeak aphorism
through the ages

Some historical specimens

In itself, an art is sound and flawless, so long as it is entirely true to its own nature as an art. – Socrates

Art imitates nature. – Aristotle

Art is a power reaching its ends by a definite path, that is, by ordered methods. – Cleanthes

As in painting, so in poetry. – Horace

There must be art in any subject in which the man who has received instruction is the superior of him who has not. – Quintilian

The wisdom of the artist is sufficient explanation of the wisdom exhibited in the arts. – Plotinus

It is the duty of Art to perfect and exalt Nature. – Bacon

In a truly beautiful work of art the content should do nothing, the form everything. – Schiller

There is nothing [. . .] in which the power of art is shown so much as in playing the fiddle. – Samuel Johnson

The value and rank of every art is in proportion to the mental labour employed in it, or the mental pleasure produced by it. – Reynolds

Any purpose perverts art. – Benjamin Constant

It is in works of art that nations have deposited the richest intuitions and ideas they possess. – Hegel

Art is a mediator of the inexpressible. – Goethe

The work of art – like any other product – produces a public conscious of its own peculiar beauty and capable of enjoying it. – Marx

In every art we are always obliged to return to the accepted means of expression, the conventional language of the art. – Delacroix

Art is the only domain of the mind in which a man may say: 'I will believe if I want to, and if not, I shall not believe.' – Baudelaire

Art is by itself a kind of religion. – Victor Cousin

A work of art is a corner of creation seen through a temperament. – Zola

All art is either infection or education. – Ruskin

Art is indefinable. – Proudhon

What business have we with art at all unless all can share it? – William Morris

In the processes of art we shall find, in a weakened form, a refined and in some measure spiritualized version of the processes commonly used to induce the state of hypnosis. – Bergson

All art constantly aspires towards the condition of music. – Walter Pater

Art alone, in which form is inseparable from content, can be passed on whole to posterity. – Renan

Art in our society has become so perverted that not only has bad art come to be considered good, but even the very perception of what art really is has been lost. – Tolstoy

All art is quite useless. – Oscar Wilde

An art which does not have emotion as its basis is not an art. – Cézanne

Artists are, above all, men who wish to become inhuman. – Apollinaire

The artist has the power to give the lifeless machine-made product a soul. – Walter Gropius

Some of the grandest and most overwhelming creations of art are still unsolved riddles to our understanding. – Freud

Science states meanings: art expresses them. – Dewey

Art is essentially an expression of love. – Lewis Mumford

There is no such thing as abstract art. – Picasso

Every utterance and every gesture that each one of us makes is a work of art. – Collingwood

Art is an intensification of reality. – Cassirer

Art is the sedimented history of human misery. – Theodor Adorno

Art – this is nothing more than a word to which nothing real any longer corresponds. – Heidegger

We don't want our works to say 'art' immediately. We want them to become art. – Gilbert and George

INTRODUCTION

1

Artspeak and necessity

Of all human works, the work of art seems to be the most fortuitous.

Hippolyte Taine

The title of Ernst Fischer's controversial book *The Necessity of Art* (Fischer 1963) was always a provocation to those accustomed to thinking of works of art as pleasing but nevertheless inessential adjuncts to the life of society and the individual. The common assumption that art belonged in the domain of leisure pursuits left little room for 'necessity'. Perhaps leisure itself might be regarded as necessary for mental and physical health in daily life. But this was not the kind of necessity that Fischer had in mind. Nor, apparently, was he thinking of the psychological compulsion that might lead an individual artist to 'need' to express some inner conviction or emotional state.

Reading Fischer's book when it first appeared, at a time when all kinds of post-war 'revolutions' in art were already in full swing, was a puzzling experience. At one level it was possible to think one understood what the author was arguing, and yet in the end be far from sure what he thought art was. Although much of his discussion could be followed without difficulty, at the same time it seemed to be based on terms and assumptions for which no satisfactory explanation had been provided. Thus while it could not be doubted that Fischer believed, for example, that art was a form of 'work' in the Marxist sense, that it had its origins in primitive magic, and that various works of Shakespeare and Beethoven were 'works of art', nevertheless it was still far from evident why Fischer thought all this qualified as 'art'. In his book many things were said *about* art, but there was nevertheless a curious reluctance to explicate the author's notion of art any further. A very innocent or ignorant reader, who had no acquaintance at all with the many specific examples to which Fischer referred, would nevertheless, if intelligent, have found it easy enough to summarize Fischer's claims – provided the word *art* itself remained undefined. In various passages it might even have been possible to substitute three asterisks for the letters *a-r-t*, while leaving the main thesis reasonably clear. So that exactly what Fischer meant by *art* – or whether he had any exact concept of art at all – in a way ceased to matter. Much the same book (albeit with different examples) might have been written by someone who thought Shakespeare a feeble dramatist and Beethoven's music much overrated. Fischer seemed to assume that the usually accepted canonical works of art and forms of art in the Western tradition were indeed rightly so regarded, but without ever explaining why they were, nor what this showed about art in general. In brief, in his exposition the term *art* (and a few other terms frequently associated with it) seemed to be used not so much for purposes of clarification but to occlude further inquiry. It was as if they were always accompanied by an invisible footnote which read: 'Explanation stops here'.

The fact that an important book about art can be written in this way suggests that if there is a topic in this field more fundamental than the necessity of art, it must be *the necessity of artspeak*, i.e. the availability of a taken-for-granted terminology in which to discuss and identify certain works and activities *as art* (whatever that might be), together with a ready-made rhetoric of praise and blame with which to evaluate them. But about the necessity of artspeak, Fischer had nothing to say at all, even though his own book was a masterly exemplification of it.

Fischer's failure in *The Necessity of Art* either to recognize or to address the question of artspeak might perhaps be explained by reference to the development in the twentieth century of another artspeak genre: the dictionary or glossary of art terms. When supplemented by biographical and technical or historical entries, the art dictionary begins to swell into the art handbook and eventually into the art encyclopedia. It might be suggested that Fischer and other writers feel no need to define the basic terms they use or justify the examples they cite, because anyone in doubt can easily have recourse to reference books which supply the relevant information.

The artspeak dictionary is in itself a particularly interesting genre. It trades on the post-Renaissance prestige of lexicography, associated indelibly in the public mind with the establishment of authoritative linguistic norms. Dictionary definitions are regarded as *reliable*. What the dictionary includes or excludes suffices to indicate a certain cultural status: there is no need to say anything more about the bona fides of the item other than that it is 'in' (or 'not in') the dictionary. By adopting the dictionary format, artspeak acquires the extra dimension of a mode of communication in which to be referred to is already a guarantee of authenticity, while silence is doubt or condemnation.

In view of this it is all the more interesting to observe the reluctance of some such dictionaries and comparable works of reference to address the central question of defining the term *art*. For example, Kenneth McLeish, author of a popular *Companion to the Arts in the Twentieth Century*, which covers architecture, poetry, fiction, film, music, painting, sculpture and theatre, writes airily: 'I have excluded such culturally programmatic but artistically contentious subjects as photography, fashion and television' (McLeish 1985: 10). But he offers no explanation of why photography, fashion and television are 'artistically contentious'. Nor does he give any account of what he takes the general critera for inclusion among the arts to be.

A similar case is the *Dictionary of Art and Artists* by the two Courtauld-trained historians Peter and Linda Murray (Murray and Murray 1991). It first appeared in 1959 and has now run through six editions. So presumably it has met with the approval and recommendation of a substantial number of those who have been working in the arts in English-speaking schools and universities in the second half of the twentieth century. But while this dictionary includes a substantial article on Rembrandt, it has none on his European contemporaries Lully and Molière. Why not? Presumably because Lully and Molière do not count as 'artists' in the Murrays' world of art. But when one tries to discover what the Murrays think an 'artist' is, one draws a blank. Their dictionary has no entry under either *art* or *artist*. A reader wishing to find out what conception of art the Murrays are working with will not get much help from their preface either, where they merely say that they have restricted their dictionary to 'the arts of painting, sculpture and engraving in Western Europe and North America, and to a period beginning about the year 1300 and continuing up to the present day'. They admit, with quite astonishing candour, that 'one good reason for this restriction is that we are almost totally ignorant of the arts of other periods and places.' And to cap this they omit to mention any other 'good' reason. Clearly, if ignorance was ever a qualification for writing about art, by their own admission they are well qualified. They are seemingly indifferent to the blatant ethnocentricity that such an exclusive approach to 'art' both relies on and promotes.

To measure the implications of this kind of academic expertise, it is relevant to compare it with comparable fields of endeavour. It would be odd indeed to open a dictionary of *Sport and Sportsmen* and find an introduction stating blandly that only tennis, baseball and rowing were included, on the ground that the authors knew nothing at all about any other form of modern sport, let alone about the sporting activities of earlier times or other parts of the world. No publisher would tolerate this, or risk it either. But in the field of art it becomes explicable if the sceptics are right in supposing that one of the functions of artspeak is, precisely, to establish a privileged status for certain works and their creators, while fudging or begging the question 'What is art?'

The Murrays' own dialect of artspeak illustrates this perfectly. For example, they pronounce weightily on Picasso: 'No man has changed more radically the nature of art.' But what is this 'nature of art'? And why does their entry on Picasso make no mention of the fact that Picasso produced not only paintings, engraving and sculpture but ceramics, costume designs and even plays? Was he an artist only in the first three activities, but not in the latter three?

As soon as such questions are raised, it becomes apparent that artspeak as currently practised is not just a neutral discourse. Its vocabulary has not been providentially supplied by disinterested lexicographers in case it might be needed. Something more manipulative is going on here. And that puts the study of artspeak on a different plane from the study of sportspeak or of other technical terminologies dedicated to specialist pursuits.

To take another example, it is not difficult to detect a certain embarrassment about what to count as 'art' in *The Oxford Companion to Art* (Osborne 1970). The editor, Harold Osborne, tries to justify its arbitrary exclusions by an appeal to semantics:

> In planning what to include in it the word 'art' has been given the narrower meaning in which it denotes the visual arts generally but excludes the arts of theatre and cinema and the arts of movement such as dance. (Osborne 1970: v)

This casuistic explanation verges on self-contradiction. However one defines the 'visual' arts – and that itself is far from straightforward – theatre and dance, to say nothing of the film, are nothing if not spectacles. To talk about the 'visual' arts (but of course without theatre, dance and film) is rather like talking about agriculture minus grain and vegetable crops: it makes no sense.

Worse, however, follows. Osborne claims that his aim has been to cover 'human artistic endeavour through all time and throughout the world', but that in order to do this in a 'manageable compass' he found it necessary to ignore 'practical arts and handicrafts such as metal-work, textiles, furniture, book design, etc.' Then why not exclude also practical arts and handicrafts such as sculpture, painting and print-making? Apparently stricken with doubt about his own rationale, Osborne confesses that 'over the greater part of human history no clear distinction has been made between arts and crafts'. Quite understandably, one might add, for it is only a modern artspeak distinction. Furthermore, Osborne concedes, 'the distinction between the useful or practical and the fine arts is both a recent and a fluctuating one'. So why, Osborne's reader feels like asking, do you need to pay so much respect to it?

It is at this point in his apologia that Osborne plays his trump card. He will break free from his own self-imposed straitjacket by (sometimes) including material that does not fall within the confines of 'fine art'. Bravo! But why venture on these daring expansions of the artistic domain? Because, Osborne explains rather awkwardly, 'some of the practical arts, and in particular architecture and ceramics, bulk so importantly in our knowledge of the artistic development of certain peoples and cultures that their complete exclusion was out of the question.' This evasively worded excuse plunges yet deeper into the quagmire. How, we ask, could architecture and ceramics possibly be relevant to the 'artistic development' of certain cultures unless these activities were also part of 'human artistic endeavour'? Here we have a classic example of the art expert tripped up by his own artspeak, and of an artspeak uncomfortably at odds with itself.

The situation is even more puzzling in the biggest art reference work published in recent times. This is the thirty-four-volume *Dictionary of Art* (1996), edited by Turner. Here there is no editorial explanation of the scope of the work. Instead there is a perfunctory article on *Art*, not by an artist but by a philosopher (Richard Wollheim). It points out, somewhat apologetically, that there is no consensus on how to define the term. Wollheim goes on to raise the question of why this should be, and writes:

> One of the reasons why the question remains in such an unsettled state is that it has been common practice, over a wide range of disciplines on which it impinges, to ignore it. (Wollheim 1996: 505)

This shrewdly worded observation could be read as a thinly veiled criticism of the failure by the editor and publishers to provide any rationale for their own rather arbitrary selection policy. Allocating approximately one page to the question of defining *art* (in the context of a publication running to thousands of pages) is already a comment about the importance/unimportance of the question. It is a question that cannot be fudged by cross-referencing to articles on art in China, art in Africa, art in such-and-such a period. That is a strategy for evading rather than addressing the basic question.

In these cases one confronts in the end exactly the same puzzle as in Fischer's book. Much is said, in considerable detail, about various forms and works of art. But nothing is said about why or how they all count as examples of art. It almost seems that this is a question deliberately avoided, or as if the profusion of examples given rendered that question superfluous. If the latter genuinely *is* the lexicographer's assumption, then there is a very dubious layer of semantic theory underlying the lexicography of artspeak. One can no more define the term *art* by listing examples of it than one can define the term *dinner* by producing restaurant menus. What still needs explaining is why the examples *are* examples.

*   *   *

'Is modern art necessary?' is the title of an essay included by Rudolph Arnheim in his book *Toward a Psychology of Art*. Here Arnheim speaks of various kinds of necessity. There is 'the public's need for visual enlightenment, stimulation, and spectacle'. Arnheim laments the fact that in modern society this need is not being satisfied by 'artists who could give clarity, weight and depth' but instead by 'the brutalities of commercial entertainers' (Arnheim 1966: 344). Then there is the more basic necessity to provide a recognizable reflection of the everyday world. Arnheim claims that 'faithful likenesses fulfill a legitimate need even though their connection with art has become tenuous'. This need is 'strong, elementary, and down-to-earth in that it is part of people's practical intercourse with the things of this world' (Arnheim 1966: 349). This in turn links up with the more general necessity that arises from what Arnheim holds to be art's permanent and principal function: that of 'making the nature and meaning of human existence visible and audible'. Furthermore, 'never before the gradual advent of modern art in the nineteenth century has art professed and practiced this principal function collectively and explicitly as it does now'. Those who blazed the trail were such figures as Beethoven, Cézanne, Flaubert and Ibsen, who engaged in art in a new way, i.e. one that had not been open to previous generations of artists. What was new was that these men did not 'work for anybody, except, possibly, for everybody'. Their great mission has been carried on by today's artists.

> Having nobody's ax to grind, the art of our time is perhaps hardening itself with a hermit's exercises of isolation, starvation, and nightmare for the task of serving a new generation – not as an entertainer and not even as a public relations officer for democracy, but as the indispensable demonstrator of truth. (Arnheim 1966: 351)

It is the word *indispensable* here which supplies the answer to the original question asked: 'Is modern art necessary?' The necessity, in short, arises from the assumption that if the artist does not take up the burden and challenge of demonstrating 'truth', no one else in modern society will.

What exactly is the 'truth' to be demonstrated poses another problem, and one which will not be pursued here. Whatever Arnheim means (and I am not sure I understand what he means), his exposition of it depends verbally on the relationship between two undefined terms; namely *art* and *truth*. So whatever Arnheim thought he was arguing about the necessity of art turns out in practice to demonstrate the necessity of artspeak.

*   *   *

Artspeak is an open-ended range of discourse, which comes in a variety of demotic as well as academic registers. But it is instantly recognizable the moment we realize we are being pressed, either overtly or tacitly, to accept the attribution of the status of 'art' (whatever that might turn out to involve) in some particular instance; or, alternatively, to deny that status. The negative function of artspeak, as recent debates well illustrate, is often as important as its positive function. All of which begins to suggest that, whatever else it may be, artspeak is not 'unnecessary' at all, but supplies a rather crucial form of social validation and rejection for certain types of product and activity.

Nor should anyone suppose that artspeak is the prerogative of those professionally engaged in the arts. There are scientists who are quite capable of 'turning on' artspeak when the occasion demands, as the following two excerpts illustrate. The first shows the biologist E. O. Wilson in full 'scientific' flow:

> In one property of the electron, its magnetic moment, theory and experiment have been matched to the most extreme degree ever achieved in the physical sciences. The magnetic moment is a measure of the interaction between an electron and a magnetic field. More precisely, it is the maximum torque experienced by the electron divided by the magnetic induction acting on it. (Wilson 1998: 53)

The second is the same writer in the same book a few chapters later:

> Artistic inspiration common to everyone in varying degree rises from the artesian wells of human nature. Its creations are meant to be delivered directly to the sensibilities of the beholder without analytic explanation. Creativity is therefore humanistic in the fullest sense. Works of enduring value are those truest to these origins. (Wilson 1998: 237)

That the first of these passages is a factual explanation, while the second is romantic waffle, is not the point. Scientists are also capable of writing romantic waffle about science; but the language in which they write it could hardly be mistaken for artspeak.

Before proceeding further, one or two other linguistic caveats are necessary. The fact that *artspeak* is an English word (even if not yet officially recognized in the *Oxford English Dictionary*) should mislead no one into supposing that artspeak is an exclusively English phenomenon. That would be just as absurd as supposing that art was a cultural category confined to the English-speaking world. The word *art* has generally recognized translation equivalents in other European languages (*arte*, *Kunst*, etc.). These 'equivalents' are loosely anchored by reference to a range of products and activities familiar throughout Western culture. But exactly how far this translatability extends across non-European languages and cultures is one of the most contentious issues that any serious investigation of artspeak today has to reckon with.

Another caveat is that if an investigation of artspeak is to be conducted with any semblance of impartiality (which is not the same as a suspension of critical judgment), it is important to conduct it in such a way as not to prejudge whether something qualifies as a 'work of art'. This applies even when, and especially when, the expression *work of art* is commonly used to describe it. A similar observation applies to the word *artist*. The credentials of this term will be, in many readers' minds, inextricably bound up with those of the term *art* itself. But if we are to view these controversial matters dispassionately, it seems essential not to restrict the application of the term *artist* to those whose endeavours have already been judged in advance to be 'works of art'. For the same reason, it is important to keep open such questions as whether works of art can be produced by small children, or by the insane, or by machines, or by members of societies too remote from our own for us to have any idea what – if anything – was 'in the mind' of their makers. As regards the well-documented activities of bowerbirds, let alone laboratory experiments with monkeys and paint brushes, there is clearly a question about whether 'artistic' inclinations are the prerogative of *Homo sapiens*. If I do not pursue the latter question in this book, it is because I think it a good idea to sort out the implications of artspeak for our own species before rushing in to apply it to others.

*   *   *

The necessity of which Fischer wrote, as a Marxist, was intimately connected with his conviction that 'art is necessary in order that man should be able to recognize and change the world' (Fischer 1963: 14). What I have been arguing so far is the case for recognizing another – overriding – necessity: the communicational necessity of the relationship between art and language about art. One may keep an open mind about whether art is necessary either in Fischer's sense or in Arnheim's; but whether it is or not has no direct bearing on arguments relating to the necessity of artspeak.

Nevertheless, it would be absurd to claim that it is possible to mount an investigation of artspeak without making any assumptions whatsoever concerning art. The question is, rather, what minimal assumptions can be made about art which will not distort the inquiry in some way.

In any society which treats works of art as subject to discussion and critical evaluation we cannot ultimately have a satisfactory theory of art without a theory of artspeak. We recognize many different artistic endeavours (poetry, music, painting, etc.), but we also recognize a supercategory ('art(s)') into which all fall. Any attempt to separate art from artspeak (by, for instance, treating one as the concern of art historians or aestheticians and the other as the concern of linguists) is not merely defective but self-stultifying; for *art as a cultural supercategory is a product of artspeak*. This last step – the creation of the supercategory – may seem at first sight 'unnecessary' (although in a rather different sense from that in which either Fischer or Arnheim conceived of 'necessity'). But is it unnecessary? And if not, what kind of necessity are we dealing with here? These are questions that will lead us in the following chapters into what turns out to be a very complex network of interrelated issues.

It is important to be clear at the outset that the sense in which art is necessary (if it is) does not, necessarily, coincide with the sense in which artspeak is necessary (if it is). That way of putting the point is, of course, too clever by half. But it should not (necessarily) be condemned on that score.

The whole notion of distinguishing between a practical necessity and (what some call) a logical necessity is itself an artifact of a certain view of the arts and language. We cannot assume that words like *art* and *necessity* somehow descend into the back yard of Western culture out of a clear blue sky. These are not pristine conceptual tools luckily put at our disposal through the workings of some benign linguistic Providence, even though that is sometimes the impression given in the writings of both philosophers and art critics.

Part I
TRADITIONAL ARTSPEAK

2

Artspeak in antiquity

Every art we follow . . . may be held to aim at some good or end.

Aristotle

The foundations of modern artspeak were laid in antiquity. Many of its terms come down to us encumbered with a heavy load of historical baggage. But the etymological core of the matter, although complex, is not obscure. The English word *art* is directly descended from a Latin word (*ars*, pl. *artes*) which could be applied in the days of Julius Caesar to virtually any activity requiring training, together with skill in the practical exercise of what had been taught. For the Romans, gymnastics was an art, medicine was an art, public speaking was an art, sculpture was an art and war was an art. An exactly parallel state of affairs obtained in Plato's Greece, where the corresponding term was *techne* (pl. *technai*).

This ancient notion of artistic activity already tells us something important about the kind of society that gave rise to it, as Marx was to point out much later: it was a society economically based on the division of labour. Marx held that the development of particular talents in certain individuals, and their corresponding suppression in the population at large, was also a result of the division of labour. But whether he was right about that is another matter (Klingender 1943: 28–9). Professional specialization in the various arts, and professional rivalry between specialists, was universally taken for granted in antiquity. Occasionally we hear of individuals excelling in very diverse arts. Hippias of Elis boasted before the crowds at the Olympic games that not only had he mastered every branch of knowledge, including geometry, music, literature, the study of the natural world, and politics, but had made with his own hands the ring on his finger, the cloak he was wearing, and the boots on his feet (Cicero, *de Oratore* II, xxxii, 127). If all this was true, then Hippias was a remarkably versatile master of the arts of his time. But he must also have been an exception (as his boast itself implies).

The original uses of the terms *ars* and *techne* thus seem to arise from and reflect early rivalries in the ancient world of trades and professions, where the claim to specialized skills and superior workmanship would have been an important factor in establishing a reputation and a successful practice. In Homer the notion of this kind of superiority is readily applied to practical crafts such as metalwork and shipbuilding. Pollitt attributes to the Sophists its extension 'to include not only practical crafts but also the less concrete intellectual and emotional activities by which a man practiced "virtue" or "excellence" in his society' (Pollitt 1974: 34).

The notion of artistry as trained skills survives to the present day, to the extent that the term *art* can still be applied to the application and cultivation of such skills in a wide variety of activities, whether displayed on the football pitch or the stage of public politics. According to Janaway, who discusses Plato's view of the arts at some length, in adopting this modern usage 'clearly we do not mean thereby to embrace these activities among "the arts"' (Janaway 1995: 9). But, *pace* Janaway, it would be an extremely odd usage indeed if we saw no connexion at all between the skills thereby praised and what Janaway evidently admits to his own roster of 'arts' (which, he says, includes music, literature, drama, painting, sculpture, dance and others unnamed). Presumably what lies behind Janaway's objection is that he would not nowadays expect someone described as an 'art dealer', or a building said to be an 'art gallery', or an exhibition advertised as an 'art exhibition', or – to take his own example – a newspaper page called the 'arts page', to have anything to do with some of the wide range of things classified as 'arts' in antiquity. The way Janaway looks at the terminological question views it through the wrong end of an etymological telescope. For what is controversial is not whether professional carpenters or footballers or wrestlers or politicians can be credited with arts which they have mastered, but the restriction which nowadays goes along with the application of terms like *art gallery, art exhibition*, etc. That restriction seems to imply that certain kinds of skill and product have a privileged artistic status. But which skills and products these are, and whether claims for their privileged status can be upheld, are questions which cannot be settled by a simple-minded appeal to dictionary definitions or current usage. They are questions which engage the whole theory of the arts as it has developed throughout the Western tradition.

Artspeak, as the form of discourse in which such questions are posed and debated, inevitably has a semantics pervaded with social assumptions concerning the value and function of the arts. This has been so right from the beginning. In antiquity there was no parity of esteem between the arts. Some were highly regarded, others depreciated or even despised; and this disparity is directly reflected in the artspeak of the day. It can be seen most obviously in the division that the Romans drew between two broad classes of artistic activity. On the one hand there were the 'liberal arts' (*artes liberales*), which meant arts that could honourably be practised by a free citizen (or a 'gentleman', as it might have been put centuries later in England). On the other hand there were the 'illiberal arts' (or *artes sordidae*), which were fit only for slaves and the lower classes. A similar classification was already familiar to Aristotle, who recognizes certain branches of knowledge as *eleutheriai* (i.e. appropriate to, or the concern of, a free citizen), as opposed to the banausic or mechanical arts. This did not mean that no slaves ever engaged in liberal arts or no free citizens in the illiberal variety; for this was primarily an artspeak distinction, not a legal distinction, even though at certain times and places there might have been particular prohibitions in force. (Vasari in the sixteenth century evidently believed that Roman cities debarred slaves from working as painters (Bull 1965: 28); but this may have been because he anachronistically retrojected his own view of painting as a liberal art into Roman times. Alexander, according to Pliny, forbade any portrait of himself other than by Apelles. But this was a matter of patronage rather than social distinction.) Any prohibition of the form 'Art x may not be practised by individuals of class y' is in any case likely to have been the consequence rather than the basis of distinguishing between arts that were liberal and arts that were not.

The question of what lay behind this general division is more complicated. For instance, it is not immediately obvious whether certain arts were held in low esteem *because* they were done by slaves, or done by slaves because they were held in low esteem (Hauser 1962: 103). What seems clear is that the distinction between liberal and illiberal arts had little to do with financial rewards, as the case of painting shows. Painting did not count as a liberal art. But the best painters were well remunerated. Pliny comments on how valuable the most highly prized paintings had become and cites the example of a king of Lydia paying its weight in gold for a painting by Boularchos. He also tells us how Zeuxis became so wealthy that he had his name woven into his cloaks in letters of gold. Plutarch notes that Polygnotos, although a famous painter, accepted no money for painting the Stoa Poikile in Athens and thereby showed his patriotic love for the city. Admiration for the work, however, does not necessarily go with prestige for the artist. Arnold Hauser quotes Seneca's remark that although we offer prayers and sacrifices before the statues of the gods, we despise the sculptors who made them (Hauser 1962: 107). Plutarch says that no one, on seeing the statue of Zeus at Olympia, ever wanted to be Phidias; an observation which was eventually to be echoed, upstaged and subverted by Picasso's dictum that 'It is not what the artist does that counts, but what he is' (Bernadac and Michael 1998: 35–6). On the other hand, it would be facile to suppose that we are dealing with a simple transposition from the social standing of the practitioners to the status of the art. The fact that even emperors, including Nero, Hadrian, and Aurelius, were keen amateur painters did not ensure the promotion of painting to the ranks of the liberal arts. Nor, on the other hand, did their indulgence in painting as a pastime bring disgrace on these eminent personages.

This did not prevent artspeak from becoming pervaded with various strains of snobbery, both social and intellectual. We learn a great deal about this from Cicero, one of the most consummate snobs of his age. In *De Officiis* (I, xlii, 150–151) he gives detailed consideration to the question of how one may honourably earn a living (*quaestus*). According to Cicero, some occupations are respectable (*liberales*), others demeaning or vulgar (*sordidi*). The latter class includes all livelihoods which incur the ill-will of others, such as being a tax-gatherer or a usurer, and all paid work in which one is paid for labour (*opera*) rather than for expertise (*artes*). Retail traders are also on Cicero's blacklist, but not wholesale importers. A moral reason – but a very specious one – is given for this: retail business is intrinsically dishonest (selling something for more than it is worth), whereas shipping goods from abroad brings benefits which the whole country would not otherwise have. All the mechanical arts are *sordidae*, because no workshop (*officina*) has anything honourable in it. Worst of all, says Cicero, are those arts that cater for pleasures of the senses. Condemned under this head are fishmongers, butchers, cooks, poulterers, perfume-makers and dancers. Examples of approved arts are medicine, architecture, teaching and – perhaps most surprising of all – agriculture. No occupation, proclaims Cicero, is more worthy of a free man (*nihil homine libero dignius*) than agriculture. At first sight this might seem to conflict with the commonly held view that the distinction between liberal and illiberal arts reflected the low esteem in which manual labour was held. The explanation of Cicero's praise of agriculture is probably due to his respect for the traditional image of the sturdy Roman farmer as the backbone of the nation. But in the vast estates of Cicero's day all the hard work was done by slaves and the art of agriculture was an art of farm management.

The question of manual labour also arises in connexion with other arts. Explaining why painters and sculptors were accorded a lower status than poets, Arnold Hauser writes:

> First of all, the sculptor or painter works for reward and makes no attempt to hide the fact, whereas the poet is looked upon as the guest-friend of his patron, even at times when he is utterly dependent upon him. Then, too, the sculptor and the painter have to work with dirty materials and tools whereas the poet goes about with clean clothes and hands – all of which counted for more than one might think in the eyes of an untechnical age. But most important of all is the fact that the sculptor or painter is obliged to be doing manual work that involves bodily effort and the performance of many wearisome tasks, while the labours of the poet are certainly not obvious to the eye. (Hauser 1962: 102–3)

No less a luminary than Leonardo would later use his own version of the 'dirty job' argument to prove that painting was superior to sculpture (Blunt 1940: 54–5). For anyone interested in the history of artspeak, it is worth noting in passing that this question of mental versus physical effort – thus appealing to the intellect as opposed to the senses – crops up again in a quite different context in the twentieth century. Discussing his early work in an interview in 1946, Marcel Duchamp said: 'I wanted to put painting once again at the service of the mind.' In his view, the nineteenth-century painters, beginning with Courbet, had put too much emphasis on the physical aspects of painting. 'The more sensual appeal a painting provided – the more animal it became – the more highly it was regarded.' 'I was endeavoring to establish myself as far as possible from "pleasing" and "attractive" physical paintings.' (Chipp 1968: 392ff.) The same idea is taken one stage further by the more recent school of 'conceptual art'. For the conceptualists, art is essentially a mental activity: any involvement in the physical handling of materials is incidental and secondary. Hence Lawrence Weiner's much-quoted pronouncement that a work of art could exist simply in the form of proposals in his notebook, until a client came along and asked him to make it. Weiner later claimed that it did not matter whether he made the work or not. No one in antiquity goes quite as far as that. The form of snobbery from which Duchamp and the conceptualists suffer, although superficially similar to one that we recognize in Cicero, is based on a different notion of culture. What motivates the modern attitude is not distaste for getting one's hands dirty but the desire to be taken seriously as an 'intellectual' (a category that did not exist in Cicero's day).

That Greeks and Romans were very conscious of the difference between mental and manual skills is hardly open to doubt. But whether Hauser is right about the reasons underlying the ranking of the arts in the ancient world is another question. A case could be made out for saying that whether artists get their hands dirty or enjoy a privileged relationship with their patron/ employer are matters of secondary importance, symptoms rather than causes.

This does not rule out the possibility that in the artspeak of Cicero's day symptoms were being commonly confused with causes. But in order to see what alternative explanation is available we need to go back beyond Cicero's muddled list of prejudices to the clearer thinking of Aristotle. Nowadays the most frequently quoted Aristotelian pronouncements about the arts come from his *Poetics*. But in order to understand Aristotle's basic position concerning artistic activities it is far more relevant to read his *Ethics* and *Politics*.

For Aristotle, as for Plato, all human pursuits need a justification. The arts are no exception. There is no such thing as a form of activity which supplies its own *raison d'être*. Aristotle would have found the modern doctrine of 'art-for-art's-sake' incomprehensible; or at least an insult to human intelligence. At the very beginning of the *Nicomachean Ethics* he makes the point (*Nicomachean*

Ethics 1094a) that the arts are too diverse to have any single purpose in common. (So – the implication is – it is vain to seek to pin down any grandiose abstraction such as 'the' universal goal of art.) Nevertheless, by virtue of their relationship with one another, certain groups of arts form hierarchies. That is to say, some are subordinate to others. This is because one art may be directed towards a goal which already presupposes the existence of another art, which in turn may presuppose the existence of another. One of the examples Aristotle gives is the art of bridle-making. There would be no point in making bridles at all unless people rode horses. But the art of horsemanship would not be cultivated unless it had some importance in other activities; for instance, in warfare. Nor is the art of war important in itself, but only because war serves political objectives. And so on. From this it would seem to follow that if one wishes to understand what determines the purpose and methods of any given art, it is first of all necessary to examine how it relates to other arts.

For Aristotle, however, that is the beginning rather than the end of the inquiry. The arts are interrelated in certain specific ways, and none is independent of all the others. Collectively, the arts serve society. Therefore one must consider the function of particular arts or groups of arts as they affect the well-being of society. The master art of all is politics. This is what determines – or should determine, in a well-run society – which arts should be cultivated and by which groups in society. Now society, for Aristotle, is organized on the basis of relationships between its members, and there are four classes of membership to be taken into account. The four classes in question are those of (1) free men, or masters, (2) women, (3) children, and (4) slaves. The relationship between one free man and another will necessarily be different in kind from the relationship between a free man and his wife, or his children, or his slaves. It is nature, not human endeavour, that assigns an individual to one or other of the four classes in question. In a prosperous, healthy society the members of these four classes will follow such pursuits as are consonant with or required by their relationships with other members.

Given this set of assumptions, it is not difficult to see why, for Aristotle, certain arts would be appropriate or inappropriate for certain classes within society. If a master tries to do a slave's work, he will be neglecting his own responsibilities as a master. If a woman tries to do her husband's work, she will be neglecting her own household duties. Children cannot in any case do the work of adults and slaves cannot do their master's work. But if all do their own tasks properly, the household will prosper.

The primary responsibility of a master is to ensure adequate provision for the well-being of his own household. But there are also responsibilities which arise from the more general needs of the community. The state needs, for instance, soldiers to protect it, as well as judges and administrators. So the question that arises is how the free man may fulfil both his personal and his social duties, and what training or education he needs to do this. The general answer seems clear enough: he will need to engage in whatever studies and forms of training lead to this end. Such arts as satisfy these criteria are the liberal arts – those which enable a free man to fulfil his responsibilities honourably.

Aristotle notes, however, that this does not solve the practical problem of whether it is better for all free men to share in the provision of all the services that the community needs, or for some to specialize (*Politics* VII, ix). Different solutions may be adopted in different circumstances. But it is necessary for those who undertake some form of public service to have the leisure that enables them to do this. Aristotle seems to think that this in practice rules out farmers, mechanics and merchants, even though their activities are essential if the community is to flourish.

Although Aristotle does not develop it, we already see here the rudiments of a theory of necessity for the arts. There would be two levels of necessity: one determined by the interdependences between the arts themselves ('Art *a* is necessary because without it Art *b* could not exist') and a higher level determined by the needs of society. This, however, leaves a question-mark hanging over many of the arts. Aristotle's attitude to music (*Politics* 1339a–1342) provides an illustration. He is cautious about the notion that music is needed for purposes of entertainment, because he deplores the idea that amusing oneself is a worthy end in life. He is more sympathetic to the idea that music serves a useful educational purpose in respect of moral training and the cultivation of the mind. But he refrains from arguing that music is necessary for those ends.

A different light is thrown on the question of necessity by the arguments that Quintilian deploys in Book II of his *Institutio Oratoria* to demonstrate that oratory is an art. Quintilian does not himself doubt this for a moment (one would hardly expect anything else from Rome's foremost authority on public speaking); but he nevertheless feels obliged to prove the point. He therefore considers the possibility that oratory is not an art at all but a natural gift. In other words, is teaching necessary? The question itself reveals that, as far as Quintilian is concerned, the fundamental opposition is one between art and nature, between what one is trained to do and what comes spontaneously. And one awkward piece of evidence is said to be 'that uneducated persons, barbarians and slaves, when speaking on their own behalf, say something that resembles an *exordium*, state the facts of the case, prove, refute and plead for mercy just as an orator does in his peroration' (*Institutio Oratoria* II, xvii, 6). So if these untutored individuals can speak eloquently for themselves without any guidance except their own common sense, where does that leave the status of oratory? Quintilian's reply is that 'everything which art has brought to perfection originated in nature'. If it were otherwise we should have to deny that medicine, building and music are arts, since these too have a basis in nature; and to deny medicine, building and music the status of arts, he implies, would be absurd. The arts, on this view, are necessary in order to perfect our natural gifts. The question of how we are to use our natural gifts, whether in their perfected or unperfected state, does not arise. This is the professional teacher's view of necessity, not the philosopher's.

In putting his case, Quintilian does not overtly invoke the distinction between the liberal and the illiberal arts, but there is an indirect reference to it in his allusion to barbarians and slaves. This implies that there are certain things that non-citizens are not allowed to do and takes us back to the idea that the liberal arts were liberal because being a free citizen was a necessary requirement for engagement in the occupations to which such arts were relevant.

Quintilian goes on to consider which subdivision of the arts oratory belongs to. He proposes three subdivisions. First, there are arts which are directed not to action, but to observation and knowledge. These are the 'theoretical' arts, and the example he gives is astronomy. Second, there are arts whose end is action, the performance of which leaves nothing further to be done. These are the 'practical' arts, and his example is dancing. Third, there are arts which aim at the completion of a visible task. These are the 'productive' arts, and his example is painting. It is interesting that Quintilian uses Greek terms (*theoretike*, *praktike* and *poietike*) as designations for his three kinds of art, which suggests that this was a classification familiar to him from Greek rather than Roman sources.

Oratory, according to Quintilian, is generally reckoned to belong to the practical arts. However, he adds that in his view it also has elements of the theoretical and the productive. In support of this he produces a curious argument. Eloquence is still in the orator's possession, even if he is silent, just as a retired doctor is still master of the art of medicine, even though he no longer practises it. At the same time, by writing speeches, even if he does not deliver them, the orator creates a product – the text. So altogether oratory partakes of all three types of art. It strikes one as odd that Quintilian does not press this analysis further and point out that many arts besides oratory might be regarded as having three components: a theoretical basis, a practical activity and a range of resultant products.

*   *   *

By the time Quintilian wrote, the term *ars* in Latin, like *techne* in Greek, was also commonly applied not just to the art itself but also to relevant treatises and manuals of instruction. This is a development that would only have been possible in a literate society. That umbilical connexion with literacy was to have profound consequences later for the whole of the Western tradition. It promoted theory above practice. That is to say, the arts tend to become identified with those forms of expertise that can be made explicit verbally (and for preference in writing), as distinct from those that depend on knacks and methods that can only be picked up by observation and imitation.

The origins of this development are obscure. We know that quite a number of the early Greek sculptors wrote treatises on sculpture – Menaichmos, Xenokrates, Antigonos and Pasiteles, for example. None of these works has survived, but they were available to Pliny when he wrote his *Natural History*. As early as the sixth century BC, practising architects had written on architecture, and from the fourth century BC a whole series of Greek painters wrote about painting.

We are evidently dealing with a cultural situation in which reputations come to be based not only on the works of art produced but, increasingly, on what is written *about* them. And along with this comes the notion that in all forms of endeavour, true knowledge manifests itself not only in actual practice but in being able to explain the practice by setting down in writing the principles of it. The alliance between work of art and work of theory dates back at least as far as Polykleitus's famous 'Canon', of which Pliny wittily, but justly, observed that here the sculptor had vindicated the author (*artem ipsam fecisse artis opere indicatur*). Pliny evidently thought that not many sculptors were good enough to practise what they preached.

None of this entirely explains what eventually emerged in antiquity as the agreed roster of the liberal arts. Varro, Cicero's contemporary, had written an influential encyclopedic work (the *Disciplinae*, now lost) devoted to the nine most important branches of knowledge: grammar, logic, rhetoric, geometry, arithmetic, astronomy, music, medicine and architecture. The first seven of these eventually survived as the 'liberal arts' curriculum of the medieval schools and universities. That reduction to seven was already established by the early fifth century AD, when Martianus Capella wrote his allegorical didactic treatise *De Nuptiis Mercurii et Philologiae*, of which a book is devoted to each of the seven. It was a work which, for all its turgidity, remained a landmark in thinking about the arts throughout the middle ages.

*   *   *

Different arts in antiquity gave rise to different kinds of writing, addressed to different readerships. This has not escaped the attention of modern scholars. The arts of sculpture, painting and architecture, according to Pollitt, sponsored (1) 'compilers of tradition', who collected from many sources 'biographical, technical, and anecdotal information' about these arts and their practitioners, (2) 'literary analogists', comprising rhetoricians and poets who looked to sculpture, painting and architecture as providing analogies to, or even inspiration for, literary works, (3) 'moral aestheticians', including Plato, Aristotle and other philosophers concerned with the effects of these arts on human behaviour, and finally (4) the artists themselves, who wrote technical and critical treatises on the arts they practised (Pollitt 1990: 6–9). Similarly, for the art or arts of music, Barker distinguishes between (1) writings which describe or evoke the activities of music-making and composition, (2) writings by philosophers and social commentators on the role of music in education and in society in general, and (3) the technical works of harmonic and acoustic theorists (Barker 1984: 1–3).

Such classifications as these might be further subdivided. The list of classes might also be augmented; for example, by adding in the case of architecture a class to accommodate surviving written specifications for actual buildings, such as Philon's arsenal in Piraeus, built in the fourth century BC (Pollitt 1990: 199–202). But these classifications, which answer to the interests of modern scholarship, can hardly be taken as identifying linguistic categories of artspeak. For one thing, the technical terms which still puzzle authorities today, such as *tetragonos* in sculpture or *nomos* in music, were doubtless less opaque to the public of the ancient world. Furthermore, any distinction between 'lay artspeak' and 'technical artspeak' tends to cut across classifications based on the point of view of the writer. Thus, for instance, even if there is good reason for classifying Plato among the 'moral aestheticians', that does not alter the fact that Plato's important arguments about the arts are couched in terms that anyone can understand. It is not so much that he deliberately avoids technicalities as that technicalities are totally irrelevant to what he is arguing. In that respect there is not a great deal of difference between the artspeak of Plato's dialogues and the artspeak of Horace's *De Arte Poetica*, even though intellectually they are worlds apart.

On the other hand, however, there are also areas of ancient artspeak where one encounters nothing but the elaboration of technicalities. The art of grammar (*techne grammatike, ars grammatica*) is a good example. The earliest surviving grammatical treatise from the ancient world, that of Dionysius Thrax (Lallot 1989), is a glossary of technical terms, doubtless corresponding to contemporary teaching practices. And this points to a far more fundamental artspeak distinction. In other words, here we have a form of artspeak to be mastered as a *precondition* for engaging in the art at all. A student could not be expected to analyse a Greek sentence unless equipped verbally with a metalanguage for that purpose, whereas a musician might play the lyre by ear, without understanding Stratonicus's teachings on *ta harmonika*, or even knowing the names of the seven strings.

The predominant conviction in the Graeco-Roman world is that an activity does not fully become an art until someone has worked out a theory, however crude, to go with the practice. And the best way of establishing such a theory is to set it down in writing so that people can judge for themselves whether theory and practice match or not.

*   *   *

Plato, however, was a sceptic where writing was concerned (Harris 2000: 17ff.). One recurrent theme in Plato's teaching is that, in order to be genuine, an art must be based on knowledge: otherwise, it is a sham. Socrates deploys this argument in the *Phaedrus* to attack rhetoric as practised in his day, when handbooks of rhetoric were already commonplace (Kennedy 1963: 57ff.). According to Socrates, unless persuasion is based on truth, it is a deception. Otherwise, rhetoric

> is not an art at all but a knack which has nothing to do with art. There is not nor ever shall be, as the Spartan said, a genuine art of speaking which is divorced from grasp of the truth. (*Phaedrus* 260; Hamilton 1973: 73)

By the same token, not any old 'how-to-do-it' manual automatically fulfils the criteria for an 'art'. A recipe book is not *eo ipso* an 'art' of cookery. There is an interesting discussion of this point in the *Gorgias*, where Socrates maintains that medicine is a *techne* but cookery is not (*Gorgias* 464–466). A good doctor has to understand both what is wrong with the patient and how a particular treatment will put it right. What is needed is a grasp of the reasons underlying cause and effect. The cook simply knows from experience how to flatter the palate, i.e. knows that certain combinations of food taste good while others do not; but has no idea of why this is so. Maybe Socrates is overestimating Greek medicine and underestimating Greek cookery. But the relevant point here is the rationale he provides for distinguishing the two.

In Plato's last work, the *Laws*, an interesting passage on the art of medicine distinguishes two ways of treating the sick (*Laws* 720). One is the way of the free-born doctor, the other the way of the slave. The latter is assumed to have acquired his remedies by observation and practice, not by the study of nature, which is the way of the former. Slave doctors are useful as auxiliaries, because they can give first-aid to slaves and act as assistants to the free-born doctor; but only the free-born doctor, treating the ailments of free citizens, will investigate each case thoroughly, enter into dialogue with the patient, and eventually prescribe according to an understanding of the nature of the individual problem. This is the highest form of medicine. Here we see an explicit – and very early – link between a genuine knowledge of the art and the social status of its practitioner.

Whether the doctors of Plato's day saw their art in this perspective is a moot point. Nevertheless, it is clear that there emerged in antiquity the notion of art as *a form of knowledge in which purposeful execution is guided by genuine understanding of the principles underlying the activity*. The true artist, as distinct from the assistant who has merely copied his master blindly, is able to apply expertise creatively. By understanding the principles, a master of the art can solve unexpected problems rationally, whereas all his assistant can do when the usual methods fail is proceed by trial and error.

*   *   *

Given this emphasis on theory and reason, the apparently puzzling superiority of the poet over the painter falls into place. For in antiquity language was regarded as the primary manifestation of human rationality. The *locus classicus* on that topic is the following passage from Isocrates.

> In most of our abilities we differ not at all from the animals; we are in fact behind many in swiftness and strength and other resources. But because there is born in us the power to persuade each other and to show ourselves whatever we wish, we not only have escaped from living as brutes, but also by coming together have founded cities and set up laws and invented arts, and speech has helped us attain practically all of the things we have devised. For it is speech that has made laws about justice and injustice and honor and disgrace, without which provisions we should not be able to live together. By speech we refute the wicked and praise the good. By speech we educate the ignorant and inform the wise. We regard the ability to speak properly as the best sign of intelligence, and truthful, legal, and just speech is the reflection of a good and trust-worthy soul. (Kennedy 1963: 8–9)

The term translated here as 'speech' is the Greek *logos*, which designates not only the capacity for articulate discourse but the rational faculty underlying language in all its forms. It is *logos* which distinguishes humanity from all other living species, and it is *logos* which provides the basis for the Classical definition of the human being as 'the rational animal'.

The argument about the arts would then go as follows. Given the primacy of *logos*, the arts become subject to a natural hierarchy, depending on whether they manifest more or less of *logos*, i.e. are more or less language-like. If this is so, the pre-eminence of the arts which are language-based needs no further justification. The skill of the poet is a skill with words. The Greek reverence for Homer provides ample evidence of the value that was placed on the poet's art.

Plato was the first thinker original enough to question that value in any serious way. Other controversial themes underlying Western artspeak can also be traced back as far as Plato. The most important of these is the relationship between art and nature. Although Plato seems to conceive of the world as having been created by a kind of divine artist-craftsman (*demiourgos*), he has little respect for the artist-craftsmen of Athens. It is paradoxical, given Plato's enormous influence on later apologists for art, that Plato's basic attitude to the arts of his day was one of deep and unremitting suspicion, particularly towards all arts based on imitation. These, for Plato, included poetry, painting and sculpture, and the suspicion was motivated by his judgment that these were forms of deception or illusion. As such they diverted attention from reality to mere appearances, and hindered the mind in its search for truth.

Plato's most celebrated example (*Republic* X) is the case of the painter painting a picture of a bed. Cornford explicates this as follows:

> A picture of a bed is a two-dimensional representation of the appearance of a solid object seen at a certain angle. The object itself is only a particular bed, which, as a part of the material world, is not a wholly real thing, since it comes into being and perishes and is perpetually changing [. . .]. This actual bed, however, is nearer to reality than the picture, because it is one of many embodiments of the essential nature common to all beds. (Cornford 1941: 315)

Thus what is produced by the art of painting is not 'the real thing', but something at two removes (at least) from it.

This analysis is what allegedly underlies Plato's supposed 'fear of art' (Wind 1985: 47) and his notorious 'banishment of the artists' from his ideal state (Murdoch 1977), where he objected to their harmful effects on the education of the young. According to Collingwood, however, this reading of Plato is a mistake based on the misinterpretation of certain passages in the *Republic* (Collingwood 1938: 46ff.). Collingwood is doubtless right, but does not seem to realize that these misinterpretations are not due to the incompetence of individual scholars and translators. They are systematic errors, attributable to the built-in biases of modern artspeak, which retrojects a generalized concept of 'art' quite alien to Plato's mode of thought.

The fact is that Plato is here engaged in his own battle of the arts; a battle directed against the art of poetry, of which Homer was traditionally accepted in the Greek world as the foremost exponent. Perhaps the most telling passage in the *Republic* is that in which Homer is posthumously challenged to name any society in which the poet, as distinct from the lawgiver, has been responsible for advocating courses of conduct that 'will make men better [. . .] as individuals or as citizens' or make any country 'better governed thanks to your efforts' (Cornford 1941: 322). For Plato, recourse to the poets as a source of wisdom or inspiration for human conduct was the antithesis of philosophy, which seeks to know the truth by a process of rigorous intellectual inquiry in the Socratic manner.

What coloured Plato's view of these matters was his metaphysical conviction that reality is located not in the everyday world about us but in the timeless domain of immaterial and eternal Forms or Ideas. Depending on one's evaluation of this metaphysics, what Plato has to say about the supposedly mimetic arts may thus appear to be philosophically profound or egregious nonsense. What interests the historian of artspeak is how strands of this profundity or nonsense (depending on one's assessment) continue to survive long after the Graeco-Roman view of the arts had been replaced by a quite different one. And this requires some consideration of what happened to the arts and artspeak in medieval Europe.

Before proceeding to that, however, it is worth noting how, right from the beginning of the Western tradition, artspeak emerges as a linguistic weapon in an ongoing war waged between different parties, all of whom are competing for public attention and prestige not only in the practical business of making a living but in a debate about education and the right way to run society and one's own life. It is a debate about values and the sources of value. It is a debate about evaluating the contributions made by the cultivation of certain skills. As noted above, it is a debate which already presupposes a society committed to a division of labour. Nowhere in that debate does anyone seriously advocate that we should all, individually, try to cultivate on our own account the arts of poetry, painting, medicine, music, politics, war, etc. In short, the concept of 'art' is *ab initio* the concept of a professionally divided society and it becomes, increasingly, the concept of a literate society. Writing about it is as influential culturally as producing actual works of art. It is in this situation that artspeak, far from passively reflecting the practice of artists, begins to determine what practices shall be granted the status of arts.

3

With glory not their own

Art has been reborn and reached perfection in our own times.

Vasari

The history of artspeak in the European middle ages was shaped by two major developments: the Christianization of culture and the textualization of knowledge. Two powerful medieval institutions, the church and the university, tended to pull in opposite directions as far as the arts were concerned. Whereas the artspeak of the universities continued to be based on the Classical ideal of reason, the artspeak of the church introduced a new set of values altogether. The ecclesiastical artspeak of the middle ages appealed to a double figure of speech: it assimilated worldly riches to spiritual values and, at the same time, the accumulation of ecclesiastical wealth to the glorification of the name of God. The academic artspeak of the middle ages equated the study of the arts with the acquisition of knowledge, and the acquisition of knowledge in turn with the study of ancient texts in which this knowledge was deemed to be preserved.

*   *   *

From late antiquity onwards, Western education became essentially an education based on literacy. The liberal arts were identified with the seven subjects of the normal university curriculum. It is no coincidence that these arts happened to be the arts in which theory and practice matched best: or, to put it slightly differently, the liberal arts were those areas of expertise which had the best theoretical writings to back them up: grammar, logic, rhetoric, arithmetic, geometry, astronomy and music. With the possible exceptions of architecture (Vitruvius) and medicine (Hippocrates, Galen), none of the 'illiberal' arts could boast an Aristotle or a Euclid.

Practising any of the liberal arts thus required a university education (a titular relic of this surviving in the modern 'Bachelor of Arts' degree).

Automatically this drove a deep social wedge between arts that were open to the illiterate and arts that were not. The liberal arts, as the medieval universities taught them, did not include what would nowadays be regarded by many as artistic vocations *par excellence*; for example, painting and sculpture. But they did include subjects such as geometry and astronomy which would not nowadays be reckoned as arts at all. In short, what the medieval education system did was redefine the liberal arts as higher branches of learning, resting on the works of Classical authorities.

Important as the textual basis of education was, however, it does not entirely explain the closed medieval inventory of liberal arts; for there were certainly authoritative texts available for study in other areas (for example, agriculture, with authors including Cato, 'who first taught agriculture to speak Latin', Varro, Columella and Palladius). The key to the universities' concept of liberal arts lies in the division between the *trivium* (grammar, logic and rhetoric) which consisted of arts that were language-based, and the *quadrivium*, based on numbers (with astronomy and music both being treated, in effect, as branches of applied mathematics). It is this partition of the curriculum which reflects unmistakably the extent to which, in the universities at least, the arts had come to be regarded as both applications and developments of human reason, rather than utilitarian pursuits or pleasurable recreations. Activities which had neither a verbal nor a numerical foundation, or demanded a subordination of these to extraneous objectives (as, for instance, agriculture and architecture), fell outside the universities' basic educational brief.

*   *   *

The church took a different view. When in the fourth century AD the emperor Theodosius made Christianity the official state religion, he altered the fate of the arts in Europe more profoundly than could have been imagined at the time. Throughout antiquity the state had been their most powerful patron; but now it was joined by a patron whose influence would be no less dominant in the centuries to come.

The ecclesiastical artspeak of the middle ages is based on the premiss that all human skills are endowed by God, and that therefore the glorification of God is the highest service to which such skills could – and should – aspire. The effect of this was twofold. In the first place, Christianity being a book-based religion, the copying and diffusion of sacred texts, commentaries and other works associated with them became an important priority. To this extent the Christianization of culture reinforced the textualization of knowledge in ways which would have been inconceivable had Christianity had no Bible. On the other hand, all the ancient authorities revered in the universities were pagans as far as the church was concerned. Even the teachings of Aristotle were at various times condemned as heretical, and the whole of Classical literature was seen to be imbued with values that were quite un-Christian. Since Latin was the language of the medieval church in Western Europe, and the best models of Latinity were Classical texts, this posed a problem which the ecclesiastical authorities never quite solved.

In the second place, since Christianity was a religion for the masses and the masses were illiterate, the church encouraged those forms of art through which the Biblical message might be brought home to the people visually. This involved ignoring the Decalogue's prohibition on making 'graven images', and giving priority to strengthening the faith of the faithful. The case for this policy was made out by Pope Gregory in the seventh century AD. But this too was not without problems. A visual image of God verges on a contradiction in terms if God is deemed to be invisible. Early in the fourth century AD Eusebius had condemned the representation of Jesus in Biblical scenes, on the ground that such images reduce the Saviour to the status of a mere man. Basil and Gregory of Nyssa, on the other hand, recommended this practice (in the interest of enlightening the illiterate), as did the Council of Nicaea in 787. But the issue of 'iconoclasm' continued to arouse passions. As late as the ninth century, the emperor Theophilus punished a painter of religious pictures by branding his hands.

This controversy provides the first clear example in the European tradition of a conflict arising between the communicational utility of certain forms of art and the doctrinal implications of the forms themselves. Artspeak is deeply involved in setting up such a conflict. For the problem turns essentially on the assumption that the artist is engaged, by definition, in a mimetic enterprise. Without that assumption, no conflict arises. As historians of the iconoclast controversy point out, what is involved is whether the image is regarded as a mere picture (in which case it can be held to function as a harmless visual aid) or whether in religious art the image is regarded as an 'emanation from the archetype' and thus 'possessed of an inherent sacramental value and power' (Conybeare 1910). This is an issue that Plato, for one, had never considered. Its echoes were to be heard for many centuries in the Christian world, right down to the Reformation and beyond.

The development of religious iconography at various levels in the churches and cathedrals of Europe eventually became one of the most striking manifestations of culture in the history of the West. Religious authorities were willing to spend money on whatever arts contributed to such purposes. Thus Abbot Suger of St-Denis enthuses in the twelfth century about his new church windows illustrating Biblical texts:

> Now, because [these windows] are very valuable on account of their
> wonderful execution and the profuse expenditure of painted glass and
> sapphire glass, we appointed an official master craftsman (*magistrum*) for
> their protection and repair, and also a skilled goldsmith for the gold and
> silver ornaments, who would receive their allowances and what was
> adjuged to them in addition, viz., coins from the altar and flour from the
> common storehouse of the brethren [. . .]. (Panofsky 1979: 77)

Not the riches of Zeuxis, evidently; but a reasonable living in twelfth-century
France, plus the protection of one of the most powerful ecclesiastics of the day.

In the preceding century we hear of Desiderius, the great abbot of Monte
Cassino, sending envoys to Constantinople

> to hire artists who were expert in the art of laying mosaics and
> pavements. (Holt 1957: 13)

Leo of Ostia tells us that

> the degree of perfection which was attained in these arts by the masters
> whom Desiderius had hired can be seen in their works. One would
> believe that the figures in the mosaics were alive and that in the marble
> of the pavement flowers of every color bloomed in wonderful variety.
> (Holt 1957: 13)

Encouraged by this success, Desiderius evidently decided to reintroduce
these arts:

> And since *magistra Latinitas* had left uncultivated the practice of these
> arts for more than five hundred years and, through the efforts of this
> man, with the inspiration and help of God, promised to regain it in our
> time, the abbot in his wisdom decided that a great number of young
> monks in the monastery should be thoroughly initiated in these arts in
> order that their knowledge might not again be lost in Italy. And the most
> eager artists selected from his monks he trained not only in these arts but
> in all the arts which employ silver, bronze, iron, glass, ivory, wood,
> alabaster, and stone. (Holt 1957: 13)

Two points that emerge from Leo's approbatory account are particularly
relevant here. One is that it is difficult to imagine a medieval university
embarking on anything comparable to Desiderius's programme; that is to say,
inviting a band of experts from abroad to come and train students in the
'illiberal' arts. The other is that this reintroduction of lost skills is evidently

regarded as meeting with divine approval. In other words, in the eyes of God – and under appropriate ecclesiastical direction – the illiberal arts are no less acceptable than their liberal sisters.

This is confirmed by the increased esteem accorded to architecture. As Erwin Panofsky points out:

> After Hugues Libergier, the master of the lost St.-Nicaise in Reims, had died in 1263, he was accorded the unheard-of honor of being immortal-ized in an effigy that shows him not only clad in something like academic garb but also carrying a model of "his" church – a privilege previously accorded only to princely donors. And Pierre de Montereau – indeed the most logical architect who ever lived – is designated on his tombstone in St.-Germain-des-Prés as "*Doctor* Lathomorum": by 1267, it seems, the architect himself had come to be looked upon as a kind of Scholastic. (Panofsky 1951: 26)

Whether or not one accepts Panofsky's more ambitious parallel between Gothic architecture and scholasticism, this medieval respect for the master craftsman working for the church is certainly a far cry from the disparagement reflected in Seneca's remark about honouring the statues of the gods but despising their makers.

On reading medieval descriptions of church buildings, altars, reliquaries and other religious artifacts, it seems at first sight that Christianity takes over an artspeak vocabulary that differs little from the secular artspeak of late antiquity. What excites admiration seems to be size (in the case of buildings and other objects), costliness and rarity (in the case of materials), detail and intricacy (in the case of workmanship), and verisimilitude (in the case of depiction). Thus, for example, Robert de Clari's description of Saint Sophia in Constantinople mentions hardly anything, apart from miraculous properties, that would not have featured if he had been describing some royal palace.

> The church of Saint Sophia was entirely round, and within the church there were domes, round all about, which were borne by great and very rich columns, and there was no column which was not of jasper or porphyry or some other precious stone, nor was there one of these columns that did not work cures. There was one that cured sickness of the reins when it was rubbed against, and another that cured sickness of the side, and others that cured other ills. And there was no door in this church and no hinges or bands or other parts such as are usually made of iron that were not all of silver. The master altar of the church was so rich that it was beyond price, for the table of the altar was made of gold and precious stones broken up and crushed all together, which a rich

emperor had had made. This table was fully fourteen feet long. Around the altar were columns of silver supporting a canopy over the altar which was made just like a church spire and it was all of solid silver and was so rich that no one could tell the money it was worth. The place where they read the gospel was so fair and noble that we could not describe it to you how it was made. Then down through the church there hung fully a hundred chandeliers, and there was not one that did not hang by a great silver chain as thick as a man's arm. And there were in each chandelier full five and twenty lamps or more. And there was not a chandelier that was not worth at least two hundred marks of silver. (Holt 1957: 83)

There is nothing here, apart from the reference to cures, which suggests any spiritual dimension in the assessment of the objects described. Doubtless it will be said that crusaders like Robert de Clari looked upon Constantinople through the eyes of looters rather than through the eyes of Christians. And evidently what impresses Robert about Saint Sophia, and is meant to impress his reader, is the magnificence and expensiveness of what he sees. He describes a church which seems to have employed the arts in order to demonstrate that its wealth is not inferior to that of any temporal ruler, and the language he uses to describe it is the artspeak of money and power.

By the time of the Fourth Crusade, the riches of Saint Sophia had long been legendary in Western Europe. In the twelfth century we find Abbot Suger at St-Denis, who is so fond of telling us what expense has been lavished on his own church and its treasures, wondering enviously whether his hoard matches that of Saint Sophia, and asking travellers to compare them. But at least we glimpse a less crassly materialist side to Suger when he muses upon his splendid collection.

Often we contemplate, out of sheer affection for the church our mother, these different ornaments both new and old; and when we behold how that wonderful cross of St. Eloy – together with the smaller ones – and that incomparable ornament commonly called "the Crest" are placed upon the golden altar, then I say, sighing deeply in my heart: *Every precious stone was thy covering, the sardius, the topaz, and the jasper, the chrysolite, and the onyx, and the beryl, the sapphire, and the carbuncle, and the emerald*. To those who know the properties of precious stones it becomes evident, to their utter astonishment, that none is absent from the number of these (with the only exception of the carbuncle), but that they abound most copiously. Thus when – out of my delight in the beauty of the house of God – the loveliness of the many-colored gems has called me away from external cares, and worthy meditation has induced me to reflect, transferring that which is material to that which is immaterial, on the diversity of the sacred virtues: then it seems to me that I see myself dwelling, as it were, in some strange region of the universe which neither exists entirely in the slime of the earth nor entirely in the purity of Heaven; and that, by the grace of God, I can be transported from this inferior to that higher world in an anagogical manner. (Panofsky 1979: 63–5)

A modern authority on Suger suggests that he

foreshadowed the showmanship of the modern movie producer or promoter of world's fairs, and in acquiring pearls and precious stones, rare vases, stained glass, enamels and textiles he anticipated the unselfish rapacity of the modern museum director [. . .]. (Panofsky 1979: 14)

Before swallowing this, one might wish to reflect on the extent to which the point depends rhetorically on casting Suger retrospectively in roles that modern artspeak has made stereotypical. The oxymoron 'unselfish rapacity' is particularly worthy of note: more art is better, however acquired. Suger himself took good care to juxtapose to the verb *adquisivimus* the justificatory adverbial phrase 'with the devotion due to the blessed Denis' (*beato Dionysio debita devotione*).

An apologist for the good abbot might doubtless have been able to make out a case for saying that his art treasures were after all symbols for other-worldly riches, and thus aids to meditation; so that although the artspeak of the church at first sight appears to imply a very materialistic outlook and scale of values, all the qualities of the art objects thus described have to be under-stood as metaphorical. The case for such an apologia would presumably rely on pointing out that such frequently invoked concepts as richness, splendour and preciousness are independently applied to heavenly things and holy visions of them. Thus making a bejewelled golden reliquary for the dry bones of a saint may reflect the limitations of merely human imagination, but, given those limitations, it is an entirely appropriate and reverent gesture.

Sophistry of that order, however, would not have deceived at least one of Suger's contemporaries. In no uncertain terms Bernard of Clairvaux inveighs against

the vast height of your churches, their immoderate length, their super-fluous breadth, the costly polishings, the curious carvings and paintings which attract the worshipper's gaze and hinder his attention [. . .]. (Holt 1957: 19)

Bernard dismisses the excuse that all this display is 'for God's honour'.

> To speak plainly, doth the root of all this lie in covetousness, which is idolatry, and do we seek not profit, but a gift? If thou askest: "How?" I say: "In a strange fashion." For money is so artfully scattered that it may multiply; it is expended that it may give increase, and prodigality giveth birth to plenty: for at the very sight of these costly yet marvelous vanities men are more kindled to offer gifts than to pray. Thus wealth is drawn up by ropes of wealth, thus money bringeth money; for I know not how it is that, wheresoever more abundant wealth is seen, there do men offer more freely. Their eyes are feasted with relics cased in gold, and their purse-strings are loosed. They are shown a most comely image of some saint, whom they think all the more saintly that he is the more gaudily painted. Men run to kiss him, and are invited to give; there is more admiration for his comeliness than veneration for his sanctity. Hence the church is adorned with gemmed crowns of light – nay, with lustres like cart-wheels, girt all round with lamps, but no less brilliant with the precious stones that stud them. Moreover we see candelabra standing like trees of massive bronze, fashioned with marvelous subtlety of art, and glistening no less brightly with gems than with the lights they carry. What, think you, is the purpose of all this? The compunction of penitents, or the admiration of the beholders? O vanity of vanities, yet no more vain than insane! (Holt 1957: 20)

Throughout the middle ages there is no more trenchant indictment of the church's use of the illiberal arts than this.

*   *   *

Such criticisms, understandably, would cut no ice with the artists involved, who were only too pleased with the enhanced standing that collaboration with the Sugers of the day brought them. A revealing example of this is to be found in what is generally acknowledged to be one of the outstanding pieces of Romanesque sculpture: the tympanum of the cathedral of St Lazarus at Autun (Grivot 1976: 3–8). The subject is the Last Judgment. Here we see Christ as judge presiding with serene impassivity over the fates of the saved (on his right) and the damned (on his left). The sculptor has 'signed' his work in Latin: *Gislebertus hoc fecit.* But instead of hiding this claim modestly in a corner of the composition, Gislebertus has positioned his name prominently in the centre, immediately below the towering figure of Christ. Given that the Christian church had replaced Plato's *demiourgos* by the Biblical God as creator of the universe, one might have expected this bold juxtaposition to be regarded as inappropriate or even sacrilegious. But presumably it was not. On the contrary, it must have been approved or even encouraged by the church authorities. It shows a level of recognition of the sculptor as 'maker' (*hoc fecit*) at least on a par with the recognition accorded to authors allowed to append their name to their work in a manuscript colophon.

There could hardly be a clearer example of how the church acted as a counterbalance to the hegemony of the universities as regards recognition of the arts. The indispensable armies of masons, sculptors and architects were the artists who stamped the authoritative imprint of religion on the towns and villages of medieval Europe. They erected the working monuments to Christianity. The products of their practical skills, seen by all, made it possible for an illiterate population to come to terms with a Bible that they could not read and a Latin they had never been taught. Here communication enters the picture. The message was in the end the key to salvation. And whatever conveyed that message and strengthened faith in it was of the highest value.

That conclusion is confirmed, although in a quite different way and in quite different circumstances, by another celebrated example: the Lindisfarne Gospels (now in the British Library in London). Its history shows that this remarkable manuscript, made about the beginning of the eighth century AD in honour of St Cuthbert, was from the beginning regarded as one of the most important possessions of the Lindisfarne monastic community, perhaps second in importance only to the relics of St Cuthbert himself. Three men are credited with its making. The text was copied and illustrated by Eadfrith. The book was made and bound by Ethelwold and Billfrith. The fact that the names of all three have been preserved is indicative of a collaboration between equals. Three arts are recognized and given their due; whereas today two of them would be demoted to the status of mere crafts.

In the tenth century, however, an interlinear translation in Northumbrian was added by one Aldred, presumably because the Latin original was no longer easily understood. Although the translation is itself an important source of philological knowledge concerning early English, the fact remains that to modern eyes its crude addition to the older work is little short of an act of vandalism. No one today, owning or entrusted with the keeping of a unique copy of a *livre d'artiste*, would spoil it by trying to squeeze in another text beside the original. Aldred's crabbed black writing has nothing to recommend it when compared to Eadfrith's elegant half-uncial script and meticulous designs. A superb manuscript composition has been ruined. Why? The answer tells us a great deal about medieval Christian values. All other considerations, artistic as well as non-artistic, are subordinate to one thing: the Christian message. Here again communication enters the picture. It is better that the message be understood than that anyone should admire a work of art for its own sake. For the monks of Chester-le-Street it was more important to have a comprehensible text than an incomprehensible one, however brilliant the workmanship. It is almost as if the translation were felt to be a 'repair' needed in order to restore the lost value of the original. That simple but striking fact points to a crucial difference between the role of the arts in the middle ages and the role of the arts today.

*   *   *

No less striking is the difference between the worldly attitude to the arts taken by a Suger in the twelfth century and the doctrinaire stance the church would adopt after the Council of Trent in the sixteenth. The vicissitudes of Michelangelo's *Last Judgment* bear witness to the latter (Blunt 1940: 103–36). Vasari mentions that a picture of St Sebastian by Fra Bartolommeo had to be removed from a church because it inspired impure thoughts in members of the congregation (Blunt 1940: 117). Presumably this was not Fra Bartolommeo's artistic aim. It needed a significant shift of perspective for the authorities to place unintentional effects before the intrinsic worth of the picture as a work of religious art.

In brief, it would be a mistake to imagine that the Christian church ever had a consistent position on the role of the arts *vis-à-vis* religion. The church never embraced the arts unconditionally, even while treating artistic creation as a God-given gift. What was approved and what was condemned varied according to the ecclesiastical politics of the period. But what remains constant is that when the church said 'Jump!' those artists dependent on ecclesiastical patronage had little option but to jump.

By the time of the Renaissance, the priorities enshrined in the universities' narrowly academic view of the liberal arts were being challenged on all sides. Curiously, however, the distinction itself between liberal and illiberal arts remained uncontested: the argument was about which arts belonged in which category. Furthermore, the old identification of 'liberal' with social superiority – in the sense in which a 'free man' was socially superior to a slave – also remained in place. One of the most interesting confirmations of this comes from the fifteenth-century masons' code known as the *Articles and Points of Masonry* (Holt 1957: 101–4). Here the fourth article prohibits enlisting apprentices who are 'born from bondage blood'. Two reasons are given. One is that this might cause trouble between the master mason and the apprentice's lord. But the second is that masonry is in any case an art that 'took its beginning from great lords' children freely begotten': in other words, it is a 'liberal' art in the ancient sense.

There are various cases of special pleading by the practitioners of one form of art to raise their own status. A notable example is Leonardo da Vinci's attempt to prove the superiority of painting over poetry. Although poetry was not itself among the canonical seven liberal arts of the universities, it presupposed mastery of those arts of verbal expression that were so numbered. Hence a demonstration that painting was an art in no way inferior constituted a challenge to the whole supremacy of language-based skills. According to Leonardo:

> Painting is poetry which is seen and not heard, and poetry is a painting which is heard but not seen. These two arts, you may call them both either poetry or painting, have here interchanged the senses by which they penetrate to the intellect (*penetrare all'intelletto*). (Richter 1949: 58)

What Leonardo goes on to say may strike the modern reader as even more questionable:

> Whatever is painted must pass by the eye, which is the nobler sense, and whatever is poetry must pass through a less noble sense, namely, the ear, to the understanding (*al senso comune*). Therefore, let the painting be judged by a man born deaf, and the poem by one born blind. If in the painting the actions of the figures are in every case expressive of the purpose in their minds, the beholder, though born deaf, is sure to understand what is intended, but the listener born blind will never understand the things the poet describes which reflect honour on the poem, including such important parts as the indication of gestures, the compositions of the stories (*istorie*), the description of beautiful and delightful places with limpid waters through which the green bed of the stream can be seen, and the play of the waves rolling through meadows and over pebbles, mingling with blades of grass and with playful fishes, and similar subtle detail which may as well be addressed to a stone as to a man born blind who never in his life has seen what makes the beauty of the world, namely, light, shade, colour, body, figure, position, distance, nearness, motion, and the rest – these ten ornaments of nature. But the deaf man who has lost a sense less noble, even though he may thereby be deprived of speech (for never having heard anybody talk he could not learn any language), will understand all the actions of the human body better than one who can speak and hear, and he will therefore be able to understand the works of painters and recognize the actions of their figures. (Richter 1949: 58–9)

Here is Leonardo challenging the academic artspeak of the middle ages, and urging recognition of a hierarchy of forms of art based on a hierarchy of the human senses. It goes without saying that any such reform is quite incompatible with the universities' conception of the liberal arts. What is particularly piquant – and humorous – about Leonardo's challenge is his decision to base it on a Classical *topos*. For Leonardo was by no means the originator of the idea that painting and poetry are sister arts. The parallel goes back to classical antiquity, and is often summed up in the tag from Horace: *ut pictura poesis* ('as in painting, so in poetry'). But the way Leonardo develops this thesis shows that he is actually concerned to establish the inferiority of poetry. His first assumption is that the visual sense is 'more noble' than the auditory sense. His second assumption is that painting is figurative painting, and in particular involves the depiction of nature and the human form. His third assumption is that poetry is oral, and likewise involves the description of nature and the human form. His fourth assumption is that anyone born blind can have no genuine grasp of the properties of space or of the form and behaviour of matter in space. His fifth assumption is that language is not essential for our understanding of the visual world. All these assumptions are open to question.

How seriously Leonardo intended the argument to be taken is a moot point. He seems to forget that the art which appeals directly and exclusively to the ear is not poetry but music, and that poetry is as much concerned with the invisible world as with the visible. His case is based on the partial overlap of subject-matter in certain types of poetry and certain types of painting. In short, as a piece of artspeak it is thoroughly unconvincing. But, as in many other cases of dubious theorizing, there is something interesting to be learnt from it.

Why is Leonardo driven to these rather grotesque intellectual contortions? Because, like other Renaissance painters, he was concerned to rescue painting from the low esteem with which, as a non-verbal art, it was still regarded by many contemporaries. Rather than simply argue for parity of status, Leonardo goes on the offensive and tries rather rashly to prove that painting is superior to poetry. That attempt – even if done with tongue in cheek – would be quite inexplicable without the context of an educational tradition which had assumed for centuries that words and numbers held the keys to the highest forms of human knowledge.

*   *   *

It was not the rather specious arguments advanced by Leonardo that constituted the important challenge to the language-based arts but the Renaissance discovery or rediscovery of principles of perspective. This proved to be a significant breakthrough, at least as regards the status of painting. Whether understanding perspective actually produced 'better' pictures was of relatively small importance beside the consideration that it at last put the painter on a par in certain respects with the grammarian and the mathematician.

Although the problem of perspective had been recognized in the ancient world, as is evident from brief comments in Vitruvius's treatise on architecture and his references to writings by others on this subject, it is unclear that any theoretical solution had been worked out until the Renaissance.

There is a contrary view (White 1956) which maintains that there is 'no valid ground for doubting the existence in antiquity of a theoretically founded system of vanishing point perspective'. The controversy cannot be pursued here. What can be said is that if there ever was such a system, the details of it seem to have been lost to subsequent generations. Giving credit for the solution of the 'perspective' problem to Brunelleschi, Uccello or any other candidate is a problem for historians. But as regards its implications for artspeak, history's witness is indisputably Alberti.

Alberti held that painting was 'the best and most ancient ornament of things, worthy of free men' (a clear claim to inclusion among the liberal arts). He begins his influential treatise *De Pictura* of 1435 by saying that he will 'take first from the mathematicians those things with which my subject is concerned'. His underlying assumption is the Aristotelian premiss that the external world is 'the same' for all, but that each observer views it from a unique vantage point. Furthermore, as soon as the observer changes position with respect to the external world, what is seen alters accordingly and consistently (i.e. in a mathematically demonstrable way). It is on this basis that Alberti develops his theory of monocular perspective and the visual 'cone'. He is not in the least worried by what worried Plato; namely, that painting captures only the external appearances of things. On the contrary, Alberti is only too glad to demonstrate that external appearances are exactly what the painter can capture, and by methods no less 'true' than those of the poet or the mathematician. He jokes that Narcissus was the inventor of painting. 'What else can you call painting but a similar embracing with art of what is presented on the surface of the water in the fountain?' (Alberti 1966: 64). Plato would doubtless have agreed, but found that deplorable instead of stimulating.

Alberti does not hesitate to conduct his discussion in a technical vocabulary which includes such terms as 'quadrangle', 'pyramid', 'diagonal', 'polygon', 'cuspid', 'centric point', etc. and even says that 'one who is ignorant in geometry will not understand these or any other rules of painting' (Alberti 1966: 90). It was here that the basis was laid for all modern dialects of artspeak in which the medieval priorities enshrined in the university curriculum are no longer taken for granted, and painting has displaced poetry as the paragon form of art.

This was the crucial turning-point, even though Alberti himself may not quite have realized what he had succeeded in doing. His achievement was to establish painting in a position to which poetry could not lay claim. It gave the painter a new and powerful voice in the forum of artspeak. The domain of the mathematician was that of the quantifiable and the calculable. The domain of the poet extended beyond the quantifiable to sensory experience in general. But it was far from clear how to bridge the gap between these domains. Perspective, as explained by Alberti, provided precisely such a bridge. It linked the abstract truths of geometry to the empirical realities of vision.

Whether it actually did this, or only appeared to, has been debated by modern scholars (Kubovy 1986). But what mattered was that the claim seemed plausible. Even though later Italian theorists such as Lomazzo and Zuccaro rejected in principle the dependence of painting on mathematics (Blunt 1940: 144–5), they did not disprove the optics involved. The importance of this for later artspeak cannot be overestimated. For if there is a common theme running incessantly through Western discourse about art, it is the subservience to nature of all forms of art. At any period we might wish to select for inspection, this is the *communis opinio*. Even Apollinaire, championing the cubists, wrote: 'Great poets and great artists have as their social funtion the constant renewal of nature's appearance in the eyes of men' (Breunig and Chevalier 1980: 63). Artspeak, in the Western tradition, is wedded to the notion that there is a special relationship between the arts and nature. This relationship may be differently interpreted at different times; but the notion that there could be any such thing as art *except* in contradistinction from nature would be incomprehensible. When nature itself is seen as art, or as the work of some divine artist (as in Pope's 'all nature is but art', or Sir Thomas Browne's 'nature is the art of God'), we are dealing with metaphor, or cosmological myth, or both. But what Alberti established – or appeared to establish – was that, in the case of painting and drawing, this was neither metaphor nor myth, but a real, direct and demonstrable link between the picture and what was depicted.

That was what was missing from the writings of his predecessors. No one who has read Cennino Cennini's *Libro dell'Arte*, followed by Alberti's *De Pictura*, can fail to realize that these two works move in entirely different intellectual worlds. The artspeak of both engages with technicalities, but in Cennini's case these are such technicalities as cutting a quill for drawing, tinting papers, preparing a wooden panel, making goat glue, and many more, right down to recommending the best kind of hen's egg for paler tempera (Cennini 1933: 93–4). The *Libro dell'Arte* includes tips about how to depict dead men and wounds and water; but nothing that, by any stretch of the imagination, could be called general principles of painting or drawing. Cennini seems to assume that his apprentice already understands what a two-dimensional likeness is; and if not, so much the worse. Alberti, on the other hand, takes the problem of the two-dimensional image as the central problem that the painter has to tackle, and presents a geometrical solution to it.

It may be far from obvious to a modern mind, familiar with the achievements of photography, how radically this threatened to undermine the hegemony of the verbal arts. Hitherto the accuracy with which a painting could depict the visible world had depended entirely on the fallible eye and hand of the individual painter; while a verbal description was likewise liable to all the potential errors of attention and observation of the individual describing what nature offered for inspection. Henceforth, however, painting according to the rules of perspective could achieve optical verisimilitude with mathematical precision; whereas no such advance in technique could guarantee a similar improvement in the resources of verbal description. Nature, it began to seem, was after all more accessible to the art of the painter than to the art of the poet. That, at least, is how it must have appeared to Alberti.

Leonardo, however, belonged to a later generation. That generation had had time to realize that Alberti's case for painting had made no impression at all upon the university professors who controlled the syllabus of the liberal arts: they showed no sign of rushing to welcome professors of painting to their academic ranks. What we see in Leonardo's recourse to Neoplatonist mumbo-jumbo about the superiority of the eye over the ear is a desperate and incoherent attempt to make a theory of sense perception into a theory of art.

4

The rise and fall of beauty

A thing of beauty is a joy for ever.
John Keats

During Alberti's lifetime there was no falling off in church patronage of the arts. (If anything, it increased.) Nevertheless, Christianity had already begun to be seen historically as having discriminated against certain forms of art. The notion of the Renaissance as a 'rebirth' of art is intimately connected to this accusation. We see it quite clearly in the fifteenth-century *Commentarii* of Lorenzo Ghiberti. Ghiberti himself had been commissioned to make statues of St John the Baptist and St Matthew for Or San Michele, as well as bronze reliefs for a baptismal font at Siena; so he was no stranger to the benefits of ecclesiastical patronage. Nevertheless, the church hardly emerges with credit from his historical account, which runs as follows:

> The Christian faith was victorious in the time of Emperor Constantine and Pope Sylvester. Idolatry was persecuted in such a way that all the statues and pictures of such nobility, antiquity and perfection were destroyed and broken to pieces. And with the statues and pictures, the theoretical writings, the commentaries, the drawing and the rules for teaching such eminent and noble arts were destroyed. In order to abolish every ancient custom of idolatry it was decreed that all the temples should be white. At this time the most severe penalty was ordered for anyone who made any statue or picture. Thus ended the art of sculpture and painting and all the teaching that had been done about it. Art was ended and the temples remained white for about six hundred years. (Holt 1957: 152–3)

Ghiberti does not explain what brought about a change in the church's attitude, but dates the revival of painting from the time of Cimabue and Giotto. The accuracy of Ghiberti's account is not what is at issue here. Two things are more important for our present purposes. The first is that here we have a form of Renaissance artspeak in which it is taken for granted that by 'art' is meant (i) an active practice or practices with a social history, and (ii) a category that can be identified across time, even after a lapse of many centuries. Both assumptions are necessary in order to make sense of Ghiberti's otherwise problematic claim that art came to an end at one point in history, only to be revived at a later point. From this perspective, clearly, the mere survival of works from an earlier age does not count as artistic continuity. This is very much a 'guild' view of the arts: the guilds are implicitly cast in the role of guardians and guarantors of artistic practice.

No less important, however, is the assumption that the identity of the category 'art' across time is independent of any adventitious social forces (such as ecclesiastical approval or disapproval) which may from age to age impinge on particular practices. Recognition of this continuity, although implicit in the 'guild' view of art, goes far beyond it. In other words, it would be a mistake to treat it as no more than a projection of the guilds' view of their own importance. Evidently professional artists in fifteenth-century Italy realized that the church could as easily sponsor suppression as encouragement of the arts. Wealthy private patrons were beginning to exercise a growing influence as an alternative source of commissions. What this amounted to was that the limited religious rationale for artistic activity which had imposed certain restrictions on art in the middle ages was being challenged by broader humanist views of the artist's role in society. What was needed, in short, was a language which could both accommodate and justify a new degree of independence for the arts, but which did not cut them off from their Classical (i.e. pre-Christian) antecedents.

The secular post-Renaissance artspeak that eventually emerged was based on a small number of key concepts, of which 'beauty' was by far the most important. Although the notion of beauty plays no part in his theory of perspective, Alberti had striven to make it relevant to the aims of painting, architecture and sculpture. As Blunt points out (Blunt 1940: 15ff.), the way Alberti did this was to qualify the goal of imitating nature by imposing on the artist the additional duty of selecting from nature only its most beautiful creations and ignoring what was ugly. Alberti rejects the view that ideas of beauty vary according to changes in fashion and taste.

[. . .] Alberti believes that man recognizes beauty not by mere taste, which is entirely personal and variable and judges of attractiveness, but by a rational faculty which is common to all men and leads to a general agreement about which works of art are beautiful. Beauty, in fact, is detected by a faculty of artistic judgement. (Blunt 1940: 17)

In his treatise on architecture (*De Re Aedificatoria*) Alberti develops his account of beauty by claiming that recognition of the beautiful involves disregarding whatever in nature goes to extremes or exceeds normal proportions. Blunt comments:

> This identification of the beautiful with the typical in nature implies a belief in the Aristotelian view of nature as an artist striving towards perfection and always hindered from attaining it by accident. According to this view the artist, by eliminating the imperfections in natural objects and combining their most typical parts, reveals what nature is always aiming at but is always frustrated from producing. Alberti has simplified Aristotle's views on this point, for he arrives at the type-beauty by a process of more or less arithmetical averaging, whereas in Aristotle some faculty nearer to the imagination is involved. (Blunt 1940: 18)

What evidently motivated Alberti's theory was the desire to weld the ancient notion of art as imitation to the humanist assumption that it falls to the artist to find in nature itself – not in the demands of church or society – the highest ideal of art. Beauty was the answer proposed. This answer was to dominate European thinking about the arts for three centuries. But since a great deal that nature offers for imitation is by no stretch of the imagination beautiful, this was an answer that was bound to cause problems. And whether it could be reconciled with the demands of religion upon the arts was in any case another question.

*   *   *

Beauty, nevertheless, had a long reign in European artspeak. As late as 1929 the *Encyclopædia Britannica* was still reassuring its readers that 'the function of art is the creation of beauty' (*Encyclopædia Britannica*, 14th ed., vol. 2, p. 441). But in so doing that learned work was speaking a language already out of date. Twentieth-century artspeak was no longer bound by the constraints that had obtained in the philosophical debates of the eighteenth and nineteenth centuries, when the notions of art and beauty had become almost impossible to disentangle. The twentieth-century reaction was stated succinctly by Herbert Read, when he complained that the 'identification of art and beauty is at the bottom of all our difficulties in the appreciation of art' (Read 1949: 17). That identification was a hangover from the Renaissance. Between the generations of Alberti and of Read we can trace the rise and fall of beauty, one of the most curious episodes in the history of Western artspeak.

If the identification of art and beauty is a mistake, as Read supposed, it is certainly not a mistake of which Plato or Aristotle were guilty. The criterion of beauty plays little or no role in their thinking about the arts at all. Iris Murdoch may be overstating the case when she says that 'beauty as a spiritual agent, in Plato, excludes art' (Murdoch 1977: 32) and suggests that the kind of designs found on 'unpretentious wallpaper' is about as much as Plato would have approved for the citizens of his Republic (Murdoch 1977: 19); but it is clear that for Plato beauty has more to do with love than with artistic aims or practices. *Kallos* is the object of *eros*.

For Aristotle too beauty does not seem to feature as a distinct artistic objective. In his view it is associated particularly with the idea of proportion between parts. Thus he argues in chapter 7 of his *Poetics* that it is not possible for a very minute creature or an immensely large creature to be beautiful. In the first case this is because the creature is too small for the human eye to distinguish its proportions, and in the second case because the eye cannot take it in all at once. But this curious excursus into the theory of beauty is simply in the interests of making the rather humdrum analogical point that a good story must be neither too short nor so long as to defeat the memory of the audience. It is useless, as one modern analyst has observed, 'out of the fragmentary observations that Aristotle has left us, to seek to construct a theory of the beautiful' (Butcher 1951: 162).

Whether the ancient doctrine that art imitates nature was rightly understood by those who later tried to reinstate it in post-Renaissance Europe is open to question. What ancient writers say in many places makes it difficult to believe that we are dealing with anything as simplistic as 'making a copy of' natural forms, colours, etc. For although recognizing 'mimetic arts' (*mimetikai technai*) as a class seems immediately to imply that there are non-mimetic arts as well, the notion of mimesis also seems to be applied to cases where there is no obvious or straightforward attempt to copy anything. Thus music and dancing are treated in antiquity as mimetic.

All this is at first sight puzzling, until it is realized that possibly the ancient doctrine that art imitates nature is best construed as meaning that the artist, in order to make anything at all, must follow the *methods* of nature. This applies just as much to making some mundane utilitarian object for everyday use as it does to making a statue of Zeus to stand in the temple at Olympia. In both cases the methods of nature have to be followed because attempts to run counter to them will result in failure. Human making, in short, – in whatever domain it may be – cannot go 'against' nature.

Striking support for this interpretation comes from the way in which – bizarrely, it may seem, to modern readers – Socrates in Plato's *Cratylus* presents his argument for a mimetic theory of names. He assumes that names must originally have been 'made' or 'given' and seeks to inquire into the rationale of this process. The hypothetical creator responsible is referred to simply as the 'law-giver' or 'name-giver' (*nomothetes*). How, then, were names originally

made? Socrates supposes that, like anything else, names might be well made or
badly made. He proceeds to argue that the same principles apply to the making
of names as to other kinds of making. And the secret of this process is to
conform to the requirements laid down by nature. It is useless to try to cut
something if the instrument is not sharp, because that runs counter to the
nature of cutting, or to burn something that is not by nature combustible.

> Socrates: [. . .] The artisan must discover the instrument naturally
> fitted for each purpose and must embody that in the material of which
> he makes the instrument, not in accordance with his own will, but in
> accordance with its nature. He must, it appears, know how to embody in
> the iron the borer fitted by nature for each special use.
> Hermogenes: Certainly.
> Socrates: And he must embody in the wood the shuttle fitted by nature
> for each kind of weaving.
> Hermogenes: True.
> Socrates: For each kind of shuttle is, it appears, fitted by nature for its
> particular kind of weaving, and the like is true of other instruments.
> Hermogenes: Yes.
> Socrates: Then, my dear friend, must not the law-giver (*nomothetes*) also
> know how to embody in the sounds and syllables that name which is
> fitted by nature for each object? Must he not make and give all his names
> with his eye fixed upon the absolute or ideal name, if he is to be an
> authoritative giver of names? (*Cratylus* 389 C, D; Fowler 1926: 27)

Whatever one may think of this argument today, it is clear that we are
dealing with a strategy of imitating nature in the sense of copying or conforming to the way nature does things. We have to bore, weave, etc. in the
manner in which nature teaches us that such things can be done. This is a
pragmatic maker's strategy, in which beauty and the appreciation of beauty
play no part, except – self-evidently – in those cases where the maker wishes
to make something beautiful. Whether names are 'beautiful' or not is a
question that does not even arise.

Now part of the problem with bringing beauty into the picture at all, at
least in modern times, is that according to popular wisdom beauty is 'in the
eye of the beholder'. This appears to make its recognition – and hence the
recognition of any work of art based on beauty – a purely subjective matter.
For many people, therefore, disagreements about art and beauty are in the end
futile, because the individual is the ultimate arbiter in every particular case
and no one can judge on behalf of anyone else. However, this subjective
notion of beauty is not that which was automatically accepted either in the
Renaissance or in earlier discussions of the subject.

It is with 'the last great philosopher of antiquity' that beauty comes seriously into the reckoning as a feature of art. For Plotinus, in the third century AD, beauty, far from being in the eye of the beholder, 'is of the Divine and comes Thence only' (*Enneads* V.8.13). The Soul 'includes a faculty peculiarly addressed to Beauty' (*Enneads* I.6.3). There is a 'Principle that bestows beauty on material things' (*Enneads* I.6.2). This Principle 'is something that is perceived at the first glance, something which the Soul names as from an ancient knowledge and, recognizing, welcomes it, enters into unison with it' (*Enneads* I.6.2). The notion that beauty emanates from a divine source is manifestly relevant to the iconoclastic quarrel that caused such bitterness in the early Christian church.

Plotinus compares two blocks of stone, lying side by side. One is uncarved and the other sculpted into the form of a god or a beautiful human figure. The stone sculpture, he argues, is not beautiful *as stone*, for in that respect it is no better than the uncarved block. The beauty resides in the idea or form introduced by the sculptor and not in the material itself. But that beauty in turn comes from within the sculptor and is transferred to the stone only imperfectly, depending on how well the sculptor has been able to overcome the resistance of the material. Plotinus rejects the notion that the mimetic arts are to be disparaged for imitating and points out that their creative scope goes far beyond just copying what the artist sees. Thus Phidias's *Zeus* (probably the most famous statue in Graeco-Roman antiquity) was not based on observation but upon the sculptor's own idea of what Zeus would look like if he chose to make himself visible. For Plotinus beauty in nature is likewise a reflection of some creative source. This source is divine, and the divine is itself transcendent beauty, 'a beauty beyond all thought'.

From this mystico-religious point of view, Plato would seem to have got hold of the wrong end of the stick about art and imitation. In artistic mimesis one should see not the benighted attempts of human beings to mimic, but the residual and imperfect (but still marvellous) transference of superhuman inspiration through specially gifted human agents. This implies a complete reversal in the role of the artist, bringing it into line with a view which was to be much more congenial to later theories of artistic 'genius'.

*   *   *

Post-Renaissance attempts to shift evaluation of the arts from a basis in reason or service to God to a new basis in beauty were a leap from the frying pan into the fire; and they have muddled much subsequent thinking on the subject. Beauty eventually became the focal point of what is nowadays called 'aesthetics'. The term *Aesthetik* was invented in 1735 by the German philosopher Alexander Gottlieb Baumgarten, who originally conceived the field as covering that part of psychology concerned with sensory experience and feelings (the term being coined from a Greek word meaning 'perception'). It was not long, however, before aesthetics came to be considered as more particularly focused on inquiry into the nature of art and beauty. In the late eighteenth century the third edition of the *Encyclopædia Britannica* (1797, vol.2) informed its readers that

> the general theory of the polite arts is nothing more than the knowledge of what they contain that is truly beautiful and agreeable; and it is this knowledge, this theory, which modern philosophers call by the Latin name of *æsthetica*.

An important figure in reconciling the doctrine that art imitates nature with a theory of beauty was the French philosopher Charles Batteux, who published an influential book on the arts in 1746 (*Les Beaux-Arts réduits à un même principe*). As the medieval universities had done, Batteux established a hierarchy among the arts, but on a rather different basis from the medieval one. According to Batteux, the arts fall into three classes. There are arts that serve the practical needs of humanity. There are arts designed to give pleasure. And there are arts that do both. The first of these classes Batteux called the 'mechanical arts' and the second the 'fine arts' (*les beaux-arts*). These are: music, poetry, painting, sculpture and dance. The third class of arts, which are designed both for utility and for pleasure, includes architecture and eloquence.

Batteux is concerned only with the fine arts, and these, as the term *beaux-arts* implies, he conceives as concerned with beauty in its various forms. But, like all other arts, the *beaux-arts* are based on nature. According to Batteux, the arts are related to one another and to nature as follows. The mechanical arts exploit nature as it is; the fine arts do not exploit nature but imitate it; and arts of the third class both exploit and improve on nature. So nature is the foundation of all arts. It will be seen from this that Batteux construes the notion of 'imitation' in a way that is hardly compatible with the broader interpretation of mimesis discussed above. What the fine arts do, according to Batteux, is transfer features observed in nature to objects in which those features *do not naturally occur*. In this sense, imitation runs counter to nature. Batteux's simplest example is sculpture. Here the sculptor transfers, for example, the features of the human form into a block of marble, which does not itself possess those features naturally. It is the same example as Plotinus uses, but minus Plotinus's metaphysics.

*   *   *

Why did it seem plausible to philosophers of Batteux's generation to claim that certain arts are set off from others by their engagement in the pursuit of beauty? This cannot be understood without taking into account that during the eighteenth century artspeak comes increasingly into competition with sciencespeak over a whole range of human activities. The categorial distinction between 'art(s)' and 'science(s)' has become one of the axiomatic foundations of modern Western culture. But during the middle ages such a distinction had been unclear, to say the least. Much terminological uncertainty was the result. Robert Kilwardby's thirteenth-century treatise *De ortu scientiarum* might just as well have been called *De ortu artium*. For Leonardo, there was already a distinction between arts and sciences, although his attempts to clarify this distinction are not among the most lucid passages in his writings. He claims that no human investigation can be called a true science (*vera scientia*) unless it be capable of mathematical demonstration (Richter 1949: 23). But whereas he counts painting as a science, being based on geometry, he denies this status to sculpture, on the rather curious ground that all the sculptor has to do is measure the limbs of the figures in order to represent them accurately (Richter 1949: 94).

Even Bacon does not draw the distinction between sciences and arts very clearly or consistently. It is true that he contrasts 'sciences' with 'arts mechanical', but apparently on the basis of their characteristic forms of development.

> [. . .] in arts mechanical the first deviser comes shortest, and time addeth and perfecteth; but in sciences the first author goeth farthest, and time leeseth and corrupteth. (Bacon 1605: I.iv.12)

He cites artillery, sailing and printing as examples to substantiate the first point, while the second is illustrated by the way in which 'the philosophies and sciences' of Aristotle, Plato, Democritus, etc. were misunderstood and 'imbased' by later commentators. This seems to suggest that whereas the arts proceed by empirical trial and error over a period of time, the sciences are set up fully constituted through the insights of great thinkers. But that is hardly borne out by the way in which, elsewhere in *The Advancement of Learning*, Bacon refers to inquiries which have not yet been 'reduced' to a science. He writes, for instance, of the 'philosophical' study of words that it is currently handled '*sparsim*, brokenly'; but adds, 'though I think it very worthy to be reduced into a science by itself' (Bacon 1605: II.xvi.4).

On the subject of 'the science of medicine', he says that 'if it be destituted and forsaken by natural philosophy, it is not much better than an empirical practice' (Bacon 1605: II.ix.1), and elsewhere complains that it is only a 'conjectural' art, which leaves much room for 'imposture'.

For almost all other arts and sciences are judged by acts, or masterpieces, as I may term them, and not by the successes and events. The lawyer is judged by the virtue of his pleading, and not by the issue of the cause; the master of the ship is judged by the directing his course aright, and not by the fortune of the voyage; but the physician, and perhaps the politique, hath no particular acts demonstrative of his ability, but is judged most by the event; which is ever but as it is taken: for who can tell if a patient die or recover, or if a state be preserved or ruined, whether it be art or accident? (Bacon 1605: II.x.2)

Not only does Bacon astonish us by this assimilation of medicine to politics, but he offers no criteria by which one might begin to distinguish a 'scientific' cure from mere quackery. It is even open to question whether Bacon thinks such criteria are available.

By the second half of the eighteenth century, however, we find Joseph Priestley in no doubt at all about the difference between arts and sciences, or about the relationship between them.

All *Art* is founded on *Science*, or the knowledge of the materials employed in them and their fitness for the uses to which they are applied. And though many arts were found out by accident, without any previous knowledge of those parts of nature on which they depend, it is useful to trace arts to their natural principles, and to be able to comprehend the reason of the beneficial effects they have in practice: for this knowledge leads to the means of perfecting and extending the arts. (Priestley 1762: 4–5)

The difference between Priestley and Bacon is not merely a difference of century. Priestley, unlike Bacon, was an experimental chemist. He continues:

Thus *Medicine* is the art of curing diseases, and though the methods of cure, in most particular cases, might be found out by chance, and many tollerably successful practitioners never trouble themselves about the theory of Physic, yet cures certainly depend upon the nature of the human body and of the medicines applied to it: since their mutual action, with the beneficial consequences of it, must have been agreeable to the usual course of nature: and it is worthy the attention of the professors of that art to consider it as a science, to trace out the natural causes of the disorders of the human body, to understand the properties of the several articles of the *materia medica* they make use of, and consider their mutual influences; since, knowing the subject they act upon, and those they act with, they may be better able to predict and procure any desired event. (Priestley 1762: 5–6)

Although Priestley is concerned to define what a 'science' is, his definition marks a watershed in Western artspeak. It is a clear adumbration of the modern polar opposition between art and science, which depends on setting apart what can be known through strictly controlled and verifiable observation of nature, and what cannot. Whatever in the old domain of art could be assigned to the former category would be thus assigned: the rest would be relegated to an inferior status, in search of some different rationale. It was in that situation that beauty seemed to many to offer the foundation for such a rationale, and hence an alternative to the burgeoning programme of the natural sciences.

*   *   *

In France the same problem was tackled head-on in the eighteenth century in Diderot and d'Alembert's monumental *Encyclopédie ou Dictionnaire Raisonné des Sciences, des Arts et des Métiers* (1751). The title itself leads one to expect an attempt to justify the three key terms *science, art* and *métier*, and the editors do not shirk it. What was to become the classic Enlightenment statement of the definition and function of the arts is set out in the *Discours préliminaire*.

> This concludes our enumeration of the principal forms of knowledge. If we now envisage all of them together, and look for general viewpoints which will serve to distinguish them, we find that the purely practical ones have as their aim the execution of something, while others, merely speculative, confine themselves to the examination of their object and the contemplation of its properties; and finally others derive from the speculative study of their object the use to which it may be put in practice. Speculation (*spéculation*) and practice (*pratique*) constitute the principal difference distinguishing the *Sciences* from the *Arts*; and it is roughly on that basis that one or the other of these names has been given to each of our forms of knowledge. However, it must be confessed that our ideas on this topic are not entirely fixed. Often it is hard to know which name to give to most of those cases where speculation unites with practice; and there is, for example, daily dispute in the schools over whether Logic is an art or a science: the problem might be quickly resolved by answering that it is both simultaneously. How many questions and troubles would be spared if we at last settled the meaning of words in a clear and precise manner! (*Encyclopédie*, 1751: I. xii)

This last remark about definitions is an echo of Locke, one of the Enlightenment's intellectual heroes. (The question of whether logic is a science or an art is taken up again in the article *Logique*, and there dismissed as 'puerile', the reason being, apparently, that it can be considered either, depending on how you define the terms *science* and *art*.) The argument in the *Discours préliminaire* continues as follows:

> In general the name *Art* can be given to any system of knowledge that can be reduced to rules that are positive, invariable and independent of caprice or opinion, and it would be permissible to say in this sense that several of our sciences are arts, when considered in their practical aspects. But as there are rules for the operations of the mind or soul, so there are too for those of the body, that is to say for those restricted to external bodies and needing the hand alone for their execution. Hence the division into liberal (*libéraux*) and mechanical (*méchaniques*) Arts, and the superiority accorded to the former over the latter. (*Encyclopédie*, 1751: I. xii–xiii)

At this point the *Discours préliminaire* introduces one of the favourite hobby-horses of the *Encyclopédie*: the injustice of the low esteem in which manual labour is held and the concomitant injustice of the way those who spend their lives in manual labour are treated.

Finally, the liberal arts are subdivided as follows:

> Among the liberal Arts that have been reduced to principles, those which aim at the imitation of Nature have been called fine Arts (*beaux Arts*), because their main objective is pleasure (*agrément*). But that is not the only reason which distinguishes them from the more necessary or more useful liberal Arts, such as Grammar, Logic and Morals. These latter have fixed, established rules, that any man may pass on to another: whereas the practice of the fine Arts consists mainly in invention which follows none but the laws of genius; the laws that have been written down respecting those Arts apply strictly to their mechanical part; their effect is like that of the Telescope, helpful only to those who can see. (*Encyclopédie*, 1751: I. xiii)

As an example of Enlightenment artspeak, the whole of this discussion is revealing. Beauty is allowed in only under the auspices of *agrément*; not as a motivating force in its own right. And at last, but no less grudgingly, we see an acknowledgment that superior forms of art owe something to a factor that goes beyond either utility or rationality. It seems to pass unnoticed by the editors of the *Encyclopédie* that, as soon as we think about its implications, their reluctant appeal to 'genius' brings the whole rule-based taxonomy of arts and sciences tumbling down.

                    *   *   *

Letting genius out of the bottle was probably the biggest mistake ever made in attempts to construct a rational theory of art. Just how disastrous its consequences might be was not yet obvious to the Enlightenment thinkers, and did not become fully apparent until the twentieth century. They may have thought it was harmless enough, because Plato had recognized the phenomenon many centuries earlier, without apparently letting it play havoc with his theory of art. In the *Phaedrus* Socrates argues that there is such a thing as 'possession by the Muses'.

> When this seizes upon a gentle and virgin soul it rouses it to inspired expression in lyric and other sorts of poetry, and glorifies countless deeds of the heroes of old for the instruction of posterity. But if a man comes to the door of poetry untouched by the madness of the Muses, believing that technique alone will make him a good poet, he and his sane compositions never reach perfection, but are utterly eclipsed by the performances of the inspired madman. (*Phaedrus* 245; Hamilton 1973: 48)

What must not be overlooked is the condition Plato imposes on this recognition of superior achievement: it is a form of madness. The whole passage is part of an argument designed to show that madness is not necessarily evil. For Plato, however, madness is something we cannot understand, just as we cannot understand how oracles are able to prophesy or spells work miracle cures. So there is no point inquiring into it.

That will not do at all for the *philosophes* of the eighteenth century. And by construing 'taste' as the passive counterpart of 'genius' they make things even more difficult for themselves. Do you have to be mad to appreciate a good poem?

*   *   *

Immanuel Kant did not immediately succumb to what one acerbic critic calls 'the Baumgarten corruption' (Dixon 1995). That is to say, he did not at first accept the legitimacy of applying the term *aesthetic*, in defiance of its etymology, to matters of artistic judgment. As Dixon points out, there is a dismissive footnote in the *Critique of Pure Reason* which puts Baumgarten down in no uncertain terms:

> The Germans are the only people who at present use this word to indicate what others call the critique of taste. At the foundation of this term lies the disappointed hope, which the eminent analyst, Baumgarten, conceived, of subjecting the criticism of the beautiful to principles of reason, and so of elevating its rules into a science. But his endeavours were vain. (Kant 1787: 42)

By the time he wrote his *Critique of Judgment*, however, Kant had changed his mind and there plunges headlong into the aesthetics of taste. The trouble with explaining art by reference to beauty (as in the case of the *beaux-arts*) is that the concept of beauty is no less – and perhaps more – problematic than the concept of art itself. Kant in the *Critique of Judgment* drew a distinction between two kinds of beauty. Kant, like Alberti, did *not* think beauty was in the eye of the beholder. For him, that was an idea based on confusing what is beautiful with what gives pleasure. But pleasure is entirely a personal matter, whereas beauty is not.

> As regards the *agreeable* everyone acknowledges that his judgment, which he bases on a private feeling and by which he says that he likes some object, is by the same token confined to his own person. Hence, if he says that canary wine is agreeable he is quite content if someone else corrects his terms and reminds him to say instead: It is agreeable to *me*. This holds moreover not only for the taste of the tongue, palate, and throat, but also for what may be agreeable to any one's eyes and ears. To one person the color violet is gentle and lovely, to another lifeless and faded. One person loves the sound of wind instruments, another that of string instruments. It would be foolish if we disputed about such differences with the intention of censuring another's judgment as incorrect if it differs from ours, as if the two were opposed logically. Hence about the agreeable, the following principle holds: *Everyone has his own taste* (of sense). (Kant 1790: I.i.1. §7)

Thus far, Kant is merely confirming traditional wisdom: *de gustibus non disputandum*. But he continues:

> It is quite different (exactly the other way round) with the beautiful. It would be ridiculous if someone who prided himself on his taste tried to justify [it] by saying: This object (the building we are looking at, the garment that man is wearing, the concert we are listening to, the poem put up to be judged) is beautiful *for me*. For he must not call it *beautiful* if [he means] only [that] *he* likes it. Many things may be charming and agreeable to him; no one cares about that. But if he proclaims something to be beautiful, then he requires the same liking from others; he then judges not just for himself, but for everyone, and speaks of beauty as if it were a property of things. (Kant 1790: I.i.1.§7)

Many people will doubt that Kant is right about this, but let us leave that issue on one side. He then goes on to claim that there are two kinds of beauty. One of these he calls 'free beauty' (*pulchritudo vaga*) and the other 'dependent beauty' (*pulchritudo adhaerens*). In the case of free beauty there is no concept of what the object ought to be like. In the case of dependent beauty, on the other hand, there is; and beauty is relative to an idea of perfection in that kind of object. He supplies the following examples:

> Flowers are free natural beauties. Hardly anyone apart from the botanist knows what sort of thing a flower is [meant] to be; and even he, while recognizing it as the reproductive organ of a plant, pays no attention to this natural purpose when he judges the flower by taste. Hence the judgment is based on no perfection of any kind, no intrinsic purposiveness to which the combination of the manifold might refer. Many birds (the parrot, the humming-bird, the bird of paradise) and a lot of crustaceans in the sea are [free] beauties themselves [and] belong to no object determined by concepts as to its purpose, but we like them freely and on their own account. Thus designs *à la grecque*, the foliage on borders or on wallpaper, etc., mean nothing on their own: they represent [*vorstellen*] nothing, no object under a determinate concept, and are free beauties. What we call fantasias in music (namely, music without a topic [*Thema*]), and indeed all music not set to words, may also be included in the same class.
>
> When we judge free beauty (according to mere form) then our judgment of taste is pure. Here we presuppose no concept of any purpose for which the manifold is to serve the given object, and hence no concept [as to] what the object is [meant] to represent; our imagination is playing, as it were, while it contemplates the shape, and such a concept would only restrict its freedom.
>
> But the beauty of a human being (and, as kinds subordinate to a human being, the beauty of a man or woman or child), or the beauty of a horse or of a building (such as a church, palace, armory, or summerhouse) does presuppose the concept of the purpose that determines what the thing is [meant] to be, and hence a concept of its perfection, and so it is merely adherent beauty. (Kant 1790: I.i.1.§16)

Again, many may question Kant's analysis, but the kind of distinction he is drawing is very relevant to one kind of thinking about artistic judgment. For it is the basis of one way of trying to justify distinguishing between arts and crafts. The crux of the matter is whether the product is to be judged in relation to function or in relation to something else. A pair of shoes may be a good (i.e. well made) pair of shoes without necessarily being pretty, elegant, attractive, or having any of the qualities one associates with being pleasing to the senses, except possibly that they should be comfortable to wear. But as soon as people begin to think more about how shoes look than whether they are well made or not, then arguably they are beginning to judge them as art objects rather than as products of craftsmanship.

Whatever one may think of Kant's account of beauty, it would be perverse to claim that great painters, for example, have been solely concerned with the depiction of beautiful things or the production of beautiful decoration. And no less perverse to claim that great poets have had no other end in view than describing beautiful scenes or actions or people. These considerations point to a serious lacuna in the attempt to establish a mimetic theory of art solely on the basis of beauty.

Batteux, like Alberti, had attempted to meet this difficulty by claiming that refined forms of art imitated only *la belle nature* (hence *les beaux-arts*). This (supposedly) emancipated the artist from slavish imitation of whatever nature might offer. The editors of the *Encyclopédie* were taken in by the notion of *la belle nature* too. In the *Discours préliminaire* we are told that human beings have two kinds of feeling (*sentiment*) that preside over their judgments. One is directed towards moral truth and is called 'conscience'. The other kind of feeling is:

> particularly concerned with the imitation of *la belle Nature* and what are called 'beauties of expression' (*beautés d'expression*). It is enraptured by sublime, striking beauties, discerns with subtlety hidden beauties, and rejects mere appearances thereof. Often it will even pronounce severe judgments without bothering to go into the reasons in detail, because these depend on a mass of ideas that are difficult to develop on the spur of the moment, and even more difficult to convey to others. It is to this kind of feeling that we owe taste and genius, distinguished one from the other in that genius is the feeling that creates, and taste the feeling that judges. (*Encyclopédie* 1751: I. xiv)

Here we see the *Encyclopédistes* struggling with a theoretical dilemma thrown up by their own artspeak. Having let genius out of the bottle, they try to control it by putting it under the aegis of the imagination (which, as far as they are concerned, is one of the three basic mental capacities of mankind; or, as they put it, the three 'different ways in which the soul operates on the objects of its thoughts', the other two being memory and reason). But this actually makes matters worse. It forces them to the conclusion that there are only three 'general objects' of human knowledge. The first two are History (presided over by the memory) and Philosophy (presided over by reason). And the third is *les Beaux-arts*, these being 'born of the imagination'. Reason takes priority over imagination, they explain, because imagination is a creative faculty, and before the mind can create anything it has to reason about what it already knows. As a piece of *a priori* psychology, this is hardly convincing.

Less convincing still is their assumption that even genius operates according to rules, but that these rules have not so far been satisfactorily ascertained.

Thus in the imitation of Nature, even invention is subject to certain rules; and these are the rules which mainly form the philosophical part of the *Beaux-arts*, hitherto somewhat imperfect, because it can only be the work of genius, and genius prefers creation to discussion. (*Encyclopédie* 1751: I. xvi)

The assumption seems to be that if only we could get a genius to introspect, reflect and tell us how exactly the great work of art was produced, it would emerge that it was after all produced according to rules, although different rules than those followed in more mundane examples of art. It is interesting to note what is happening to the concept of 'rules' (*règles*) in the course of this discussion. In typical Enlightenment fashion, it slides almost imperceptibly down the slippery slope from 'precept' to 'constitutive order'. The former was the basis for the traditional concept of art, while the latter provides the ground for believing that even genius can be reduced to rationality. The difference is that 'rules' of one kind are conscious, formulable, and testable while 'rules' of the other kind are not. Believing adamantly in both is, to be sure, an impressive display of faith in a rational, rule-governed universe (whether thus ordained by God or by Nature). But it is not exactly an impressive demonstration of humble empiricism.

More awkwardly, it involves construing imagination as a kind of speeded-up intuitive reasoning, rather than as a separate faculty. Even the *Discours préliminaire* is obliged to admit that scientists use imagination. 'Imagination in a Geometer who creates is no less active than in a Poet who invents.' But again this admission is accompanied by no recognition of the damage inflicted on the whole structure of human knowledge as the *Encyclopédie* presents it. For if imagination – and hence both 'genius' and 'taste' – are also involved in the development of science, its allegedly special role in the arts – and specifically the *Beaux-arts* – seems to be undermined. We no longer see clearly why the *Beaux-arts* are *beaux*, or why geometry is not included in their number. More particularly since 'rational' figures – the circle, the equilateral triangle, the sphere – were and are widely regarded as intrinsically beautiful.

*   *   *

The other problem with invoking beauty to explain the *beaux-arts* was that many works of art seemed dedicated to representing things that were by no stretch of the imagination 'beautiful'. One way of dealing with this that became popular in the artspeak of the eighteenth century was to invoke, alongside and *contrasting with* beauty, the notion of 'the sublime'. This expression (frowned on by Johnson in his *Dictionary* as a Gallicism) was the usual English translation of the Greek *hupsos*, as it occurred in the title (*Peri hupsous*) of an anonymous rhetorical treatise long attributed mistakenly to Longinus and probably dating from the first century AD (Roberts 1907: 1–23). Whether the term *sublime* is a misleading translation of *hupsos* is a question scholars have raised: its use seems in part to be based on the fact that the usual Latin title for this treatise was *De Sublimitate*. Roberts points out that there are seventeenth-century English translations such as *Of the Height of Eloquence* (John Hall, 1662) and *Of the Loftiness or Elegancy of Speech* (John Pulteney, 1680) and gives it as his opinion that it is to be regretted that these titles 'have not held their ground' (Roberts 1907: 210). He suggests that the title of Edmund Burke's well-known *Philosophical Enquiry into the Origin of our Ideas of the Sublime and Beautiful* may have added to the confusion. It is certainly questionable whether Burke is discussing the same 'sublime' as his Greek predecessor, whose treatise appears to have been written in response to a work on that subject by Caecilius. Although 'Longinus' is writing in the rhetorical tradition and concerned primarily with verbal expression, it is clear that he regards the sublime as emanating from a source beyond the words themselves. It 'flashes forth' and 'scatters everything before it like a thunderbolt' (Roberts 1907: I.4). In itself it does not need the support of words. 'Sublimity is the echo of a great soul' (Roberts 1907: IX.2). Thus, for example, the silence of Ajax in the underworld (*Odyssey*, Book XI) is 'more sublime than words' (Roberts 1907: IX.2). The effect of the sublime is to overwhelm us. The question thus arises whether it is a product of art or of nature. In the view of 'Longinus', the sublime cannot be produced to order by rhetorical devices; but nevertheless there are rules of art which apply to it, and these rules can at least determine what is incompatible with the sublime.

In the seventeenth century, Boileau produced an influential translation of 'Longinus' into French and put his own gloss on the notion of the sublime. This appeared in the same year (1674) as Boileau's own *Art poétique*, a text widely regarded as the Gospel of the French neo-classicists. But a quite different interpretation of the sublime emerged when Edmund Burke revamped the idea in the mid-eighteenth century. Burke's interpretation is purely psychological:

Whatever is fitted in any sort to excite the ideas of pain, and danger, that is to say, whatever is in any sort terrible, or is conversant about terrible objects, or operates in a manner analogous to terror, is a source of the *sublime*; that is, it is productive of the strongest emotion which the mind is capable of feeling. (Burke 1759: VII)

This is at first sight quite unconvincing. What Burke has defined seems to be something considerably different both from the sublime of 'Longinus' and from the sublime of modern sensibilities. If Burke were right, one might nowadays typically expect to find the sublime in horror movies or descriptions of Nazi concentration camps. But anyone who did apply the term 'sublime' to such cases would probably be suspected of perverted inclinations.

Was Kant nearer the mark when he claimed that the beautiful and the sublime are alike in that 'we like both for their own sake' (Kant 1790: I.i.2.§23)? He goes on to argue that we need to distinguish between the 'mathematically' and the 'dynamically' sublime. The mathematically sublime is bound up with the concept of magnitude: the sublime in this sense is that which is 'absolutely great' or 'great beyond all comparison' or 'that in comparison with which everything else is small'. The dynamically sublime involves the idea of might or power. Here Kant moves closer to Burke, describing the dynamically sublime as exciting fear. (However, he is careful to stipulate that not everything that excites fear will be judged sublime.) Thus thunder and lightning, volcanoes and hurricanes are for Kant sources of the sublime; provided, that is, we can contemplate them from a safe distance and are not actually threatened by them. For this contemplation makes us realize that although we are impotent in the face of the forces of nature, nevertheless we are also superior to nature inasmuch as our mind can make its own independent judgments concerning natural phenomena. Sublimity 'does not reside in anything of nature, but only in our mind'.

In the wake of Kant, more tortuous and abstruse attempts to interrelate or distinguish the sublime and the beautiful were forthcoming from German philosophers. According to Schiller (*On the Aesthetic Education of Man*, 1795) art is the means by which it is possible to reconcile two basic instincts or drives in the human being, one towards the sensuous (*Stofftrieb*) and the other towards the formal (*Formtrieb*). This reconciliation, manifested in art, is the work of the 'play-drive' (*Spieltrieb*), with beauty or living form as its object.

> The object of the sense impulse, expressed in a general concept, may be called *life*, in the widest sense of the word; a concept which expresses all material being and all that is immediately present in the senses. The object of the form impulse, expressed generally, may be called *shape*, both in the figurative and in the literal sense; a concept which includes all formal qualities of things and all their relations to the intellectual faculties. The object of the play impulse, conceived in a general notion, can therefore be called *living shape*, a concept which serves to denote all aesthetic qualities of phenomena and – in a word – what we call *Beauty* in the widest sense of the term. (Schiller 1795: xv.76)

Beauty, asserts Schiller, as the consummation of man's humanity, is neither exclusively life, nor exclusively form, but living form. But when art attains the sublime, it becomes pure form.

> In a truly beautiful work of art the content should do nothing, the form everything; for the wholeness of Man is affected by the form alone, and only individual powers by the content. However sublime and comprehensive it may be, the content always has a restrictive action upon the spirit, and only from the form is true aesthetic freedom to be expected. Therefore, the real artistic secret of the master consists in his *annihilating the material by means of the form* [. . .]. (Schiller 1795: xxii.106)

*   *   *

Schopenhauer's artspeak is based on quite different metaphysical premisses, contrasting the world as idea with the world as will (*Die Welt als Wille und Vorstellung*, 1819; 2nd ed. 1844). The world as idea is the world we construe as an apparently orderly universe, subject to what Schopenhauer calls the 'principle of sufficient reason'. The world as will is the world as it appears in the light of our wants and needs, which arise ultimately from human deficiencies and hence from suffering. The first of these worlds Schopenhauer identifies with the world of science, while the second is the world of art. Only art is concerned with what is 'essential'.

> But what kind of knowledge is concerned with that which is outside and independent of all relations, that which alone is really essential to the world, the true content of its phenomena, that which is subject to no change, and therefore is known with equal truth for all time, in a word, the *Ideas*, which are the direct and adequate objectivity of the thing in-itself, the will? We answer, *Art*, the work of genius. (Schopenhauer 1844: III.36)

In Schopenhauer's view the function of art is communication of timeless ideas.

> It repeats or reproduces the eternal Ideas grasped through pure contemplation, the essential and abiding in all the phenomena of the world; and according to what the material is in which it reproduces, it is sculpture or painting, poetry or music. Its one source is the knowledge of Ideas; its one aim the communication of this knowledge. (Schopenhauer 1844: III.36)

This line of thinking leads Schopenhauer to defining art in the following terms:

We may, therefore, accurately define it as the *way of viewing things independent of the principle of sufficient reason*, in opposition to the way of viewing them which proceeds in accordance with that principle, and which is the method of experience and of science. (Schopenhauer 1844: III.36)

Here we can see, with the hindsight of history, a remarkable attempt to reconcile the post-Renaissance division between sciences and arts with the Platonic concept of timeless Forms or Ideas, but effected in such a way as to appropriate for the arts – not the sciences – a concern for eternal truths.

The will also plays an important role in Schopenhauer's understanding of the difference between the beautiful and the sublime. He claims:

What distinguishes the sense of the sublime from that of the beautiful is this: in the case of the beautiful, pure knowledge has gained the upper hand without a struggle, for the beauty of the object, *i.e.*, that property which facilitates the knowledge of its Idea, has removed from consciousness without resistance, and therefore imperceptibly, the will and the knowledge of relations which is subject to it, so that what is left is the pure subject of knowledge without even a remembrance of will. On the other hand, in the case of the sublime that state of pure knowledge is only attained by a conscious and forcible breaking away from the relations of the same object to the will, which are recognised as unfavourable, by a free and conscious transcending of the will and the knowledge related to it. (Schopenhauer 1844: III.39)

*   *   *

The theory of beauty was plunged into even murkier philosophical waters by Hegel. For Hegel, beauty in art is 'the representation of the absolute'. Exactly what that is supposed to mean still puzzles philosophers. Here, in short, we have a form of artspeak in which the preferred mode of explanation seems to be *obscurum per obscurius*. No light is thrown on this by Hegel's contention that the history of art in Europe has been one of steady decline since the classical period in Greece. Nor is it clarified by Hegel's restriction of 'aesthetics' to artistic beauty. The beauty of nature is thus excluded from consideration. Artistic beauty, according to Hegel, is in any case on a higher level than natural beauty, since it proceeds from the mind: 'and by as much as the mind and its products are higher than nature and its appearances, by so much the beauty of art is higher than the beauty of nature' (Hegel 1835: I.[II]). But in what sense is artistic beauty 'higher' than natural beauty? Hegel's not altogether perspicuous answer to this is:

> Mind, and mind only, is capable of truth, and comprehends in itself all that is, so that whatever is beautiful can only be really and truly beautiful as partaking in this higher element and as created thereby. In this sense the beauty of nature reveals itself as but a reflection of the beauty which belongs to the mind, as an imperfect, incomplete mode of being, as a mode whose really substantial element is contained in the mind itself. (Hegel 1835: I.[III])

As Hegel scholars have pointed out, the logic of this explanation is sadly defective (Inwood 1993: 100), but it seems to echo some of the ideas of late Mannerist art theory in Italy (Blunt 1940: 140ff.).

From the incessant wrangles that broke out concerning these matters no consensus emerges. As regards the sublime, Monk summarizes the situation in the eighteenth century by saying: 'No single definition of the term would serve in any single decade for all writers' (Monk 1935: 233). As a supplement to the doctrine of beauty, therefore, the sublime proved to be more of a hindrance than a crutch. For it left the distinction between beauty and sublimity quite unclear. And much the same might be said of various other notions, including 'the picturesque' and 'the pathetic', that tend to trail along behind the concept of beauty in critical discussions of the time.

Nor does the situation improve in the early nineteenth century. If anything, the advent of Romanticism made it worse. Keats's celebrated line 'Beauty is truth, truth beauty', Shelley's definition of a poem as 'the very image of life expressed in its eternal truth' and Coleridge's definition of beauty as 'multeity in unity' can sound like enthusiastic attempts to out-Hegel Hegel. In fact, one might say that by the time the Romantics had added their emotive contributions, artspeak in Europe had degenerated into a state where one could no longer be sure what was meant by the terms *art* and *beauty* until the individual writer had given his own definition. And often, it need hardly be added, not even then.

Part II
ARTSPEAK MODERN

Part I

MASTER GUIDING

5

Artspeak and the machine

The artist [. . .] becomes a machine harnessed to another machine.

Delacroix

Today no one doubts that the Industrial Revolution was also a cultural revolution, the most far-reaching in the history of the Western world. The dependence of modern society on the machine and its products is visible everywhere in the proliferation of tools, materials and modes of transport, not to mention the non-stop flow of mechanically relayed images, words and music that is the all but inescapable concomitant of contemporary urban life. But these were long-term consequences which did not appear overnight.

The Industrial Revolution changed Western attitudes to the arts in three fundamental ways. In the first place, it made many practitioners of the more humble utilitarian arts redundant, or turned them into factory workers. In this way it accentuated the prestige of the 'fine arts', which remained aloof from the impersonality of mechanization. At the same time, it gave rise to a nostalgia for the lost or vanishing world of traditional skills in which the trained hand and eye presided over the creation of well-made things. Thus emerged the modern concept of 'crafts', as distinct from 'arts'. By the end of the nineteenth century William Morris was already cast in the role of socialist reformer, opponent of mass production, and champion of the 'handicrafts-men'. The 'Arts and Crafts' movement was launched with the aim of rescuing the craftsman from becoming a 'a mere cog on the wheel of machinery' (Cumming and Kaplan 1991: 6).

The second respect in which the Industrial Revolution impinged on the arts was more radical. By making available new tools and techniques, it raised the question of the extent to which the whole field of artistic endeavour might be enlarged by the emergence of new creative forms impossible in a pre-machine age.

Third, by promoting the prospect that all society's practical needs would eventually be met by the products of industrialization, it ensured the success of the notion that art incurred no social responsibilities or functions. Thus art was free to exist, as Constant's famous dictum put it, solely 'for art's sake'.

*   *   *

Morris started from a conception of art that had virtually nothing in common with that of any of the nineteenth-century German philosophers. In an article published in 1885, he answered his own question 'What is art?' as follows:

> Art is man's embodied expression of interest in the life of man; it springs from man's pleasure in his life; pleasure we must call it, taking all human life together, however much it may be broken by the grief and trouble of individuals; and as it is the expression of pleasure in life generally, in the memory of the deeds of the past, and the hope of those of the future, so it is especially the expression of man's pleasure in the deeds of the present; in his work. [. . .]
>
> I repeat that the chief source of art is man's pleasure in his daily necessary work, which expresses itself and is embodied in that work itself; nothing else can make the common surroundings of life beautiful, and whenever they are beautiful it is a sign that men's work has pleasure in it, however they may suffer otherwise. (Briggs 1962: 140–1)

Here there is no appeal to 'the absolute' or other recondite abstractions, but to the familiar circumstances of everyday working-class existence. For the deplorable state of art in his day, Morris had no hesitation in blaming the fact that workers 'are forced by the commercial system to live, even at the best, in places so squalid and hideous that no one could live in them and keep his sanity without losing all sense of beauty and enjoyment of life'. He makes a point of refusing to blame the decline of art on the advance of science.

> The theory that art is sick *because* people have turned their attention to science is without foundation. It is true that science is allowed to live because profit can be made of her, and men, who must find some outlet for their energies, turn to her, since she exists, though only as the slave (but now the rebellious slave) of capital; whereas when art is fairly in the clutch of profit-grinding she dies, and leaves behind her but her phantom of *sham* art as the futile slave of the capitalist. (Briggs 1962: 142)

What exactly Morris meant by 'sham' art is not altogether clear. But one may hazard a guess that it was not far removed from what Roger Fry later called 'pseudo-art'. In an article entitled 'Art and Socialism', Fry speaks, in tones reminiscent of Morris, of 'a populace whose emotional life has been drugged by the sugared poison of pseudo-art'. According to Fry, 'in the present commercial State' we see that 'such handiwork as is not admirably fitted to some purely utilitarian purpose has become inanely fatuous and grotesque' (Fry 1920: 61). And he explains what he means by describing in detail what he sees while sitting in a railway-station refreshment room.

> The space my eye travels over is a small one, but I am appalled at the amount of "art" that it harbours. The window towards which I look is filled in its lower part by stained glass; within a highly elaborate border, designed by some one who knew the conventions of thirteenth-century glass, is a pattern of yellow and purple vine leaves with bunches of grapes, and flitting about among these many small birds. In front is a lace curtain with patterns taken from at least four centuries and as many countries. On the walls, up to a height of four feet, is a covering of lincrusta walton stamped with a complicated pattern in two colours, with sham silver medallions. Above that a moulding but an inch wide, and yet creeping throughout its whole with a degenerate descendant of a Graeco-Roman carved guilloche pattern; this has evidently been cut out of the wood by machine or stamped out of some composition – its nature is so perfectly concealed that it is hard to say which. Above this is a wall-paper in which an effect of eighteenth-century satin brocade is imitated by shaded staining of the paper. Each of the little refreshment-tables has two cloths, one arranged symmetrically with the table, the other a highly ornate printed cotton arranged "artistically" in a diagonal position. In the centre of each table is a large pot in which every beautiful quality in the material and making of pots has been carefully obliterated by methods each of which implies profound scientific knowledge and great inventive talent. Within each pot is a plant with large dark green leaves, apparently made of india-rubber. This painful catalogue makes up only a small part of the inventory of the "art" of the restaurant. (Fry 1920: 62–3)

One wonders how many readers of Fry a generation later – or even two – could put their hands on their hearts and swear that they had never seen, either in a station refreshment room or elsewhere, such a décor as Fry describes. Morris was already dead when Fry wrote this. But what he would certainly have approved is Fry's next comment: 'Not one of these things has been made because the maker enjoyed the making' (Fry 1920: 63).

Fry is doubtless a more sophisticated pleader of causes than Morris was. But in Morris's blunt rhetoric we already see a renewal of artspeak more invigorating than anything in the previous three hundred years. He is closer than anyone since Aristotle to the ancient notion of art as hands-on expertise, but to this he adds – and this is his first originality – the notion of beauty as the expression of personal pleasure in the exercise of this expertise. For him, an ugly environment automatically goes hand-in-hand with the lack of pleasure. 'This absence of pleasure is the second gift to the world which the development of commercialism has added to its first gift of a propertyless proletariat' (Briggs 1962: 142). And his second originality is linking a theory of beauty to a theory of social conditions, and in such a way that the revival of beauty is seen as an inescapable concomitant of the regeneration of society. By its own internal logic this leads straight to Morris's conclusion that 'Socialism [. . .] is the only hope of the arts'.

It is at first sight surprising that someone with Morris's views does not reject altogether the distinction between 'fine art' and what he calls 'popular art' (or sometimes the 'decorative arts', or even 'the lesser arts'). But on closer inspection it becomes clear that Morris's acceptance of an elite 'fine art', supported by wealthy patrons, is simply acceptance of a social *fait accompli*. For him the division between fine art and popular art is a symptom of a divided society:

it is only in latter times, and under the most intricate conditions of life, that they have fallen apart from one another; and I hold that, when they are so parted, it is ill for the Arts altogether: the lesser ones become trivial, mechanical, unintelligent, incapable of resisting the changes pressed upon them by fashion or dishonesty; while the greater, however they may be practised for a while by men of great minds and wonder-working hands, unhelped by the lesser, unhelped by each other, are sure to lose their dignity of popular arts, and become nothing but dull adjuncts to unmeaning pomp, or ingenious toys for a few rich and idle men. (Briggs 1962: 84–5)

This comes from the text of Morris's first public lecture (1878) and it shows his third and greatest originality: a vision of the indivisible unity of the arts, which stands in the greatest possible contrast to that pursuit of special status for a few selected arts which had preoccupied the theorists of the preceding age.

The artspeak of the eighteenth and early nineteenth centuries bears scarcely a trace of recognition of the great social changes that were already taking place. When reading the tediously abstract discussions of beauty that abound, one would hardly imagine (since the fact is never mentioned) that 'dark Satanic mills' and other features of the new industrial landscape had already invaded the paintings of the time. As Klingender points out in *Art and the Industrial Revolution* (Klingender 1968), painters of note, including Joseph

Wright of Derby and J. M. W. Turner, were clearly impressed by the changes that industry had brought to the range of paintable subjects. Ignoring the countless injunctions to select from the visible world only what was 'beautiful', these painters addressed what they saw, directly and without qualms, and clearly did not think they were compromising any artistic principle in doing so. But it is not surprising that this development is stoutly ignored by all the principal theoreticians of beauty, from Batteux to Hegel. For taking it seriously into account would have led them into a predicament. The paradox was noted by Delacroix, who exclaims in his *Journal* (15 September 1854): 'What a strange thing painting is, pleasing us by representing objects which could never please!' In brief, either a case would need to be made for claiming that part of the function of the arts involves transforming what is ugly in itself into beauty; or else it would have to be maintained that the dark, satanic mills were not so dark and satanic after all. Could they even have been sublime?

It was not simply the landscape that industrialization altered. Nor was painting the only art form to feel its effects. Both points are well illustrated by Zola's novel *Germinal* (1885). But already a generation earlier a future British prime minister had written a novel which acknowledged the miserable plight of industrial workers. In Disraeli's *Sybil* (1845) the author describes the evening exit of miners from the mine as the pit delivering its 'bondsmen':

> The plain is covered with the swarming multitude: bands of stalwart men, broad-chested and muscular, wet with toil, and black as the children of the tropics; troops of youth, alas! of both sexes, though neither their raiment nor their language indicates the difference; all are clad in male attire; and oaths that men might shudder at, issue from lips born to breathe words of sweetness. Yet these are to be, some are, the mothers of England! (Disraeli 1845: III.i)

The narrator comments:

> But can we wonder at the hideous coarseness of their language, when we remember the savage rudeness of their lives? Naked to the waist, an iron chain fastened to a belt of leather runs between their legs clad in canvas trousers, while on hands and feet an English girl, for twelve, sometimes for sixteen hours a day, hauls and hurries tubs of coal up subterranean roads, dark, precipitous, and plashy; circumstances that seem to have escaped the notice of the Society for the Abolition of Negro Slavery. (Disraeli 1845: III.i)

It is not a coincidence that the author of this passage, some thirty years later, introduced in Parliament the famous Education Act of 1876. The passage itself implicitly anticipates Morris's point: where is the scope for recognition of beauty and art in degrading lives of such 'savage rudeness'? Likewise, Morris's disdain for the aloofness of 'fine art' is foreshadowed when Disraeli in the same chapter, having just described the mine's child labourers of four and five years of age, chides the fashionable artists of his day:

Sir Joshua, a man of genius and a courtly artist, struck by the seraphic countenance of Lady Alice Gordon, when a child of very tender years, painted the celestial visage in various attitudes on the same canvas, and styled the group of heavenly faces guardian angels!

We would say to some great master of the pencil, Mr. Landseer, or Mr. Etty, go thou to the little trappers and do likewise! (Disraeli 1845: III.i)

Disraeli's targets here are not selected at random. Sir Joshua Reynolds's *Discourses*, delivered between 1769 and 1790 during his presidency of the newly founded Royal Academy, have been described as 'the first major body of artistic theory produced in England' (Rogers 1992: ix). The very conservative approach to painting that these discourses present was still regarded by many in Disraeli's day as authoritative. For Reynolds, the imitation of nature is essential to the training of a painter and the goal of that art is to capture idealized forms of beauty (a position denounced by William Blake in his annotations to the *Discourses* as 'folly'). What Disraeli's shrewd anecdote about Lady Alice Gordon draws attention to is the social level at which Reynolds looked for his models. (This is the picture of 'cherub heads' which Ruskin would later laud to the skies as 'an incomparably finer thing than ever the Greeks did': Ruskin 1869: 419.) Sir Edwin Landseer, Queen Victoria's favourite painter, had a reputation based largely on his ability to paint animals – particularly dogs – in a way that appealed to the sentimental side of the Victorian public, while William Etty specialized in idealized nudes. Both were Academicians. In this trio of cases that Disraeli has chosen to mention we see the implied criticism of a narrowness of vision characteristic of the Establishment art of the day (a narrowness not in the optical but in the social sense, although both might be said to apply to Reynolds's idealized cherubs).

What Disraeli says supports Morris's contention that the so-called fine arts have drifted out of touch with the basic conditions required for the arts to flourish. Morris writes:

I do not believe in the possibility of keeping art vigorously alive by the action, however energetic, of a few groups of specially gifted men and

their small circle of admirers amidst a general public incapable of understanding and enjoying their work. (Briggs 1962: 143–4)

This would have shocked all those who, in discussing artistic achievement,
had placed so much emphasis, both theoretically and historically, on the role
of 'genius'. Art, for Morris, is not something created by the geniuses of this
world, but by everyone. Here it is noticeable that Morris avoids the term
genius and deliberately speaks of 'specially gifted men'. They are just that:
men, and not demigods or divinely inspired individuals. Not that Morris
denies the value of their special gifts. He would no more think of belittling the
abilities of an outstanding athlete or great statesman. His point is, rather, that
special gifts alone cannot ensure the survival of the arts.

In his more pessimistic moments Morris seems prepared to envisage the
demise of the arts if social conditions do not improve. However, he proclaims
his faith in their eventual revival, with the advent of social equality:

I am so confident that this equality will be gained, that I am prepared to
accept as a consequence of the process of that gain, the seeming disap-
pearance of what art is now left us; because I am sure that that will be
but a temporary loss, to be followed by a genuine new birth of art
[. . .]. (Briggs 1962: 144)

Here, for the first time since the Renaissance, the notion of 'rebirth'
reappears in the discourse of artspeak.

*   *   *

The paradigm case of a new art form that would not have been possible before
the Industrial Revolution is photography. Although the eighteenth century
had seen advances in the techniques employed for producing and reproduc-
ing visual images, such as Senefelder's invention of lithography, they did not
pose any serious threat to the established hierarchy of the arts. Photography
did, since it deployed mechanical means in order to 'imitate nature' more
accurately and reliably than the unaided eye and hand of the painter. It is
therefore interesting to examine the reluctance which attended the acceptance
of photography as art, and in some quarters still does. When in November
2000 the Turner Prize was awarded to Wolfgang Tillmans, *The Independent*
carried a banner headline announcing that the judges had contrived yet
another 'shock' for the public: namely that 'the winner is a *photographer*'. The
last word was in italics, and the article describing the award began by spelling
out the news to its readers: 'Photography is art.' This status, according to
David Lister, the paper's Media and Culture editor, was now 'official',

following the decision of the Turner judges, who included the Director of the Tate Gallery as their chairman, to honour a photographer. There were other reasons why the award to this particular photographer might have been regarded as controversial; but the 'shock' to which *The Independent* referred was unmistakably that of at last admitting photography as an art form at all.

The furore in the art world of the nineteenth century caused by the advent of photography bears eloquent witness to the power of artspeak. For in fact various machines and mechanized processes had been used by practitioners of the arts for many centuries. (The potter's wheel is nothing if not a machine, by means of which the potter achieves a control of form and texture which would be otherwise unattainable.) Only when, with the Industrial Revolution, the concept 'mechanical' had become virtually an obscenity in contemporary artspeak was it possible for a painter like Delacroix to refer disparagingly to the daguerreotype as *'cet art de la machine'*. But the whole debate would have been groundless had it not been for the continued harping by theorists on the traditional artspeak theme of the imitation of nature. Ironically, when a machine appeared that could copy the appearances of nature with unprecedented accuracy, everyone rushed to find some more exalted or more devious function for art to fulfil. In the end, it took the camera to put Aristotle out of business.

Right from the beginning, painters had been impressed by the unmatched fidelity with which the photographic process could render visual detail. In 1839, on a visit to Daguerre's studio in Paris, the American painter and inventor Samuel Morse was astonished by it. According to Morse, in a letter published in the *New York Observer* in that year, the daguerreotype surpassed everything previously achieved as regards optical accuracy.

> [. . .] the exquisite minuteness of the delineation cannot be conceived. No painting or engraving ever approached it. (Welling 1978: 7)

What proved the point, in Morse's eyes, was that in the picture of a street that Daguerre had shown him, blurred lettering on a placard in the distance became perfectly legible under a magnifying glass.

> In a view up the street, a distant sign would be perceived, and the eye could just discern that there were lines of letters upon it, but so minute as not to be read with the naked eye. By the assistance of a powerful lens, which magnified 50 times, applied to the delineation, every letter was clearly and distinctly legible, and so also were the minutest breaks and lines in the walls of the buildings, and the pavements of the street. The effect of the lens upon the picture was in great degree like that of the telescope in nature. (Welling 1978: 7)

The comparison is telling: for who, in 1839, would dispute that the telescope is a more powerful optical instrument than the human eye? Here again the tables were turned against traditional artspeak. And that was the nub of the crisis, rather than the images that photographers managed to produce (which at that time lacked any representation of colour). Like many revolutions, it hinged on what would be admitted and what would be denied, rather than on what was actually happening. Like many revolutions, it would be won by progressives who offered little more than the defeat of an indefensible position.

In the same year, 1839, François Arago prepared a report on the daguerreotype process for the Chambre des Députés in Paris. In this report, as might be expected, the emphasis is placed on the scientific utility of the invention. Arago points out that had it been available in 1798, on the occasion of the Napoleonic invasion of Egypt (*'notre immortelle expédition'*), the labour of copying without error the millions of hieroglyphs at Thebes, Memphis and Karnak, and making pictorial records of the monuments themselves, could have been accomplished at a fraction of the cost. Like Morse, he claims that the daguerreotype surpasses in fidelity the works of the most skilful painters. In particular, since photographic images are based on known geometrical principles it would have been possible to record not only the visual appearance of the Egyptian monuments but, simultaneously, their exact dimensions, including those which would have proved difficult to ascertain by any other form of measurement. As regards the relevance of Daguerre's invention for the fine arts, Arago quotes the well-known painter Paul Delaroche (recently commissioned to execute the immense mural in the lecture theatre of the École des Beaux-Arts). The daguerreotype, according to Delaroche, carries to perfection the application of certain essential conditions of art (*'certaines conditions essentielles de l'art'*). He rejects the fear that it will prove harmful to painters and engravers, and anticipates on the contrary that it will be of great value in the preparatory work of pictorial composition. In short, it represents *'un immense service rendu aux arts'* (Frizot and Ducros 1987: 11–14).

Another prominent painter of the day, however, expressed crucial reservations. In 1850, in the preface to a book on drawing by Élisabeth Cavé, Delacroix wrote:

> The daguerreotype is more than a tracing, it is a mirror of the object; certain details, nearly always neglected in drawings from nature, assume great and characteristic importance, and thus introduce the artist to a complete knowledge of construction: the shadows and lights can be seen in their true character, that is to say with the exact degree of firmness or softness, a very delicate distinction and one without which there is no relief. One must nevertheless not forget that the daguerreotype must be

looked upon only as an interpreter (*traducteur*) whose job is to initiate us more intimately into nature's secrets; for, in spite of its astonishing reality in certain respects, it is still but a reflection of the real, a copy, in some sense false through being exact (*fausse en quelque sorte à force d'être exacte*). The monstrosities it presents are rightly shocking, although they are literally those of nature herself; but these imperfections, which the machine faithfully reproduces, do not shock our eyes when we look at the model without this intermediary; the eye, without our knowing it, corrects the unfortunate precision of rigorous perspective; it already takes on the task of an intelligent artist: *in painting, spirit speaks to spirit and not science to science*. This reflection of Mme Cavé's is the old quarrel of the letter and the spirit: it is a criticism addressed to those artists who, instead of treating the daguerreotype as advice, as a kind of dictionary, make it the picture itself. They believe they are much closer to nature when they have taken the trouble not to alter too much in their painting the result that had first been obtained mechanically. They are overwhelmed by the disheartening perfection (*la désespérante perfection*) of certain effects they find on the metal plate. The more they strive to resemble it, the more they discover their weakness. Their work is thus only the necessarily cold copy of that copy which is imperfect in other respects. The artist, in a word, becomes a machine harnessed to another machine. (Frizot and Ducros 1987: 21–2)

To the Platonistic theme of copying a copy, Delacroix here adds the extra indictment of copying *mechanically*: and this was to become a leitmotif in the accusations of those who sought to deny that photography was an art. *Mechanical* now takes on a different sense from that associated with the traditional expression *mechanical arts*. In the artspeak of the nineteenth century, *mechanical* would be a pejorative term. In other words, the scientific precision of the photographic process was turned against it: its greatest strength became its greatest weakness. But it is interesting to observe how this reversal was based on an underlying syllogism derived from an earlier period. The concept of *belle nature* already assumed that the artist must select, rather than imitate nature slavishly. Since a mechanical process, by its nature, is incapable of selection, it would follow by this reasoning that any resulting image of nature, whatever else it might be, cannot be art. Thus *mechanical* and *artistic* enter into a mutually defined semantic opposition. But concealed behind this opposition is the old assumption that art is concerned with beauty. Once this assumption is dropped – that is, if art is concerned with depicting the full range of nature and not just its perfections – then the case against photography collapses.

Elsewhere Delacroix develops his misgivings about photography and the representation of reality. In his *Journal*, on 1 September 1859, he writes:

The most confirmed realist, when he attempts to render nature in a painting, is compelled to use certain conventions of composition or of execution. If it is a question of composition he cannot take an isolated fragment, or even a series of fragments, and make a picture out of them. He is bound to set some limits to the idea if the beholder's mind is not to hover uncertainly over an area, which has unavoidably been cut out from a large whole; if it were not so, there would be no art. In a photograph of a view you see no more than a portion cut from a panorama; the edges are as interesting as the centre of the picture and you have to guess at the scene of which you are shown merely a fragment, apparently chosen at random. In such a fragment, the details have as much importance as the principal object and, more often than not, obstruct the view because they occur in the foreground. (Wellington and Norton 1951: 414–15)

This is an interesting example of the ways in which artspeak can lead almost imperceptibly into false logic. Convinced that photography, as opposed to art, is 'mechanical' in the sense discussed above, Delacroix evidently supposes that this necessarily deprives the photographer of any control over composition. It is an early example of what might be called the 'camera-cannot-lie' fallacy, which later generations would come to regard as extremely naive. But it is all of a piece with Delacroix's earlier condemnation of reducing the artist to 'a machine harnessed to another machine'. Delacroix evidently believed that the machine controls its user, rather than the user controlling the machine. This notion in turn is part of a more widespread 'mechanophobia' that developed during the nineteenth century as a reaction against the less desirable effects of the Industrial Revolution, and survives into the twentieth in such forms as Chaplin's *Modern Times* and other satires on factory production.

Delacroix maintains that it is only the fact that the human eye does *not* see things in same way as a machine-made lens that makes photographs themselves acceptable:

Photography would be unbearable (*insupportable*) if our eyes were as accurate as a magnifying glass; we should see every leaf on a tree, every tile on a roof, and on each tile, the moss, the insects, etc. (Wellington and Norton 1951: 415)

This sounds almost like a direct retort to Morse's praise of photography for operating with the fidelity of a telescope. Delacroix goes on to repeat his earlier criticism that too much accuracy distorts:

The confirmed realist corrects this inflexible perspective which, because of its very accuracy, falsifies our view of objects (*cette inflexible perspective qui fausse la vue des objets à force de justesse*).

Even when we look at nature, our imagination constructs the picture: we do not see blades in a landscape, nor minute blemishes in the skin of a charming face. Our eyes are fortunately incapable of perceiving such infinitesimal details and only inform the mind what it needs to see. Again, the mind itself has a special task to perform without our knowledge; it does not take into account all that the eye offers, but connects the impressions it receives with others that have gone before, and depends for its enjoyment on conditions present at the time. This is so true, that the same view will not produce the same impression when seen from a different angle (*saisie sous des aspects différents*). (Wellington and Norton 1951: 415)

Here is another old theme (art as the offspring of imagination) pressed into service in order to disparage photography. How, we are invited to ask ourselves, could we suppose that a machine has either memory or imagination?

For Delacroix the point about suppressing intrusive detail evidently applies to the fine arts in general, and not just to painting. Relentlessly he pursues this topic into the realms of literature. The 'inferiority' of modern writing, he claims, is due to the attempt to say everything ('*la prétention de tout rendre*'): 'the ensemble disappears, drowned in detail, and the consequence is boredom'. One might think he had in mind certain meticulous descriptions in the pages of French realist novels, and specifically those of Balzac, but in fact the examples he refers to are Cooper and Walter Scott.

It is hardly surprising that, as a leading Romantic painter, Delacroix should see photographers as allies of the realism that he opposed. (Possibly in his reference to the errors of '*le réaliste obstiné*' we should see an allusion to Courbet, who is said to have dismissed a request to put angels in a painting commissioned for a church by replying: 'I have never seen angels. Show me an angel and I will paint one.') But it is unexpected to find Delacroix described nowadays as a 'staunch supporter' of photography (Gernsheim 1988: 36). He did, however, sit on the committee set up to investigate the status of photography, whose deliberations were influential in the decision to allow photographers to submit work to the *Salon* of 1859, 'though by a separate entrance' (Gernsheim 1988: 36). Delacroix himself had even made one *cliché verre* in 1854, but does not seem to have been tempted to repeat the experiment: pusillanimous for a staunch supporter.

The same alliance between opposition to realism and scepticism concerning photography is to be found in Baudelaire. In his comments on the *Salon* of

1859, published in *La Revue Française*, Baudelaire caricatures realism in the arts as follows. The realist's creed is:

'I believe in Nature, and I believe only in Nature [. . .]. I believe that Art is, and cannot be other than, the exact reproduction of Nature (a timid and dissident sect would wish to exclude the more repellent objects of nature, such as skeletons or chamber-pots). Thus an industry that could give us a result identical to Nature would be the absolute of art (*l'art absolu*).' (Harrison, Wood and Gaiger 1998: 667)

Baudelaire identifies Daguerre as the 'Messiah' of the realists and ridicules the realists' (alleged) conviction that photography is art because it can give *'toutes les garanties désirables d'exactitude'*. Photography he denounces as 'the refuge of all failed painters'. He prophesies that once photography is allowed even to assist the painter, it will soon supplant or corrupt painting entirely, 'thanks to the natural alliance that it will find in the stupidity of the masses'. The only role Baudelaire will allow photography is one on a level with that of printing or stenography in relation to literature. It can be allowed to record ruins and preserve for posterity valuable books, prints and manuscripts. But it must not be allowed to intrude into the domain of the imagination.

What evidently worries Baudelaire most of all is the public's enthusiasm for photography. Here he comes close to taking Morris's line about 'sham' art. Baudelaire fears that familiarity with the photographic image will lead to people looking for verisimilitude where they should be looking for beauty. Artists, whether they like it or not, will respond to the public's attitude:

It is an incontestable, an irresistible law that the artist should act upon the public, and that the public should react upon the artist; [. . .]. Each day art further diminishes its self-respect by bowing down before external reality; each day the painter becomes more and more given to painting not what he dreams but what he sees. (Harrison, Wood and Gaiger 1998: 668).

There is one other consideration which doubtless counted for something in the minds of those artists hostile to the new medium. This was the relative ease with which it seemed possible to take fairly acceptable photographs (as compared with the hours of painstaking labour and training put in by the painter). Photographers did not deny this. In 1857, Félix Nadar admitted that the theory of photography could be learnt in an hour, and the practical rudiments in a day, while the actual operations involved were not beyond the most dim-witted (*'à la portée du dernier des imbéciles'*).

These shocking facts, as some might have viewed them, did not in Nadar's opinion detract in the least from the artistic skill in photography. He wrote:

> What *cannot* be taught, I will tell you: it is the feeling for light, it is the artistic appreciation of the effects produced by its varieties and combinations, it is the application of one or other of these effects, depending on the nature of the physiognomy which, as an artist, you have to capture. What can be taught far less concerns the moral intelligence of your subject, the swift tact which enables you to empathize with your models, assess them, feel your way into their habits, their ideas, according to the character of each, and enables you to produce not a banal or chance likeness, the kind of indifferent reproduction that a mere laboratory assistant might be capable of, but the most familiar and favourable resemblance, the intimate resemblance. This is the psychological side of photography, and I do not think that is a too ambitious way of putting it. (Frizot and Ducros 1987: 9)

Here Nadar gives the definitive answer to the kind of objection raised by Delacroix and Baudelaire. His example is portrait photography, but it can be applied also to landscape and other subjects. When mood, character and atmosphere are taken into account, capturing the resemblance you want is not a simple matter of pressing a button with the camera pointed in the right direction. And once this is understood, photography appears not a facile art, but a far more difficult one than painting. The photographer, unlike the painter, cannot spend hours building up his picture, stroke upon stroke. He must catch the right moment, which will determine the success or failure of the whole composition. And he cannot, unlike the painter, rely on his imagination to supply what is missing, but must by some means coax the desired image out of his subject. In this sense, the photographer's model is far more elusive than the painter's.

The other side of photography that had a bearing on its artistic status concerned the treatment of the negative. It was at first assumed that what the camera 'saw' was what the printed image showed. But at the first meeting of the Photographic Society of London in 1853 Sir William Newton read a paper in which he denounced the 'false and limited' view that 'a photograph should always remain as represented in the camera'. He recommended that the photographer should explore ways of developing his negatives 'in order to render them more like works of art' (Harrison, Wood and Gaiger 1998: 653). The realization of this possibility, together with the technique of combining several negatives in order to make a single print, dealt an even more serious blow to the claim that photography was merely 'mechanical'. In spite of all this, essentially the same flawed arguments as those advanced by Delacroix went on being repeated for generations by those opposed to admitting photography as an art form in its own right. Seventy-five years after Delacroix's death the *Encyclopædia Britannica* was still telling its readers that 'photography has no place among the arts'. Why not? Because 'it has to accept nature uncontrolled and unmodified' (Konody 1929: 441).

Even today one finds the Royal Photographic Society still feeling obliged to persuade the public that photography, *in spite of* its dependence on science, is an art form. A text at a recent (October 2000) exhibition from the RPS collection announces:

The invention of photography presented creative artists with another exciting medium of expression and definition. This new technology – mixing chemistry, physics and optics – could produce an end product of sublime artistic merit every bit as worthy as work produced with paint, pastel, pencil or chisel.

Here the subtext clearly reads: 'You wouldn't think anything coming out of a laboratory could produce real *art*, would you?'

*   *   *

Anyone who saw photography as being in competition with painting and drawing was more than likely to see it as an 'unfair' competition in which human skills of hand and eye were being pitted against a machine. That conception in turn fitted into a broader picture of industrialized society where, in every conceivable field, human beings were in competition with machines, and, in many cases, being forced to admit defeat. An understandable reaction to the sense of fighting a losing battle against the machine was to turn instead to values for which the machine could not possibly compete; and the doctrine of 'art-for-art's-sake' may be seen as one facet of this reaction. It signals a retreat of the artist into a *tour d'ivoire* (as Sainte-Beuve memorably described Alfred de Vigny's position) where the only valid criteria of judgment are deemed to be those of 'art itself'.

An obvious problem with the strategy of declaring art to be totally autonomous is that of deciding what 'art itself' is and how exactly it can be pursued for 'its own sake'. Although Kant is sometimes credited with (or accused of?) being the founder of this brand of aestheticism, this is no more than a reflection of the difficulty in determining what the core content of the art-for-art's-sake doctrine is. Does it stand opposed to art-for-beauty's-sake? If not, then its individuality as a distinctive theoretical stance is immediately compromised, and its origin gets lost amid the endless ramifications of post-Renaissance theorizing about pursuit of 'the beautiful'. Plato has also been put forward as the ultimate author of the thesis that the arts are autonomous, but the passage in *Republic* (341, D) sometimes cited to demonstrate this seems only tenuously connected with the radical stance that caused such excitement and controversy in the nineteenth century. Hegel is occasionally mentioned as a source of the doctrine, but by the time Hegel began lecturing on aesthetics in Berlin (1820), the idea that Benjamin Constant brought home from a dinner conversation with Henry Crabb Robinson (1804) and captured in the canonical slogan *l'art pour l'art* was evidently already in circulation.

Another authority commonly mentioned in connexion with that celebrated artspeak dictum is the French philosopher Victor Cousin, whose lectures *Du vrai, du beau et du bien* were given in Paris in 1817–1818 and published in 1836. But Cousin too has a prior commitment to beauty:

Art is the free reproduction of the beautiful, not of a single natural beauty, but of ideal beauty, as the human imagination conceives it by the aid of data which nature furnishes it. (Harrison, Wood and Gaiger 1998: 193)

Here we see most of the artspeak buzzwords of the preceding two centuries packed into a single definition. How Cousin conceived the 'freedom' of art is best seen from his own account of the history of art. He rejects the view that when the arts flourished in the past they were subject to the demands of the state or religion.

Ancient Greece and modern Italy are continually cited as triumphant examples of what the alliance of art, religion, and the state can do. Nothing is more true, if the question is concerning their union; nothing is more false, if the question is concerning the servitude of art. Art in Greece was so little the slave of religion, that it little by little modified the symbols, and, to a certain extent, the spirit itself, by its free representations. [. . .] In Italy as in Greece, as everywhere, art is at first in the hands of priesthoods and governments; but, as it increases its importance and is developed, it more and more conquers its liberty. Men speak of the faith that animated the artists and vivified their works; that is true of the time of Giotto and Cimabue; but after Angelico de Fiesole, at the end of the fifteenth century, in Italy, I perceive especially the faith of art in itself and the worship of beauty. (Harrison, Wood and Gaiger 1998: 193)

Now this is no revolutionary credo addressed to contemporary artists, but a historical thesis concerning the relations between artists and the society of their day. It does not in fact identify a specific doctrine at all (other than the vague reference to 'the worship of beauty'), but merely stresses the progressive independence of artists from social constraints. Cousin even warns that 'extreme liberty may carry art to a caprice which degrades it' (Harrison, Wood and Gaiger 1998: 195). The various arts, in Cousin's view, enjoy different degrees of freedom. He thinks that sculpture, painting, and especially music and poetry, are freer than architecture and the art of gardening. But all this is a far cry from the strident claim reported by Constant that *any* purpose perverts art ('*tout but dénature l'art*': *Journal intime*, 11 February 1804).

Nor does it answer to Wilde's view as expressed much later in *The Decay of Lying* (1891), where Vivian responds to Cyril's contention that art must at least express 'the temper of its age, the spirit of its time' by this vehement denial:

> Certainly not! Art never expresses anything but itself. This is the principle of my new aesthetics; and it is this, more than that vital connection between form and substance, on which Mr Pater dwells, that makes basic the type of all the arts.
>
> [. . .] Art never expresses anything but itself. It has an independent life, just as Thought has, and develops purely on its own lines. (Harrison, Wood and Gaiger 1998: 860)

But what 'its own lines' are and what kind of 'self' art expresses are none the clearer.

In some ways it is more instructive to consider how opponents of the doctrine saw it. Courbet dismissed it out of hand, describing the practice of art for art's sake as a 'pointless objective' (catalogue for his Paris exhibition of 1855: Harrison, Wood and Gaiger 1998: 372). Nietzsche (*Die Götzen-Dämmerung*, 1889) interpreted it as an objection to the subordination of art to morality, and pointed out that 'when the purpose of moral preaching and of improving man has been excluded from art, it still does not follow by any means that art is altogether purposeless, aimless, senseless [. . .]' (Kaufmann 1954: 529). Proudhon, in *Du principe de l'art et sa destination sociale* (1865) sees it as the underlying principle of both the Romantics and their predecessors: 'According to the classics and Romantics – it would be quibbling to distinguish them – art is its own end.' What this means, according to Proudhon, is the following:

> To know nothing, to foreswear reasoning, to abstain from reflection, since it would chasten verve and discourage inspiration; to have a holy terror of philosophy; such were the maxims of the proponents of art for art's sake. We do not condemn science in itself, they say; we do full justice to its utility and respectability, and we are not slow to honour its representatives. We merely claim that it is of no assistance to art; that it is, indeed, fatal to art. (Harrison, Wood and Gaiger 1998: 405)

If Proudhon is right, the emergence of the principle of art-for-art's-sake was essentially a recognition of the gulf that now separated the natural sciences from the arts, a gulf that had been growing ever wider since the Renaissance.

In a famous essay published in 1936 ('The work of art in the age of mechanical reproduction') Walter Benjamin dismissed art-for-art's-sake contemptuously as 'a theology of art' (Arendt 1969: 224). The judgment is misguided in at least three respects. It is difficult to have a theology when no one knows exactly who its theologians are or which its sacred texts might be. Secondly, theology is essentially an enterprise of exposition, commentary, interpretation and explanation; but where art-for-art's-sake is concerned all of these are commonly wanting. Finally, Benjamin's explanation of this supposed theology as a reaction against 'the first truly revolutionary means of reproduction, photography, simultaneously with the rise of socialism' is sadly out of step with the historical sequence of events. The idea makes its appearance before Niépce or Daguerre or Fox Talbot had even begun their experiments, while if we count Babeuf and his fellow revolutionaries as socialists, the 'reaction' seems to come from an odd quarter and to be thoroughly inappropriate. Nevertheless, the notion of a 'theology' is of interest, inasmuch as it reveals what latter-day opponents of art-for-art's-sake saw as objectionable. For Benjamin, 'theology', with its religious, doctrinaire and obscurantist overtones, stands as the antonym of 'science'.

One reason why that antonymy is of particular interest to the student of artspeak is that the rhetoric of art-for-art's-sake survived unchanged long after the alleged dichotomy between science and art, on the basis of which the autonomy of art was proclaimed, had been seriously questioned. Thus, to cite just one fairly recent example, Jean Duvignaud in his _Sociologie de l'art_ (1967; 3rd ed. 1984) defines artistic creation as follows:

> When we refer to the uniqueness of artistic creation, we are referring to _artistic practice_ such as it is enacted in the complex network of human relationships, of groups in conflict or alliance, and at the level of the many 'dramas' of daily experience where the _wagers_ (_pari_) that are authentic works of art are made. (Wilson 1972: 36–7)

But what, then, is artistic authenticity? Duvignaud's answer is:

> If someone were to ask how the authenticity (_authenticité_) of a work of art was to be established, we would suggest that in this context it depends on two factors: the force of conviction in a work (bearing in mind its explicit aims) and its detachment from financial, ideological and political concerns – in other words, the authentic work of art cannot serve as a justification for any other activity except itself.

This definition should enable us to eliminate from the sociology of art various 'philosophies of art' and even 'aesthetics' whenever these fail to take into account the completely independent nature (*autonomie absolue*) of artistic creation. (Wilson 1972: 37)

Here, quite explicitly, the artspeak of the early nineteenth century is being enlisted in the interests of laying the foundations for a late-twentieth-century branch of sociology.

*   *   *

Morris's exaltation of handicraft and abhorrence of the machine reflected an attitude to the arts that was not without its critics. In 1895, Rioux de Maillou, writing in the *Revue des Arts Décoratifs* on the decorative arts and the machine, posed the question: 'Which is better, a true *mechanistic* art or an art of imitation individuality?' and spoke of 'a new decorative aesthetic to be developed from the arrival of industrialisation in the field of art' (Maillou 1895: 5). Six years later, in a similar vein, Henry van de Velde argued for the overdue recognition of engineers as artists, and waxed enthusiastic over perambulators, bathroom fittings, electric lamps and surgical instruments as being 'among the modern inventions which attract by their beauty' (van de Velde 1901: 33). Hermann Muthesius, in *Das Englische Haus*, ridiculed the hand-made kitchen furniture on show at the Arts and Crafts Exhibition:

This new furniture differed from the genuine kitchen pieces in that it was ten times more expensive because it was produced under the economic conditions of works of art. In the London Arts and Crafts Exhibition they are displayed with the claim that they are works of art, not only because their retail price corresponds to that of works of art, but also because in the catalogue, apart from the name of the 'designer' there is given the name of every single craftsman who was associated with the product. Is it any wonder that the public laughs at such exhibits? (Muthesius 1904–05: 34)

It was not long before Morris's socialist craft doctrine was being stood on its head. According to Theo van Doesburg, it was actually hand craftsmanship that had 'debased man to a machine'; whereas 'the machine, used properly in the service of cultural construction, is the only means of bringing about the converse: social liberation' (van Doesburg 1922: 93). For Moholy-Nagy, socialism and the machine were inseparable: 'Before the machine, everyone is equal' (Moholy-Nagy 1922: 95). What Fernand Léger called 'the machine aesthetic' (Léger 1923) was becoming recognized as appropriate to the arts in the modern world.

The notion that machines and machine-made forms may be beautiful finds expression as early as 1864, according to Cheney and Cheney, who cite James Jarvis Jackson's claim that:

> The American while adhering closely to his utilitarian and economical principles, has unwittingly, in some objects to which his heart equally with his hand has been devoted, developed a degree of beauty in them that no other nation equals. His clipper-ships, fire-engines, locomotives, and some of his machinery and tools combine that equilibrium of lines, proportions, and masses, which is among the fundamental causes of abstract beauty. (Cheney and Cheney 1936: iii)

When the first exhibition of 'Machine Art' was held in New York in 1934 at the Museum of Modern Art it included such items as hydrometer jars, dental instruments, billiard balls, an X-ray machine, a telescope, a saucepan, a cash register and an outboard propeller. The Foreword to the exhibition catalogue (written by Alfred Barr) quoted from Plato's *Philebus*:

> By beauty of shapes I do not mean, as most people would suppose, the beauty of living figures or of pictures, but, to make my point clear, I mean straight lines and circles, and shapes, plane or solid, made from them by lathe, ruler and square. These are not, like other things, beautiful relatively, but always and absolutely.

Barr continued:

> The beauty of machine art is in part the abstract beauty of "straight lines and circles" made into actual tangible "surfaces and solids" by means of tools, "lathes and rulers and squares." In Plato's day the tools were simple handworker's implements but today, as a result of the perfection of modern materials and the precision of modern instruments, the modern machine-made object approaches far more closely and more frequently those pure shapes the contemplation of which Plato calls the first of the "pure pleasures."
> Machines are, visually speaking, a practical application of geometry. Forces which act in straight lines are changed in direction and degree by machines which are themselves formed of straight lines and curves. The lever is geometrically a straight line resting on a point. The wheel and axle is composed of concentric circles and radiating straight lines. The watch spring is a spiral. Sphericity and circularity are the geometrical characteristics of a ball bearing. Screws, bearing springs, and propellors are various – and variously beautiful – applications of the helix and helicoid. (Barr 1934)

Alberti himself could hardly have taken exception to any of this, had he been acquainted with watch springs and ball bearings. What is ironic is that the terms in which machine art was first presented to the New York public should have been largely borrowed from an artspeak that antedated the Industrial Revolution.

6

The flight from meaning

All art constantly aspires towards the condition of music.
Walter Pater

The Age of Reason (as exemplified in the *Encyclopédie*) had at least tried to impose some kind of rationale on the extravagances of artspeak. But it proved to be a losing battle. The more closely Reason became identified with Science, and Science in turn with Technology, the more inevitable it became that there would break out, sooner or later, a revolt. Since Reason in all its forms pre-supposes stability of meanings, the most radical revolt against Reason is always one which rejects meanings lock, stock and barrel, or else subjects them to the arbitrary dictates of individual caprice. The doctrine of art-for-art's-sake allowed for both. It provided a foundation for all registers of freethinking artspeak that were anti-Enlightenment and/or anti-Science.

It is no coincidence that the emergence of this doctrine should be concomi-tant with the popularity of the notion that the paradigm form of art is music, as memorably summed up in Pater's much-quoted dictum. That dictum, however, cannot be properly understood without reference to its context, which is Pater's essay on the school of Giorgione. Pater's claim is that 'one of the secrets' of this school is its 'dexterous choice' of subject matter, allowing the 'perfect interpenetration of the subject with the elements of colour and design' (Pater 1877: 95). It is the selection of 'ideal instants' which is the key; that is, instants which 'seem to absorb past and future in an intense con-sciousness of the present.'

Quite what that has to do with music is not altogether obvious until we realize that the point of departure for Pater's tortuous argument is the analysis of the distinction between painting and poetry that had been proposed by Lessing more than a hundred years before (*Laokoon*, 1766), and which Pater mentions briefly at the beginning of his essay (Pater 1877: 83). Lessing claimed to base his case on 'first principles' and reasoned as follows:

If it is true that painting and poetry in their imitations make use of entirely different means or symbols (*Zeichen*) – the first, namely, of form and colour in space, the second of articulated sounds in time – if these symbols indisputably require a suitable relation to the thing symbolized, then it is clear that symbols arranged in juxtaposition can only express subjects (*Gegenstände*) of which the wholes or parts exist in juxtaposition; while consecutive symbols can only express subjects of which the wholes or parts are themselves consecutive.

Subjects whose wholes or parts exist in juxtaposition are called bodies (*Körper*). Consequently, bodies with their visible properties are the peculiar subjects of painting.

Subjects whose wholes or parts are consecutive are called actions (*Handlungen*). Consequently, actions are the peculiar subject of poetry. (Lessing 1766: XVI)

Historians have pointed out that Lessing was not the first to draw this distinction, but his influential version of it has come to be 'invoked as an oracle' (Mitchell 1986: 97) by theorists of quite different persuasions. The first thing to be said about it (although it is not often said, and certainly not said by Pater) is that Lessing's second conditional is false. That should have sufficed to dispose of the matter, had it not been that both in Lessing's day and in Pater's its falsity was concealed by the general acceptance of a certain theory of meaning. Worse still, however, is that even if it were not false, the conclusion Lessing draws would not follow.

One modern commentator observes that 'Lessing's choice of space and time as the first principles for generic distinction of the arts was an especially canny move'; for it had the effect of seeming to ground his argument 'directly in natural necessities' (Mitchell 1986: 104). In this respect Lessing was following in a long line of theorists who sought to present the necessity of artspeak as deriving directly from everyday common sense, rather than as a form of special pleading. But it is one thing to claim – uncontroversially – that works of art have these two dimensions available, and quite another to insist *therefore* on a distinction between 'spatial' arts and 'temporal' arts. This leads fairly quickly to saying things about the arts 'that make little or no sense' (Mitchell 1986: 103).

Behind Lessing's specious argument from natural necessity lies an older quarrel about the relative superiority of the verbal and non-verbal arts. This is what Pater clearly has in mind when he appeals to Lessing as an authority. For he says that in the appreciation of painting in particular 'the false generalisation of all art into forms of poetry is most prevalent' (Pater 1877: 84). This, he contends, 'is the way of most spectators, and of many critics' who are incapable of recognizing 'true pictorial quality': this latter resides in the 'inventive or creative handling of pure line and colour' (Pater 1877: 84). The objectionable fallacy, according to Pater, is in turn a version of a more general mistake, which is:

> to regard poetry, music, and painting – all the various products of art – as but translations into different languages of one and the same fixed quantity of imaginative thought, supplemented by certain technical qualities of colour, in painting; of sound, in music; of rhythmical words, in poetry. (Pater 1877: 83)

Why is this a mistake? Because, according to Pater, in this way

> the sensuous element in art, and with it almost everything in art that is essentially artistic, is made a matter of indifference; and a clear apprehension of the opposite principle – that the sensuous material of each art brings with it a special phase or quality of beauty, untranslatable into the forms of any other, an order of impressions distinct in kind – is the beginning of all true aesthetic criticism. (Pater 1877: 83)

The question-begging use of the adjective 'true' here is enough to indicate – were it not otherwise obvious – the exact point where Pater's brand of artspeak substitutes rhetoric for reason. And that is not without interest. For if we take what Pater says at face value, the bottom line is this: what is objectionable about the view he rejects is not that it undermines art but that it sabotages *the form of artspeak* he wishes to promote ('all true aesthetic criticism'). Here we see, perhaps for the first time in the Western tradition, what comes close to an admission that what counts is not so much the work of art as what you can say about it.

Music itself does not feature in Lessing's argument at all: its introduction is Pater's own handiwork. A clumsy move, since music is the temporal art *par excellence*. Any melody requires the temporal succession of notes for its articulation. A synchronous presentation of them produces nothing recognizable as a compressed tune, but merely a cacophony. So at first sight it would seem that if all art aspires to the condition of music, then all arts must aspire to be temporal arts. But this is not what Pater means. On the contrary, that would be disastrous for his eulogy of Giorgione and Giorgione's followers.

In what sense does this 'aspiration' to the condition of music manifest itself? In order to help himself over this rather major conceptual hurdle, Pater borrows a piece of abstruse terminology from German artspeak: the word *Anders-streben*, which he glosses as 'partial alienation from its own limitations'.

Thus, some of the most delightful music seems to be always approaching to figure, to pictorial definition. Architecture, again, though it has its own laws [. . .] yet sometimes aims at fulfilling the conditions of a picture, as in the *Arena* chapel; or of sculpture, as in the flawless unity of Giotto's tower at Florence; and often finds a true poetry, as in those strangely twisted staircases of the *châteaux* of the country of the Loire [. . .]. Thus, again, sculpture aspires out of the hard limitation of pure form towards colour, or its equivalent [. . .]. (Pater 1877: 85)

These are more than 'mere figures of speech', asserts Pater (as if suddenly waking up to the fact that that is precisely what they are). But what more they are than fanciful indulgence in metaphor he leaves unexplained.

The example is interesting not only because the appeal to *Anders-streben* is an impudent case of artspeak coming to its own rescue interlinguistically (if it makes no sense in English, try German), but because when even this desperate rescue bid fails, that failure is passed off as a success, by the simple rhetorical strategy of leaving the reader unenlightened. And here, for the first time, long in advance of Picasso or the Dadaists or James Joyce, we see artspeak rehearsing an intellectual technique that would become pivotal to the success of later generations of artists and critics. The technique in question can be summed up as: *the more inexplicable, the better*. The critic who described Pater's style as 'too austerely magnificent to be always persuasive' was missing the point by a wide margin.

Paterspeak comes in direct line of descent from Schiller, who proclaims:

Music in its loftiest exaltation must become shape, and act upon us with the tranquil power of the antique; the plastic and graphic arts must become music, and move us through their immediate sensuous presence; poetry in its most perfect development must, like musical art, take powerful hold of us, but at the same time, like plastic art, surround us with quiet clarity. It is just in this that perfect style in any art reveals itself – that it is capable of removing the characteristic limitations of that art, without however removing its specific excellences [. . .]. (Schiller 1795: xxii.105)

The corollary of this, for Schiller, is:

In a truly beautiful work of art the content should do nothing, the form everything. (Schiller 1795: xxii.106)

In the hands of Pater, this blatant *non sequitur* is developed into a verbal technique that is ready for service in any artistic emergency. Psychologically, it is a style that wrongfoots the reader. It says: if you do not see my point, *tant pis*. It is your aesthetic sensibility that is at fault, not mine. For art critics and art theorists, that was tantamount to a licence to print their own money. Not the least of the irony in all this was the fact that Pater, while protesting verbally *against* the adoption of poetry as a model for the non-verbal arts, enlisted metaphor as his preferred artspeak mode of argument. That may have owed something to his sympathy with the pre-Raphaelite movement. But it opened a Pandora's box of viruses, from which modern artspeak has never recovered.

Pater was also evidently familiar with Schopenhauer's 'metaphysics of music' (the title of a chapter in *The World as Will and Idea*). According to Schopenhauer, music is quite different from all the other arts. Music is a 'universal language'. (Schopenhauer never mentions non-Western musical traditions.) Its universality

> is by no means that empty universality of abstraction, but quite of a different kind, and is united with thorough and distinct definiteness. In this respect it resembles geometrical figures and numbers, which are the universal forms of all possible objects of experience and applicable to them all *a priori,* and yet are not abstract but perceptible and thoroughly determined. All possible efforts, excitements, and manifestations of will, all that goes on in the heart of man and that reason includes in the wide, negative concept of feeling, may be expressed by the infinite number of possible melodies, but always in the universal, in the mere form, without the material, always according to the thing-in-itself, not the phenomenon, the inmost soul, as it were, of the phenomenon, without the body. (Schopenhauer 1844: iii.52)

This description of music in Kantian terms is followed by an attempt to put it in the terms of medieval logic. Although melodies are to a certain extent, 'like general concepts, an abstraction from the actual', nevertheless music, unlike concepts, 'gives the inmost kernel which precedes all forms, or the heart of things.'

> This relation may be very well expressed in the language of the schoolmen by saying the concepts are the *universalia post rem*, but music gives the *universalia ante rem*, and the real world the *universalia in re*. (Schopenhauer 1844: iii.52)

Predictably, Schopenhauer has nothing but contempt for 'programme music', such as Haydn's *Seasons*, and operas in which the music is subordinated to the libretto, so that the words become 'the chief thing and the music a mere means of expressing it, which is a great misconception and a piece of utter perversity' (Schopenhauer 1844: iii.52). Later in the century, exactly the opposite view would be championed by Ruskin, for whom 'passionate music', untempered by words and thought, quickly becomes 'brutal' and 'meaningless' (Ruskin 1869: 343). What links Schopenhauer and Ruskin, however, is their common preoccupation with the problem of what music 'means', and what relationship obtains between the meaning of music and the meaning of words. For Ruskin, the contest between Apollo and Marsyas symbolizes the struggle between music under the control of words and music uncontrolled. The flaying of Marsyas is a punishment not so much for challenging the gods as for deliberately abusing the power of music.

The explanation Schopenhauer gives for the special status of music is that it rests on the relationship between music and the will.

> Music is distinguished from all the other arts by the fact that it is not a copy of the phenomenon, or, more accurately, the adequate objectivity of will, but is the direct copy of the will itself, and therefore exhibits itself as the metaphysical to everything physical in the world, and as the thing-in-itself to every phenomenon. We might, therefore, just as well call the world embodied music as embodied will. (Schopenhauer 1844: iii.52)

This last statement must count as one of the most remarkable artspeak pronouncements in the Western tradition. If we are trying to understand the curious logic that drove Schopenhauer to this conclusion, the first point to grasp is that he is utterly committed to the Platonic view that the (fine) arts are essentially mimetic. Works of art derive their meaning from their mimetic function. But music presents a problem. What does a melody imitate? (Other than in 'perverse' cases where the composer has used it to mimic or suggest other audible effects.) It appears to imitate nothing. And yet instinctively we feel it to be meaningful nevertheless, even though we cannot say what its meaning is. Moreover, great music moves us deeply and immediately, without the intervention of any 'explanation' of what it means and without our understanding how or why it does so. Consequently, reasons Schopenhauer, its mimetic function must be of a different order from that of the other arts. It does not represent either things in the visible world or concepts, as painting and sculpture do. But that leaves only one option left within the framework of Schopenhauer's philosophy. It is a 'direct copy of the will itself', without any intermediary mimesis.

What Pater seems to have made of all this was something simpler but no less opaque. Dispensing with the philosophical underpinnings that are so important in Schopenhauer, he conceived of music as the limiting case of an art in which the meaning *is* the form. The dictum that 'all art constantly aspires towards the condition of music' might be glossed as: 'art is best when it succeeds in eliding the distinction between form and content'. That distinction, as theorists of Pater's generation were beginning to realize, was a millstone around the critic's neck. The *critic's* neck – it should be emphasized – not the artist's. Unless the artists were like Delacroix, who made verbal notes of 'possible' paintings (i.e. of their content) before proceeding to paint them. For Pater, Delacroix – or painters like Delacroix – would presumably have been misled about their art by construing it in terms of some 'fixed quantity of imaginative thought' which then had to be 'translated' (when they had time) into paint on the canvas. The days when any quick splodge of paints (or excrement) could be titled 'Day by the seaside' or 'Study No.1' and exhibited for sale in a London gallery were still far away. But not all that far, once artspeak had disposed of the awkward traditional dichotomy between form and content.

The emancipation from meaning that music offered would eventually be taken one step further by *avant-garde* twentieth-century composers (Boulez, Cage) committed to 'indeterminate music' (Griffiths 1983). Here the score is incomplete, allowing performers maximum freedom to impose their own interpretations; or else the sequence of notes is settled by 'aleatory' procedures such as tossing a coin. That, at least, upstages Schopenhauer (unless one is prepared to believe that coins fall heads or tails according to the will of the composer).

In the sphere of literature, the dichotomy between form and content was challenged by Mallarmé's ground-breaking *Un coup de dés jamais n'abolira le hasard*, composed towards the end of the poet's life, but not published until 1914. Here we see what one critic describes as an attempt 'to emulate the capacity of music to express meanings simultaneously rather than in the linear sequence enforced by typographical conventions' (McClure 1982: 390). Mallarmé himself in the brief preface to the poem refers to it as a score (*partition*). But that is, perhaps intentionally, inaccurate. For we know how to read a musical score (or else it is not much use to us); whereas how to read Mallarmé's disjointed poem is a puzzle. Evidently we are *not* intended to read it in the way we would if it were presented in 'normal' typography. In his deliberate dislocations of the lines, the spacing and changes of type face, the unexpected juxtapositions, the poet makes it impossible for us to divorce the verbal content of the poem from its materialization on the page. In short, the typography becomes part of the poem, and not merely a printed representation of it. It could be argued that there is still a verbal meaning 'in there', to be extracted from the words; but whatever sense the reader can make of that is transformed by its projection into another field, which is visual, not aural. In Mallarmé's case, the flight from meaning leads into a new dimension of art; but it was a flight from the 'old' meaning of poetry nonetheless. Pater, who died before its publication, would doubtless have acclaimed it as an outstanding example of the possibilities of *Anders-streben*.

*   *   *

Pater might also, had he lived to see it, have regarded cubism in the same light; that is to say, as an attempt to take painting beyond its natural limits and into another sphere of art. Apollinaire sounds almost Pateresque when he says of the cubists that theirs is 'an entirely new art which will stand, with respect to painting as envisaged heretofore, as music stands to literature' (Breunig and Chevalier 1980: 59; Chipp 1968: 222).

The fact that in *Les peintres cubistes* Apollinaire re-uses earlier material, together with the fact that the title was a last-minute addition, possibly on the insistence of the publisher, have led some to the conclusion that Apollinaire 'was not an apologist for the Cubist movement' (Chipp 1968: 220). But this hardly squares with the impression the book makes on the reader. Whether, or to what extent, Apollinaire spoke *for* the cubists themselves is another question. According to Duchamp, Apollinaire was 'always talking about things he knew nothing about', and there has been a tendency to see *Les peintres cubistes* as 'a poem on painting' (Raynal's assessment: Breunig and Chevalier 1980: 166) rather than a serious work of art criticism. But this is to miss the point. Together with André Salmon's *La jeune peinture française* (1912), and *Du cubisme* (1912) by the two painters Albert Gleizes and Jean Metzinger, *Les peintres cubistes* shows the foundations of cubist artspeak in the process of being laid.

The ground plan is plain to see. A critical discourse in which the cubist revolution could be explained to a suspicious or hostile public needed to address problems of identity, on the one hand, and problems of meaning on the other. Who were the cubists? What did their art 'mean'?

The accusation that the work of the cubists was meaningless was common at the time. Braque's paintings were described by Louis Vauxcelles in 1908 as 'aggressively unintelligible' (Breunig and Chevalier 1980: 178). Louis Perceau in 1913 spoke of cubists pursuing a dizzy path towards their ideal of *obscurité* and endeavouring, with each exhibition, to advance the limits of incomprehensibility (Breunig and Chevalier 1980: 162). Pro-cubist artspeak sought to counter these charges in two ways: first, by producing art-historical validations which would situate the cubist approach as meaningful within a certain tradition, and second, by offering theoretical validations to show that the aims of this approach were in fact neither unintelligible nor perverse.

The problems of identity were more intractable, partly because the cubists had been caught on the wrong foot at the outset by being forced to accept the derogatory artspeak label *cubisme*. Nevertheless, a name was needed: one cannot defend an anonymous school, for then no one is sure who is being defended or against what. 'Schools disappear for lack of convenient labels,' Salmon had written. He went on:

> This is annoying to the public, for it likes the schools because they enable
> it to understand clearly without effort. (Chipp 1968: 206)

This is the observation of a strategist who understands exactly how you have to play the artspeak game. It does not matter whether a group really constitutes a 'school' or not, provided the public can be offered a label that distinguishes them from rival groups (in this instance, in particular, from Fauves and Futurists).

Gleizes and Metzinger accept the label, while protesting somewhat pompously in the opening paragraph of their essay:

> The word "Cubism" is here employed merely to spare the reader any
> uncertainty as to the object of our inquiry; and we would hasten to
> declare that the idea which the term evokes – that of volume (*volume*) –
> cannot by itself define a movement which tends towards the integral
> realization of Painting. (Chipp 1968: 207)

Having entered this caveat (but proposing no alternative term), the authors almost give the game away by refusing to give a definition of what they understand by it. This was artspeak at its most feckless, taking quite unnecessary risks, but possibly in deference to colleagues who disliked the label more than they did.

Apollinaire too was a great believer in labels, for he provided no less than four: *cubisme scientifique*, *cubisme physique*, *cubisme orphique* and *cubisme instinctif* (Breunig and Chevalier 1980: 68–9). His rather cavalier attempt to define these four divisions got him into trouble with the artists in question, who evidently took the labels more seriously than Apollinaire did. But that in itself was a minor triumph for the architect of cubist artspeak. The terms were more important than the definitions. So it was with Apollinaire's invention of the verb *cubiquer*, which he quite deliberately left undefined (except, by implication, in semantic circularity: a cubist is presumably an artist *qui cubique*).

When challenged to define cubism, Apollinaire resorted to the vaguest formula that it would be possible to devise without being accused of deliberate evasion:

> Cubism is the art of painting new ensembles (*ensembles nouveaux*) with
> elements taken not from visual reality, but from conceptual reality

(*empruntés non à la réalité de vision, mais à la réalité de conception*). (Breunig and Chevalier 1980: 23)

This 'definition' is purely negative: it cautions against judging cubist paintings by their optical verisimilitude – a caveat that could equally well apply to the work of many twentieth-century non-cubists, and to many more at earlier periods.

When all else fails, a group with a collective label can always be identified extensionally, i.e. by listing its members. But problems may arise if two or more lists are in circulation. Salmon identified the leader without question as being Picasso, and associated with him Metzinger, Delaunay and Braque. Apollinaire produced a more extensive and controversial inventory of cubists, which included Gleizes, Léger, Gris, Le Fauconnier, Picabia, Duchamp and Marie Laurencin (who protested to the last that she had never been one). But if Apollinaire erred on the side of inclusiveness it was doubtless because, as with his 'definition' of cubism, he saw that it served the purposes of critical discourse better to have a generous cast of characters rather than too few. One can always then resort to subdividing them and drawing subtle distinctions between the subdivisions (as he proceeded to do in *Les peintres cubistes*).

The historical validation provided for the cubists by their apologists involved the familiar exercise of rewriting the history of art in order to situate the chosen protagonists in the mainstream. This was accompanied by an appropriate deployment of hyperbole. Salmon, for instance, invoked Shakespeare and Goethe in order to describe the qualities of Picasso. According to Apollinaire, he had 'reinvented anatomy' single-handed. More modestly, Gleizes and Metzinger trace the ancestry of cubism back to Courbet. The choice is not without significance. It relates to the theoretical justifications offered for cubism. Courbet is presented as the great 'realist' of the nineteenth century; but a realist with a fatal flaw. He was taken in by everything his eye saw:

> He remained the slave of the worst visual conventions. Unaware of the fact that in order to display a true relation (*un rapport vrai*) we must be ready to sacrifice a thousand apparent truths (*mille apparences*), he accepted, without the slightest intellectual control, all that his retina presented to him. He did not suspect that the visible world can become the real world only by the operation of the intellect (*l'opération de la pensée*). (Chipp 1968: 207–8)

The next great realist, according to Gleizes and Metzinger, was Manet, who also had many failings, but counts as a realist because 'he knew how to endow the many potential qualities concealed in the most commonplace objects with a radiant reality' (Chipp 1968: 208). Here we see emerging what was to become a Platonistic leitmotif in cubist artspeak. As if responding across the centuries to Plato's criticism that painting merely imitates appearances, the cubists were advertised as explorers who had, at long last, found a way to go *beyond* the visual surface of things to the underlying reality.

Between Manet and the cubists, however, there allegedly occurred an important schism. 'The realistic impulse is divided into superficial realism and profound realism' (Chipp 1968: 208). The 'superficial realists' are the Impressionists; 'profound realism' is reserved for the painting of Cézanne. 'To understand Cézanne is to foresee cubism.' Thus elevated to the status of immediate precursor, Cézanne too is described in enthusiastic, if somewhat vague, hyperbole. Cézanne, we are told,

> teaches us to overcome the universal dynamism. He reveals the recipro-
> cal and mutual modifications caused by supposedly inanimate objects.
> From him we have learned that to alter the coloration of a body is to
> corrupt its structure. He prophesies that the study of primordial volume
> will open unknown horizons to us. His work, a homogeneous mass,
> shifts under the glance, contracts, expands, fades or illumines itself,
> irrefragably proving that painting is not – or is no longer – the art of
> imitating an object by means of lines and colors, but the art of giving our
> instinct a plastic consciousness. (Chipp 1968: 209)

Thus realism 'plunges, with Cézanne, into the profoundest reality, growing luminous as it forces the unknowable to retreat' (Chipp 1968: 209). In short, giving Plato his ultimate put-down, painting as practised by Cézanne and his cubist successors, is no mere imitation of reality (much less of appearances), but a *revelation* of it. Like John the Baptist, Cézanne had been the prophet in the wilderness; but now, as foretold, Picasso had come.

The two authors of this Messianic scenario were already cast in the role of apostles (since the Messiah himself refused to say anything, and even to exhibit in company with his disciples). But the scenario itself raised a problem: how was it that the truth, concealed for centuries, had taken so long to be revealed? The answer involved bringing Science back into the picture, an obvious move for a generation in awe before the seemingly unstoppable advances of 'modern science'. Zola, discussing realism in art, had already prophesied in 1866 the way the wind would blow:

> The wind favours science; in spite of ourselves we are pushed towards
> the exact study of facts and things. Thus all the strong personalities who
> declare themselves come out in support of the truth. The movement of
> the age is certainly realist, or rather positivist. (Zola 1866: 120–1)

Thus: modern art = science = the search for truth. This was a platform ready-made for Picasso and his allies. The cubists were acclaimed as the first experimental 'scientists' of vision. Picasso was their leading researcher. He deliberately refused to rely – as any ordinary mortal might have done – on his amazing natural facility as a draughtsman, and instead sought to understand pictorial art at a deeper level. He 'meditated upon geometry'. Salmon described his preliminary work for *Les Demoiselles d'Avignon* as 'research' and claimed: 'Henceforth, painting was becoming a science and quite an austere one' (Chipp 1968: 202). The scientific theme was taken up by Apollinaire: for him *cubisme scientifique* and what he called *les premières toiles scientifiques* carried painting into a new domain of analysis. Picasso, he claimed, analysed objects 'as a surgeon dissects a corpse' (Breunig and Chevalier 1980: 60). And traditional geometry was no longer adequate for this new pictorial science. Just as modern mathematicians had gone beyond Euclidean three-dimensional geometry, so had the cubists. They were, in fact, already exploring the fourth dimension (*quatrième dimension*). This, according to Apollinaire, was 'space itself, the dimension of the infinite'. Or rather, it represented 'the immensity of space extending boundlessly in all directions at any given moment' (Breunig and Chevalier 1980: 61).

With this novel blend of secular pentecostalism and pseudo-science, cubist artspeak established for itself a recognizably oracular register. It outmanœuvred sceptics who complained about 'meaningless' art by invoking a deeper and quasi-ineffable level of significance.

*   *   *

Given wings by its own apologists, the flight from meaning still had some way to go. Apollinaire had remarked that the art of the cubists was not yet as abstract (*abstrait*) as they would wish (Breunig and Chevalier 1980: 60). It was, after all, still possible to recognize a few objects and figures in most cubist works, and to that extent the viewer could still make descriptive sense of them, however much the painters might protest to the contrary.

According to one version of art history, abstract art 'proper' was born on the day when Wassily Kandinsky, returning at dusk to his studio in Munich, failed because of the poor light to recognize what was depicted on a canvas leaning against the wall, but could discern only an entrancing configuration of shapes and colours. According to another version, abstract art has been practised for millennia, and in some cultural traditions might be considered a major form. These two versions are not entirely irreconcilable, but it is in the context of the former that the kind of painting developed by Kandinsky, Mondrian and others can be seen as a further manifestation of the flight from meaning. Its main concern seemed to many to be a concern to expel from the picture space anything recognizable as a depicted object, and thus focus attention on the painting itself, just as 'absolute' music – as opposed to 'programme' music – had rejected all allusions to extra-musical content and demanded priority for the composition in its own right. (The expression 'absolute music' had been coined by Wagner, and takes its place in a complex of 'apologetic and polemical formulas in Wagner's esthetics' (Dalhaus 1989: 18).)

Music meant a great deal to Kandinsky (Dabrowski 1995: 19–22). He referred to his own paintings as 'compositions'. He had been inspired to devote his life to art on hearing a performance of *Lohengrin*, and later became deeply immersed in the work of Scriabin and Schönberg. He was interested in the former's attempts to establish correspondences between musical tones and colours, and in the latter's rejection of traditional tonal and harmonic patterns. Although Kandinsky himself did not abandon the terminological distinction between 'form' and 'content', he construed content vaguely as the 'inner necessity' which impelled the artist to produce the work. This necessity, it would seem, is not fully understood, even by the artist, but simply experienced. It is 'spiritual' in nature. (The title of Kandinsky's *Über das Geistige in der Kunst* (1911) is usually translated as *Concerning the Spiritual in Art*.) Kandinsky too joins the ranks of those who look to music as pointing the way for other arts.

> Despite, or perhaps thanks to, the differences between them, there has never been a time when the arts approached each other more nearly than they do today, in this later phase of spiritual development.
>
> In each manifestation is the seed of a striving towards the abstract, the non-material. Consciously or unconsciously they are obeying Socrates' command – Know thyself. Consciously or unconsciously artists are studying and proving their material, setting in the balance the spiritual value of those elements, with which it is their several privilege to work.
>
> And the natural result of this striving is that the various arts are drawing together. They are finding in Music the best teacher. With few exceptions music has been for some centuries the art which has devoted itself not to the reproduction of natural phenomena, but rather to the expression of the artist's soul, in musical sound. (Kandinsky 1911: 19)

Here Kandinsky follows laboriously in the wake of those theorists who, a century earlier, had striven to make a place for 'an object- and concept-free instrumental music' (Dalhaus 1989: 11). For some of these, such as Tieck, music was 'the ultimate mystery of faith, the mystique, the completely revealed religion' (Dalhaus 1989: 89).

Kandinsky does not go this far, but he defends the doctrine of art-for-art's-sake as a reflection of the needs of the soul. It is:

an unconscious protest against materialism, against the demand that everything should have a use and practical value. It is further proof of the indestructibility of art and of the human soul, which can never be killed but only temporarily smothered. (Kandinsky 1911: 54)

By this circuitous route, Kandinsky's artspeak rejoins the earlier post-Renaissance discourse about beauty and genius.

The work of art is born of the artist in a mysterious and secret way. [. . .] In fact, the artist is not only justified in using, but it is his duty to use only those forms which fulfil his *own need*. Absolute freedom, whether from anatomy or anything of the kind, must be given the artist in his choice of material. Such spiritual freedom is as necessary in art as it is in life. [. . .]
    If the artist be priest of beauty, nevertheless this beauty is to be sought only according to the principle of the inner need, and can be measured only according to the size and intensity of that need.
    That is beautiful which is produced by the inner need, which springs from the soul. (Kandinsky 1911: 53–5)

*   *   *

The flight from meaning eventually reached its final destination with the Dadaists, who conceived of themselves as engaged in anti-art, and consequently set out to subvert all previous forms of artistic meaning. The Dada Manifesto of 1918 proclaimed proudly and in capital letters:

DADA DOES NOT MEAN ANYTHING.

Tristan Tzara there both explains and refuses to explain why, although he is in principle 'against manifestos', this one is necessary:

I'm writing this manifesto to show that you can perform contrary actions at the same time, in one single, fresh breath; I am against action; as for continual contradiction, and affirmation too, I am neither for nor against them, and I won't explain myself because I hate common sense. (Tzara 1918: 4)

The logic of Dadaism demanded for its own artspeak a vocabulary of meaningless terms. Kurt Schwitters' celebrated contribution was the invention of the word *Merz*.

The word "Merz" had no meaning when I formed it. Now it has the meaning which I gave it. The meaning of the concept "Merz" changes with the change in the insight of those who continue to work with it. (Chipp 1968: 384)

The paradox of words whose meaning depends solely on the 'insights' of their users leads directly into the artspeak logic which concludes with Tzara's – at first sight baffling – claim (Tzara 1921: 41): 'dada is the dictatorship of language'.

A necessary dictatorship, if artspeak is manufactured as required, to suit the needs of the manufacturer. Plato might well have retorted that he had already dealt with this linguistic problem in his *Cratylus*. But not to the satisfaction of all. Before any of the Dada manifestos had been published, Saussure's colleagues at the University of Geneva had brought out the posthumously reconstructed text of his *Cours de linguistique générale* (1916). This was to alter Western perceptions of language and put all questions of meaning in a new light.

*   *   *

That could also be said of the work of Freud, whose impact on thinking about art first made itself felt in the activity of the surrealists. They too recognized the necessity of constructing a form of artspeak which would serve as a vehicle for the explanation and defence of their iconoclastic activities. The definition of the word *surréalisme* supplied in the first surrealist manifesto reads:

SURRÉALISME n.m. Pure psychic automatism by which it is intended to express, whether verbally, or in writing, or in any other way, the real functioning of thought. Dictation (*dictée*) of thought in the absence of any control exercised by reason, and outside all aesthetic or moral preoccupations. (Breton 1924: 37)

The theoretical basis for this revolt against reason, as Breton acknowledged, was deemed to lie in Freud's 'discoveries' about the human mind. According to Breton:

We are still living under the reign of logic [. . .]. But logical procedures today are applied only to solving problems of secondary interest. The absolute rationalism which remains fashionable allows only the consideration of facts narrowly confined to our experience. [. . .] It is only, apparently, by the greatest chance that light has recently been thrown on a part of our intellectual world – and in my view by far the most important part – which was deemed to be of no interest. For this we must be thankful for the discoveries of Freud. (Breton 1924: 18–19)

Psychoanalysis was thus enlisted from the outset in support of surrealist artspeak. Freud was never consulted. As he wrote later (Gombrich 1966: 34), although he realized that he had been chosen by the surrealists 'as their patron saint', nevertheless he thought they were 'pure lunatics or let us say 95 per cent, as with "pure" alcohol.' It was not until he met Dalí in 1938 that Freud revised his opinion of surrealism, and even then expressed grave reservations.

As a critic, one might still be entitled to say that the concept of art resisted an extension beyond the point where the quantitative proportion between unconscious material and preconscious elaboration is not kept within a certain limit. (Gombrich 1966: 35)

Even for Freud, the flight from meaning in the arts had to stop somewhere.

7

Cultivating the primitive

Primitive sculpture has never been surpassed.
Picasso

The rise of social anthropology as an academic discipline in the latter part of the nineteenth century opened a new phase in the history of artspeak. Comparisons were inevitably drawn between the arts of other societies and those practised in the European tradition, and such comparisons were used to measure the relative 'advancement' of a culture.

In his world-wide survey *Anthropology* (1881) Edward Burnett Tylor devoted four chapters to what he called 'the arts of life' and a further chapter to 'the arts of pleasure'. Among the arts of life he included the making of tools and weapons, the wheel and its applications, the drill and lathe, the mill, techniques of hunting, agriculture, warfare, building and transport, costume and personal ornament, spinning, weaving, pottery, metal-working, cookery and commerce. In the arts of pleasure he included poetry, music, dance, drama, sculpture, and painting. At first sight one might be tempted to think that here, at last, is a sensible perspective on the arts, which gets away from all those Teutonic abstractions and partisan aesthetic disputes, since its categories are grounded in everyday practicalities.

However, Tylor's division, reflecting as it does the Western distinction between the fine arts and the mechanical or utilitarian arts, takes no account of how such a distinction might be drawn, if at all, in the cultures from which the anthropologist drew his examples. Tylor likewise took for granted that all these practices answer to the satisfaction of universal needs or desires common to the whole human race, rather than to the circumstances of particular societies. This made it possible for him to proceed as if any given art, anywhere in the world and at any point in time, could be judged by a single standard of development, as if it were advancing towards a pre-determined goal, the question for the anthropologist being simply how far it had progressed towards that objective. Thus for Tylor Greek painting was clearly an advance over Egyptian painting, because the Greek painters could produce 'grouped studies of real men', whereas Egyptian painting, although showing ingenuity, had not progressed that far:

> with all their clever expressiveness, the Egyptian paintings have not quite left behind the savage stage of art. In fact they are still picture-writings rather than pictures, repeating rows of figures with heads, legs and arms drawn to pattern, and coloured in childish daubs of colour – hair all black, skin all red-brown, clothing white, and so on. (Tylor 1881: ii.57)

Many might detect a typically British predilection in Tylor's inclusion of games among the 'arts of pleasure'. One seems to hear the tones of a public school headmaster in his solemn declaration:

> Games which exercise either body or mind have been of high value in civilization as trainers of man's faculties. (Tylor 1881: ii.61)

He doubts, however, whether societies 'in a low savage state' ever get beyond 'practical sports' (which serve to introduce children to skills they will need later in life) to the stage of inventing 'games of mere play'. These latter are only found 'higher up in civilization'. He might have hesitated over the words 'mere play' if he had lived to witness the behaviour of late-twentieth-century football 'supporters'.

But the art which Tylor regarded as distinguishing the civilized from the uncivilized peoples, and to which he therefore devoted a special chapter of its own, was the art of writing. Thus, as throughout most of the history of Europe, literacy was promoted to a position of special importance. Tylor's cultural bias did not stop there, however. His account of writing is based on the assumption that the 'best' system is alphabetic, and that a hierarchy of progress can be established, depending how closely other systems approximate to the alphabetic ideal. By this criterion, for instance, Japanese writing comes out as superior to Chinese, since the Japanese at least got as far as breaking words down into their recurrent syllables and selecting a single graphic sign for each. This is not quite alphabetic, but it needed only the further step of breaking down the syllable into consonant and vowel – a step which Japanese scholars never managed to take.

As to why writing should be selected as an overriding yardstick in this way, Tylor makes no bones about it. That it is right to treat the invention of writing as 'the great movement by which mankind rose from barbarism to civilization' is, for him, obvious when we consider 'the low condition of tribes still living without it'. They are unable to keep records or to 'amass knowledge' and pass it on to future generations. It is writing that 'gives permanence to history, law, and science' (Tylor 1881: i.142). Here we see the reasoning of the medieval universities transformed into a cultural criterion for humanity as a whole.

It is interesting to note that Tylor lived to see the day when the Parisian *avant-garde* acclaimed the carving of pre-literate African tribes as more sophisticated than anything produced in the European studios of Tylor's contemporaries. What Tylor thought of this is not recorded. But Tylor's attitude was no exception to a more general European habit of thought in his lifetime concerning the arts of 'lesser breeds' among the world's population. Tylor's Oxford was the Oxford of Ruskin, who had memorably condemned Indian art on the ground that 'it never represents a natural fact'.

> It either forms its compositions out of meaningless fragments of colour and flowings of line; or, if it represents any living creature, it represents that creature under some distorted and monstrous form. To all facts and forms of nature it wilfully and resolutely opposes itself: it will not draw a man, but an eight-armed monster; it will not draw a flower, but only a spiral or a zig-zag. (Ruskin 1859: 265)

This criticism makes one wonder how much Indian art Ruskin had actually seen. But his conclusion concerning the mind of the artist is unhesitating.

> It thus indicates that the people who practise it are cut off from all possible sources of healthy knowledge or natural delight; that they have wilfully sealed up and put aside the entire volume of the world, and have got nothing to read, nothing to dwell upon, but that imagination of the thoughts of their hearts of which we are told that "it is only evil continually." [. . .] They lie bound in the dungeon of their own corruption, encompassed only by doleful phantoms, or by spectral vacancy. (Ruskin 1859: 265–6)

What links Tylor, the anthropologist, to Ruskin, the art critic and educator, is not merely the pervasive ethnocentricity of their view of the arts but their deployment of an artspeak in which it is assumed without question that a direct inference can be made from typical forms of art to the corresponding mental or spiritual state of the society in which those forms flourish. In theory, the two prejudices do not necessarily coincide, but in practice they often go hand-in-hand.

*   *   *

In retrospect it is all too easy to blame Victorian thinkers for failure to recognize that a Western view of the arts is not the only possible view. But the problem that recognition poses has not gone away in the interim, i.e. in the generations that separate the Victorian era from our own. If anything, it has become more complex. The study and promotion of 'primitive art' has become a flourishing business in its own right, encouraged originally by the importance that Vlaminck, Derain, Picasso and others attached to it as a source of inspiration. But whether any of them understood much about the cultural sources and functions of the primitive artifacts they so greatly admired seems doubtful, to judge by their comments.

Picasso, for example, seems to have had a naive theory about a lost golden age of artistic vision, which primitive art preserved. He once told Sabartès:

Primitive sculpture has never been surpassed. Have you noticed the precision of engraved lines in the caves? [. . .] The Assyrian bas-reliefs still have that purity of expression. (Bernadac and Michael 1998: 167)

When Sabartès asked how that original simplicity had been lost, Picasso replied:

Because man ceased to be simple; he wanted to see further and he lost the power of understanding what was within sight. When you reflect, you stop. (Bernadac and Michael 1998: 168)

This rather crude version of the 'noble savage' myth (in which the Assyrians presumably save themselves, in spite of living in cities, by not thinking too much) is the other side of that anthropological coin on which we see the image of mankind emerging from barbarism to civilization through the development of writing. (Writing, as Derrida and others have pointed out, can easily be seen as an 'un-natural' practice, if not a perversion of the original pictography from which it – allegedly – arose.)

An essential part of this cult of the primitive, as it developed in European artistic circles in the early part of the twentieth century, was the facile assimilation of exotic objects into the categories already established in Western artspeak. (Thus anything carved was 'sculpture', anything with pigment was a 'painting', etc.) When Roger Fry in 1920 waxed enthusiastic about the art of the Bushmen of Africa he out-Picassoed Picasso in attributing its qualities to the fact that the Bushman mind was not unduly burdened by the conceptual rigours of reflection. For Fry, 'the primitive drawing of our own race is singularly like that of children' (who, the implication is, do not think very much either). Comparing Bushman animal drawings to two chariot horses on an early Greek vase, Fry explains the shortcomings of the Greek artist by the assumption that he was thinking too much about what he was doing. The Greek was

> incomparably more of an artist [sc. than the Bushman]; but how entirely his intellectual and conceptual way of handling phenomena has obscured his vision! His two horses are a sum of concept-symbols, arranged with great orderliness and with a decorative feeling, but without any sort of likeness to appearance. (Fry 1920: 82)

On this view, evidently, education tolls the knell for draughtsmanship. Warming to his theme, Fry awards the palm to the Palæolithic painters of the Dordogne and Altamira, whose work 'as far as mere naturalism of representation of animals goes' surpasses 'anything that not only our own primitive peoples, but even the most accomplished animal draughtsmen have ever achieved' (Fry 1920: 83). Then, perhaps troubled by the problem of explaining how modern *Homo sapiens* ever developed from ancestors who had no capacity for concept-formation at all, Fry modifies his thesis as follows:

> It would be an exaggeration to suppose that Palæolithic and Bushman drawings are entirely uninfluenced by the concepts which even the most primitive people must form. Indeed, the preference for the profile view of animals – though as we have seen other aspects are frequent – would alone indicate this, but they appear to have been at a stage of intellectual development where the concepts were not so clearly grasped as to have begun to interfere with perception, and where therefore the retinal image passed into a clear memory picture with scarcely any intervening mental process. (Fry 1920: 85)

Here we see an attempt to bolster unconvincing artspeak by appeal to even less convincing neuropsychology. But both in Picasso's case and in Fry's, what is interesting is the compromise to which their artspeak bears witness. Although the cult of the primitive continues the flight from meaning, by consciously opposing the rationalization of art that is represented by the academies, nevertheless it accepts the necessity for artspeak to continue to be a *rational* discourse. Hence both Picasso and Fry are led to seek reasons, however implausible, which could justify their claims concerning the superiority of the primitive. In spite of themselves they are thus drawn into formulating hypotheses about psychology and the history of culture. This is a far cry from the contemporary but self-consciously anarchistic artspeak of Dada.

It is also a far cry from the position taken by a more recent generation of anthropologists. Discussing 'Aesthetics in "primitive societies"', David Stout writes:

anthropologists have long since made it clear that the work of the adult artist in a primitive society is *not* to be equated with that of children in our own, or that it is not representative of an arrested state in human aesthetic possibilities [. . .]. (Stout 1960: 31)

Both Picasso and Fry, evidently, would have needed to revise their view of primitive art rather radically in order to count as pioneers of this more enlightened approach.

*　　*　　*

The use of such epithets as *childish* and *childlike*, however, is also common in discussions of Western paintings produced by 'untrained' painters. Too common to be dismissed as a mere reflex of professional prejudice. In a perceptive chapter on 'The Naïve Vision', Hans Hess points out:

It is also not accidental that at the beginning of the [sc. twentieth] century the art of children was being accepted and eventually cultivated. What was happening was the discovery of the primitive in one's own backyard. (Hess 1975: 92)

He goes on to comment on 'the tragi-comedy of the naïve painters' (such as Rousseau, Séraphine, Vivin, Bombois, Csontvary) who became 'the victims of a cruel joke which they could not understand'. These painters, all 'working-class or petty bourgeois and uneducated', painted as they did 'because they knew no better'. They were taken seriously by the professional artists and critics for what would have been – to the naïve artists themselves – the 'wrong reasons'. 'The discovery of the Naïve was a sort of slumming of the sophisticated' (Hess 1975: 93).

Something similar might be said of children's art, but with the caveat that this could also be taken seriously for quite different reasons. It could be regarded not as pathetic aping of sophistication, but as a psychological revelation of certain intrinsic and universal features of a primitive artistic vision. This put it in the same frame as African sculpture, at least as far as the artists of the Paris *avant-garde* were concerned.

Howard Gardner, discussing children's art from the point of view of a psychologist, cites Picasso's remark: 'Once I drew like Raphael, but it has taken me a whole lifetime to learn how to draw like children' (Gardner 1980: 141). Gardner also gives one of Picasso's preliminary studies for *Guernica* (a drawing of a horse) as an example of a deliberate attempt to 'draw like children'. Gardner is interested in the question of whether 'the young child is an artist, at least in the sense that we apply the term to the mature artist'.

Gardner's way of tackling the problem involves wheeling on a philosopher of art, Nelson Goodman (Goodman 1968), whose role seems to be to tell us what art 'really' is. We can then decide for ourselves which of the candidate cases measures up to the criteria indicated. Gardner fixes upon two of the artistic qualities Goodman identifies, 'expressiveness' and 'repleteness', and proposes to investigate whether or not children's drawings show any command of these qualities.

It is not altogether clear whether Gardner has misconstrued Goodman's definitions, or whether he has deliberately simplified them for purposes of his own inquiry. Gardner seems to assume that an expressive drawing is simply one that conveys an emotion (sadness, happiness, anger, etc.) and a replete drawing one in which the thickness, shape, shading and uniformity of line 'contribute to the work's effect'. The difficulty is, as Gardner admits, that these are somewhat elusive qualities, and different judges might assess a child's drawing differently in these respects. So in order to circumvent that problem, he turns to the results of experimental tests in which children were required to complete drawings already begun.

The objective was to determine whether the child could complete a 'sad' drawing in a 'sad' manner, a thick-lined drawing by using thick lines, and so on. The children were also tested to see whether they could recognize 'appropriate' completions, even if they could not draw such completions themselves. In all cases, the unsurprising finding was that younger children had poorer results on these tests while older children scored better. He concludes:

> While the age varies, depending on the particular "artistic" symptom under examination, children apparently acquire aesthetic sensitivity sometime during the middle years of school. (Gardner 1975: 135–6)

This is a blatant case of redefining 'aesthetic sensibility' in terms to suit the developmental psychologist. It has to be 'measurable' over a life-span. Gardner also discusses the results of tests designed to determine whether a child is able to alter a drawing in order to make it more 'recognizable' to the viewer. Again, the unsurprising results showed that five-year-old children were poor at this, but seven- and eight-year-olds considerably better.

What does all this tell us in the end about the juvenile artist? What is relevant in the present context is to note how these investigations are based on, and presumably prompted by, an artspeak muddle in the first place. In other words, 'art' was equated with 'drawing', and skill in drawing, or in spotting resemblances between drawings, was then equated with artistic sensitivity. The flawed logic seems to be as follows. Picasso is an artist. Picasso can produce drawings having the properties p, q, r, etc. If (or when) the child can produce (and/or recognize) drawings with the properties p, q, r, etc., the child is an artist too.

This is rather like supposing that tests for recognizing and joining together simple tubes of varying dimensions will reveal whether or not the child is a plumber. A crude aptitude test is being confused with engagement in a trade or vocation. But, worse still, *art* is being treated as a cover term for a collection of isolable 'artistic' potentials that exist early on in a 'primitive' form and merely have to come to maturity in the adult artist.

The question 'Is the young child an artist in the sense that the mature artist is?' is already a curious question to start with. (Cf. 'Is the aboriginal artist an artist in the sense that a Western artist is?') But, if we wish to pursue it, there is an even shrewder question to be asked at the same time: 'Is the mature artist an artist in the sense that the young child is?' (Cf. 'Is the Western artist an artist in the sense that an aboriginal artist is?') The whole puzzle is an artspeak conundrum from start to finish. It is generated by first labelling all the possible examples 'art' and then subsequently worrying about whether they 'really' are.

There is a more general point to be made about the early twentieth-century obsession with 'the primitive' (whether in foreign cultures or in children). Only in the so-called 'fine arts' would this ever have been taken seriously. No one engaged at that time in carpentry or dentistry or cartography would ever have supposed that for progress one must diligently seek out lessons to be learnt from pre-literate and pre-industrial tribes, let alone from one's own offspring. And this already tells us something about the intellectual corner into which the 'fine arts' had boxed themselves. The glorification of 'the primitive' is a signal of retreat from the ideal of progress that lay at the heart of the Enlightenment programme.

*   *   *

Although Picasso and his circle in Paris are often given credit for the 'discovery' of primitive art, they were by no means the first on the scene. As early as the 1860s the drawings of the Australian aboriginal artist Tommy McCrae were being collected by Theresa Walker, herself an artist who had emigrated from Britain in 1837 (Sayers 1994: 46–7). At the Centennial International Exhibition in Melbourne in 1888, an exhibition devoted to primitive art aroused great public interest. Under the title 'The Dawn of Art', it consisted entirely of work by contemporary aborigines. The drawings (now in the South Australian Museum) date from the 1880s. The man responsible for the exhibition, John George Knight, was neither an artist nor an anthropologist but a public servant who had in 1880 been appointed Deputy Sheriff of Palmerston Gaol in the Northern Territory. The drawings shown were by five men, whose names are known, four of them prisoners serving sentences and the fifth a native interpreter attached to the gaol.

The title of the exhibition already says a great deal about how Knight interpreted these works. He evidently saw them as evidence of initial steps along the road that 'civilized' art had long since travelled. The drawings are on paper in pencil and coloured crayon. They are almost all of birds, animals and fish, with the name of each species and its English equivalent written beside it, probably in Knight's own hand. It looks as though the artists were told to draw examples of various creatures, but what precise instructions Knight gave them it is impossible to say, or exactly why he wanted these drawings made. The native words for the birds and other creatures come from more than one aboriginal language, which presumably reflects the fact that the prisoners in Palmerston goal, which was in Darwin, had been sent there from various parts of Australia.

These works seem to have made a very favourable impression on the public and were commented on in the press. The accompanying notice at the exhibition made it clear that the drawings had been done 'without the aid of a master'. Knight was highly pleased with their reception, and wrote: 'As I predicted the drawings [. . .] attract almost undue attention, especially from real artists.' The 'real artists' he had in mind, it hardly needs saying, were not aborigines but white Australians. (For Knight's comments, as well as reproductions of some of the drawings, see Sayers 1994: 82–3.) He continues: 'The other evening Mr. Folingsby, a painter of some renown, after a careful inspection of the original works declared that the executants were all worthy of being made honorary members of the Australian Academy of the Arts.' Folingsby was in fact the man then in charge of the Australian National Gallery and its School. Whether his comment was made tongue-in-cheek it is hard to say, but Knight evidently took it at face value. There is no record of the Darwin jailbirds getting any remission of sentence by way of recompense.

The 'Dawn of Art' drawings show animals that seem curiously lifeless. The birds do not look as if they are flying, but nor are they perched on branches or rocks; similarly the animals are neither standing nor running, but they are not sitting down either. The human figures are quite stiff and schematic. The use of colour is notable too. It is not so much used to render the actual colours of the creatures as to draw attention by chromatic contrast to different parts of the anatomy. Some of the bodies have rather implausible bands of coloured stripes, which, it has been suggested, indicate particular joints of meat that were favoured in aboriginal cooking. If this explanation is correct, it would argue that what Knight's primitive artists were (sometimes) aiming at was more a diagram of the creature than a representation of what it looked like.

Critics of Knight's experiment (if that is what it was) will not be slow to point out that as an investigation of primitive art it was flawed from the outset by the fact that the materials supplied to the artists (paper, pencil, crayon) in no way corresponded to those available within the confines of indigenous aboriginal culture. From its very conception, therefore, the 'art' was forced to assume an alien European form of expression. A similar criticism dogged much later attempts to encourage aborigines to produce 'primitive' work. Knight could hardly have foreseen the day when contemporary aboriginal paintings would sell in Sydney galleries, and on the international market, for prices of which any London Academician would have been proud, not to mention many denizens of Montmartre. Those who regard such work as 'inauthentic' point to the fact that much of it was produced, like Knight's exhibition, directly at the bidding of non-aboriginals, and sometimes executed on canvases already stretched, with acrylic paints and Western hair brushes, all supplied by dealers or 'art consultants'. Such critics also point out that in authentic aboriginal settings, painting is never undertaken in order to have a visually attractive object to hang on the wall and admire. Traditionally, all abo-riginal painting was done for a specific purpose, and the purpose was usually associated with particular ceremonies in the life of the community. Once the ceremony was over, it was discarded. If it was body-painting, it was washed off. It was no longer needed. Painting was never kept for decorating the home or preserved for people to come back and look at. There was nothing in abo-riginal culture corresponding to a museum or gallery which functioned as a repository of works to be valued permanently as outstanding achievements of their own kind.

Thus throughout many discussions of primitive art in Australia one soon becomes aware of underlying themes which are often missing elsewhere. The question of artistic 'authenticity' is tied up with that of exploitation, while much of the emphasis on artistic 'originality' is motivated by an awareness of the acute pressures on aboriginal people to compromise with and copy Western lifestyles. Having destroyed so much of aboriginal culture, the Western invaders (or some of them) sought too late to preserve or resuscitate what was left; and part of that conscience-stricken programme involved lauding and conferring the occidental status of 'primitive art' on whatever could possibly be so regarded. This was doubtless felt to be morally preferable to treating aboriginal artifacts primarily as ethnographic specimens or objects of curiosity, and so emphasizing the cultural apartheid that such an approach might seem to imply.

*   *   *

The problems of artspeak cannot be avoided by modern museums and curators. In 1995 there was a major exhibition at the Royal Academy called 'Africa: The Art of a Continent'. It was subsequently put on display in an augmented form at the Guggenheim in New York the following year. In 1997 the *New York Review of Books* published an essay about this exhibition by Anthony Appiah, under the title 'The Arts of Africa'. The author was a Ghanaian living in the U.S.A., who was himself involved with organizing the American version of the exhibition. So he is not an entirely impartial witness. However, he writes about himself:

> I learned about art growing up in my hometown, Kumasi, the capital of Asante, an old Akan kingdom at the heart of the new republic of Ghana. There were paintings and drawings on our walls; there were sculptures and pots, in wood and ivory and earthenware and brass; and there were art books in the bookcases. (Appiah 1997)

Appiah evidently belonged to a wealthy and well-educated family. The first point he makes about this exhibition is that it was based on putting together two Western concepts quite foreign to most of the makers of the original objects on display, one being the idea of 'Africa' and the other being the idea of 'art'. He argues that 'Africa' is an idea invented by Western colonialists. Most of the indigenous inhabitants of that continent, he claims, do not think of themselves as 'African' but as coming from one specific region or people. In fact, the continent is culturally diverse in the extreme and the various cultures have little in common.

Art too, Appiah says, is a Western concept and it plays no role in any of these cultures. Take the case of masks. For Westerners, these are typical African art objects, largely – he suggests – because everyone knows the story of how, when Picasso saw such a mask at the Trocadero museum in 1907, it had a profound influence on his work. But in this European perspective, which was doubtless Picasso's, what was interesting about the mask was the curious way in which it depicted a human face. Whereas what is important about a mask in the culture from which it originates is not its depiction of the human face but its role in the ceremonies or other purposes for which it was made. And these may be very diverse as between the different traditions involved. Appiah gives the following examples. First, the Dan, Mano, and Weinon masks, wooden masks from Liberia, five to ten inches tall, which look like 'something you could wear to a (slightly eerie) Venetian ball', were not used as masks in the Western sense at all. They were to be kept hidden, 'destined for personal protection or enhancement'. At the initiation rites of certain Dan secret societies, the path to the gathering place was strewn with these small masks, and initiates had to pay to have them removed. At circumcisions, the knife blade might be wiped on a small mask. A tray of masks could represent the benevolent spirits of the region. Or they might be installed on personal altars. Elsewhere in the region, however, among the

Yoruba and Igbo, for example, masks *were* worn in public, in masquerades, and the wearer came to represent a god or an ancestor, through possession of the mask. Third, there are cases of using masks in masquerades for pure entertainment, as in the Guro dances of the Ivory Coast. Three Guro masks in the exhibition, one of an elderly man, one of a young woman, and the third unidentified, were made to be worn in inter-village dance competitions.

The point Appiah is making here could be put like this: the category 'African mask', which in reality does not exist, is the product of decontextualizing these objects by putting them in Western museums for people to see as curiosities, without properly understanding what it is they are looking at. Inevitably, in those circumstances, the spectator focuses on what can be seen, what these objects look like, what they have in common, and consequently treats them primarily as representations – often grotesque representations – of human faces. And since, for Western people, representation of the human face is a job for artists – in particular, painters and sculptors – the 'African mask' is automatically classed as a primitive kind of art object.

Another example Appiah gives is Asante goldweights, of which his mother was an avid collector. These are small figures or geometrical shapes, cast in brass, usually from wax originals. They were used for weighing gold dust, which was the traditional currency of the kingdom of Akan. The figurative goldweights come in the forms of people and animals, plants and tools, weapons and domestic utensils, often in arrangements that will remind an Asante who looks at them of a familiar proverb. An example Appiah discusses is a piece in the form of two crocodiles with a shared stomach. This corresponds to an Asante proverb which Appiah translates as: 'Stomachs mixed up, crocodiles' stomachs mixed up, they both have one stomach but when they eat they fight because of the sweetness of the swallowing.' This is a traditional proverb about family life. Its meaning is that what the family acquires benefits the whole family – the family has one collective stomach – but nevertheless only individual members of the family can have the pleasure of consuming what is acquired. However, Appiah adds:

> quite often among these elegant objects, so obviously crafted with great skill and care, one [. . .] has a lump of unworked metal stuffed into a crevice, in a way that seems completely to destroy its aesthetic unity; or, sometimes, a well-made figure has a limb crudely hacked off. These amputations and excrescences are there because, after all, a weight is a weight: and if it doesn't weigh the right amount, it can't serve its function. If a goldweight, however finely crafted, has the wrong mass, then something needs to be added (or chopped off) to bring it to its proper size. [. . .]

Goldweights, in sum, have many of the features that we expect of works of art. In Ashanti itself, they were appreciated for their appeal to the eye, or for the proverbial traditions they engaged. But in the end [. . .] they were weights: and their job was to tell you the value of the gold dust in the weighing pan. (Appiah 1997)

Now it could be argued that what these cases show is simply that in some cultures artistic values play second fiddle to utilitarian values. So there is no compunction about 'spoiling' a work of art in order to make it serve the utilitarian purpose that originally lay behind its making. When utility and art conflict in these instances, it is always art that is sacrificed. One is reminded of the tenth-century additions to the Lindisfarne Gospels.

However, that way of putting it already begs the question. For it describes the situation in terms of Western artspeak, where artistic values stand in opposition to utilitarian values. In cases where both sets of values cannot be satisfied simultaneously, one of them has to lose out. But the issue is whether that is how it is seen in those parts of Africa where the goldweights were made. Were these objects ever 'works of art' for their original makers and users? Does the indigenous culture have the concept of a 'work of art' at all, other than by importation from Europe through colonization?

Appiah himself clearly values the goldweights very highly. He writes:

The best of the Asante goldweights are among the splendours of African creativity. But they were not the product of a culture that valued these objects as art. Their decorative elegance was something prized and aimed for, of course; but it was an ornament, an embellishment, on an object that served a utilitarian function. (Appiah 1997)

Here, interestingly, Appiah's discussion switches abruptly from anthropological explanation into artspeak appraisal. When he refers to 'the best of the Asante goldweights', he is no longer talking about how accurate their weight is, but about what they look like in the museum showcase. When he uses terms such as 'ornament' and 'embellishment' what he is telling us is how they fit in to a well-recognized category: 'the decorative arts'. Thus Western artspeak provides a convenient pigeonhole into which these products of African craftsmanship can be slotted. But that pigeonhole is itself dependent on the recognition of a rather complicated hierarchy of art forms and a supporting theory of the value of manual labour, as Morris's discussion of 'the lesser arts' shows (Briggs 1962: 84–105). What is far from clear is that in the African case there is anything like this structure of ideas to support the recognition of such a category. Once again, all that seems to have been established is that *if* objects similar to Asante goldweights had been made and used in Western society, they would be classified as examples of decorative art. But that does not answer the question of how such things were regarded in the context of the culture to which they belong.

Appiah tells us:

It is clear that some people – chiefs among them, but also the richest commoners – had particularly fine collections of weights, and that, in using them in trade, they advertised their wealth at the same time, by displaying the superior craftsmanship of their possessions. (Appiah 1997)

This suggests a rationale for the production of these objects which is altogether different from that which Morris supplies for his decorative arts. In fact, Morris does not mention anyone amassing *collections* of decorative art objects, or the possibility of their being produced for that purpose. Doubtless in his Socialist eyes that would have established too close and unwelcome a link between the decorative arts and the rich and idle. Appiah concludes that 'in appreciating and collecting these works *as* art we are doing something new with them, something that their makers and the men and women who paid them did not do.'

*   *   *

A quite different approach to the problem is taken by William Fagg and Margaret Plass in their book *African Sculpture*. Their view is that Europeans see certain types of African woodwork, metalwork, etc. as 'art' *not* because the European eye imposes its own preconceptions on the African products but because there are in fact only a limited number of three-dimensional shapes and ways of treating them, and these few recur again and again at different times and places throughout human history. So it is not a case of projecting a specifically European vision on to non-European culture, but rather of *recognizing* the recurrence of a basic set of art patterns that are universal. They explain their project in these terms:

Our purpose is [. . .] to try what is, for us at least, a new way of looking at African art [. . .]. As ethnologists interested in art history, we are well aware that many of the styles and movements widely supposed to have developed for the first time in Europe – even 'Art Nouveau' – really represent recurrent modes in the human arts, modes which have always been available to the artist, within the limits of his human and natural environment. So it occurred to us that it would be interesting, and might be illuminating, to examine some African sculptures in relation to some of these European concepts of art and to see how far, if at all, they are applicable. Since these categories are those in which we are accustomed to think about the more familiar kinds of art, the attempt to use them in the very different conditions of African art may help us to free ourselves from the preconceptions which we unconsciously harbour about the exotic arts. (Fagg and Plass 1964: 5)

They go on to emphasize the 'immense variety of African sculptural forms'.

To a casual glance indeed it may suggest a chaotic confusion of unrestrained stylistic inventiveness such as that which obtains in the art of the Western world today. But African art is no product of romantic decadence; its image, when properly understood, is rather that of a disciplined yet flexible classicism. The apparent confusion arises simply from the fact that the art of each tribe is a separate universe; in traditional Africa the language of art is not intertribal, as the language of Western art is international. When we examine the art of a single tribe we find it to be an entity as coherent and consistent as the tribal religion and philosophy which largely inspired it. Art, in fact, like language, religion, social institutions and customary law, is one of the ways in which a tribe (by its nature an 'in-group') distinguishes itself from its neighbours. In Africa, then, art does know frontiers, and tribality is of its essence. (Fagg and Plass 1964: 6–7)

As for what these authors call, in scare quotes, 'African contemporary art', i.e. non-traditional art, it provides

merely a demonstration that Africans – who are no less well endowed with artistic genius and intelligence than people of other races – are quite capable of working in the international or Western style of art, and here [. . .] African roots are rarely discernible – not surprisingly, since their patrons are still almost exclusively European and American. In these and many other ways the people of Africa are under heavy but largely subliminal pressure to give up their birthright for a mess of pottage. [. . .]

  We do not mean that contemporary art should be discouraged, or cease to be encouraged in those fitted for it. But we do believe that Africans are still largely unaware of the immense value of their tribal art to the world and of the danger that the African values which it represents may soon become fossilized in the world's museums. (Fagg and Plass 1964: 7)

The book then gets down to business and sets about demonstrating the authors' thesis. It begins by quoting Cézanne's remark: 'You must see in nature the cylinder, the sphere and the cone.' On this they make the following comment:

> Cézanne's best-known dictum is often quoted as a kind of summary charter of the modern movement in art; and so it was. But we prefer to consider it here as the clearest explicit appreciation by the early modern artists of the nature of conceptual art, which is not modern but ancient. For people brought up under the influence of the Renaissance tradition, it is usually conceptual art – in which the artist seeks to communicate not the appearance of things but his own ideas or concepts about them – which seems to need explanation. But when we survey the whole field of man's artistic accomplishment, it is rather the Graeco-Roman-Renaissance specialization in naturalistic imitation which appears out of step with the rest of the world – even though the intensity of this specialization produced some of the greatest of all works of art. (Fagg and Plass 1964: 8)

This is virtually the opposite of the Picasso–Fry theory, according to which the 'primitive' vision is characteristically unimpeded by any commerce with concepts. Fagg and Plass then proceed to illustrate Cézanne's three archetypal geometrical forms as found in Nature by giving examples from African sculpture. These are ancient terra-cottas which show the human head modelled as a cylindrical, spherical or conical shape, according to which of the three suits the maker's purpose. The same three shapes are shown combined in the carvings of ancestor figures by sculptors of the Oron tribe. The heads are spherical, the headdress conical, and the upper torso and arms cylindrical. Throughout their book Fagg and Plass draw attention to the similarities between the work of African sculptors and those of well-known European artists, such as Brancusi, Henry Moore and Matisse, while at the same time protesting that this is not a reason for regarding the African sculpture as worthy of attention. ('We do not of course recommend that African sculptures be admired for their resemblance, superficial or not, to modern styles.') In spite of this caveat, it is rather difficult to avoid the conclusion that the reader is being invited to see the African pieces as being 'just as good as' a Brancusi, a Moore or a Matisse; at any rate, no other criteria for admiring these works are suggested.

The affinities between traditional African and modern European sculpture do not stop there. According to Fagg and Plass,

> The twentieth century has been a great one for the naming of styles in art, most of the names ending in '-ism'. But our century did not invent most of these styles, any more than Linnaeus created fauna and flora.

Rather they are to be regarded as modes which have always been available to the conceptual artist [. . .], and which have been placed at the disposal of Europe once more by the liberating effects of the modernist revolution. (Fagg and Plass 1964: 32)

They produce examples of a whole range of modern art styles already found in African sculpture; including 'cubism' in the carvings of the Niger Delta and the Congo basin, 'abstract art' in central Nigeria, 'expressionism' in the Cameroons and Angola, 'naturalism' in various places, and 'assemblage' in Mali and Liberia. But it is not only twentieth-century art styles for which they adduce African parallels: they also find examples of 'Gothic', 'Romanesque', 'Baroque' and 'Rococo'. It begins to seem that whatever feature of European sculpture one cared to mention, however recondite, Fagg and Plass would find its counterpart in some corner or other of the African continent.

Comparing this approach with that of Appiah, it is difficult to avoid the conclusion that Fagg and Plass fall into precisely those traps that Appiah mentions. They base their discussion on taking for granted the concept of 'Africa' on the one hand and the concept of 'art' on the other. As far as they are concerned, 'art' is universal: the question of whether the African objects are works of art at all in their African context is not allowed to arise. But both Appiah on the one hand and Fagg and Plass on the other – in spite of their disclaimers – are engaged in the same enterprise: applying Western artspeak distinctions to a non-Western tradition.

8

Finding the words

In the illusory babels of language, an artist might advance specifically to get lost.

Robert Smithson

As new art forms continued to emerge, modern artspeak faced the recurrent challenge of providing a vocabulary in which the innovations could be identified, discussed, criticized. At an elementary level, this kind of challenge can be met by drawing on the resources that all languages have for naming new things. Inventions are often named by their inventors or after their inventors (*daguerreotype*). Greek and Latin are pressed into service to coin quasi-descriptive designations (*lithography*). Initially, rival terms may compete before one is dropped (*heliography*, *photography*). These lexical processes are well-known and call for no special comment where artspeak is concerned.

Somewhat more problematic are cases in which a designation becomes attached to a school or movement, but no one is quite clear about what exactly this covers. One typical example, already mentioned in an earlier chapter, is that of *cubism*, originally a derogatory term, but adopted by the 'cubists' themselves, even though its etymology soon became inappropriate to their varied styles. Hence Apollinaire's valiant but in the end confusing attempt to distinguish between *cubisme scientifique*, *cubisme physique*, *cubisme orphique* and *cubisme instinctif* (Breunig and Chevalier 1980: 68–9). Nomenclatorial difficulties of this order are commonly complicated by the tendency of schools to fragment and of individual artists to shift allegiance from one movement or sub-movement to another.

Problems of a different order concern the development of terms for the particular properties of a new art form. Very often, the existing vocabulary of a neighbouring art form is drafted in to plug the gap, as in the case of photography borrowing from the vocabulary of painting. But this is an awkward type of solution, inasmuch as it can obstruct the recognition of qualities that are unique to the innovating medium. Photography suffered from this for a long time, being discussed in terms which tended to imply that it was merely a substitute for the art of painting. In some instances, this unsatisfactory situation can be prolonged indefinitely. Collage would be an example of an art form which has its own distinctive range of effects, but virtually no distinctive vocabulary by which to identify them.

The tendency for new arts to lean on old arts, and thus obscure their own originality, is well illustrated by Scriabin's attempt to introduce a chromatic dimension into opera. His *Prometheus*, first performed in Moscow in 1911, included in its score a line for *tastiera per luce*, or 'keyboard of light'. The corresponding 'instrument' was a device intended to project a moving play of colours on to a screen in the theatre. Thus one form of what subsequently became known as 'kinetic art' was initially conceptualized as a form of music, or a translation of sound into visual sensation. This goes back at least to Castel's invention of the *clavessin oculaire* in the eighteenth century, and was supported 'theoretically' by whimsical assumptions about synaesthetic correspondences between colours and sounds (Steadman 1965; Scholes 1983). Other inventions along the same lines, from Rimington's 'colour organ' to Thomas Wilfred's 'clavilux', popularized the notion that colours could be 'played' on an instrument, just as music could be. Here again we are dealing with a line of thinking that could not break free from the artspeak stranglehold.

The conceptual poverty of modern artspeak is nowhere more strikingly illustrated than by Roger Fry, who, when asked in 1928 to supply a list of 'words wanted in connexion with art' could think of only a score or so (Fry 1928). Most of these 'wanted words' identified by Fry were just English translations of already existing foreign terms (*Blütezeit, chiaroscuro, éclat, grisaille,* etc.). He did, however, detect the need for a word for 'the visual arts as a whole in opposition to music and letters'. He also felt that it was 'very desirable that distinctive words should be found for distinguishing the aesthetic from the merely useful or commercial action of inscribing forms and colours on a flat surface'. He deplored the use of the word *artist* in its 'narrower usage of aesthetic painter' and recommended that it 'should cover all kinds of aesthetic creators'. He did not like the term *art-expert* (since it had a 'distinctly commercial suggestion') and opined that the 'profession of the study of art history as contrasted with aesthetics' was 'hardly recognized in England, largely for want of a name'. And he thought it desirable that 'some word should be discovered which would classify so-called works of art which are made to please the average public and generally merely for gain'. But this amounts to more or less the sum total of his thinking on the subject.

It may be urged in Fry's defence that he was not a professional lexicographer or a linguist. But for someone who at the time was recognized as one of the foremost critics of the day, it is remarkable that he admitted to no lacunae when it came to describing the more subtle and original characteristics of the newer art forms.

*   *   *

Some might argue that the situation is quite different nowadays, when the arts have taken their own 'linguistic turn'. There is certainly more awareness, both by artists and commentators, of the importance of terminology and its theoretical implications. But that awareness does not always make for clarity: on the contrary.

To take one example, a leading exponent of 'concrete poetry', Ian Hamilton Finlay, was honest enough to admit in 1963 that the term *concrete* still puzzled him.

> I wonder if we are not all a little in the dark, still as to the real significance of 'concrete' [. . .]. For myself I cannot derive from the poems I have written any 'method' which can be applied to the writing of the next poem [. . .]. 'Concrete' began for me with the extraordinary (since wholly unexpected) sense that the syntax I had been using, *the movement* of language in me, at a physical level, was no longer there – so it had to be replaced with something else, with a syntax and movement that would be true of the new feeling (which existed in only the vaguest way, since I had, then, no form for it . . .). So that I see the theory as a very essential (because we are people, and people think, or should think, or should TRY to think) part of our life and art; and yet I also feel that it is a construction, very haphazard, uncertain, and by no means as yet to be taken as definitive. (Finlay 1963: 9–10)

Here there was recognition of a need to get to grips with language at two levels, one at the level of writing poetry and the other at the level of theorizing about poetry. But quite what the relation between these two levels was remained obscure.

Concrete poets themselves found it difficult to articulate this relationship. Pierre Garnier (to whom Finlay's letter was addressed) had tried to do so in a series of propositions including the following:

> The word is an element.
> The word is a material.
> The word is an object.
> [. . .]
> Every word is an abstract picture.
> A surface. A volume.

A surface on the page. A volume when spoken.

[...]

Visual poetry should not be 'read'. It should be allowed to 'make an impression', first through the general shape of the poem and then through each word perceived out of the whole at random.

A word which is read only grazes the reader's mind: but a word that is perceived, or accepted, starts off a chain of reactions there. (Garnier 1965)

Whatever we may think of these statements, this is at least an attempt to forge an artspeak adequate to the writer's understanding of the new enterprise. It recognizes an inevitable conflict with an old artspeak, an artspeak in which, for example, written poetry entails 'reading'. But the new artspeak rapidly gets bogged down by the inadequacy of its own linguistic terminology. It confuses words either with their inscriptions or with their sounds.

The unsympathetic way to view concrete poetry in the 1960s was to say:

Basically, it is a hybrid: an attempt to marry literary content with abstract design [...]. (Lucie-Smith 1966: 43)

But the derogatory term *hybrid* presupposes the prior existence of 'pure' strains. It disguises the fact that concrete poetry signalled not so much the deliberate 'crossing' of pure strains as the breakdown of the old categorizations that traditional artspeak had imposed upon the arts.

Another case in point was the emergence of the *lettriste* movement in France. This implicated not just poetry and painting but music too. But apologists for the movement often found themselves struggling to say exactly what *lettrisme* was. Thus in the volume on *la musique lettriste*, published in 1971 by *La revue musicale*, Albert Richard was obliged to admit, paradoxical as it might seem, that *la musique lettriste* was not, after all, music. Among his reasons were that even though the oral performance utilized the human voice for phonation, and thus made it comparable to singing, *lettriste* compositions dispensed entirely with melody and rhythmic variation. On the other hand, he argued, *lettriste* compositions were not poetry either, because their basic unit was not the word, but the (meaningless) sound (Richard 1971). And *a fortiori*, for Richard, *lettrisme* is not language (*langage*). Whether these conclusions would have been endorsed by all his colleagues in the *lettriste* camp is another matter. The interest lies in the form of the argument. Here Richard is maintaining not merely that traditional artspeak fails to accommodate *lettrisme* as an art form, but that *that failure itself* validates the recognition of a new art form. In other words, the poverty of traditional artspeak is both assumed and treated as a platform for identifying something new *as art*.

*　　　*　　　*

Perplexities of this order reached new depths with what one prominent art historian called the 'dematerialization of the art object' (Lippard 1973). This, allegedly, was a totally unprecedented development, unique in world history. Paradoxically, it acquired the already second-hand designation 'conceptual art' (previously used to identify types of painting which sacrificed exact visual representation in the interests of expressing the artist's conception of what was depicted). Conceptualist artspeak, which accompanied this allegedly new development and promoted the designation, played a key role not only in justifying the 'dematerialization' but in actually identifying the dematerialized object. 'Dematerialization' *avant la lettre* had been anticipated in 1952 by John Cage's composition for piano entitled $4'33''$, in which no notes are played. This, as one admirer solemnly observed, meant in practice that 'it could just as legitimately be performed on any other instrument(s)' (Kostelanetz 1996: 54). The most notorious of all exhibitions mounted under conceptualist auspices, by Robert Barry in Amsterdam in 1969, confronted the visitor with a sign on the door which read: 'during the exhibition the gallery will be closed'. There was no work on view.

Conceptualism ushered in a new era in the relations between the work of art and verbal comment about it. Words, under the new dispensation, became essential in the recognition of a product of artistic creativity, where the product itself could be neither heard nor seen. This move in practice promoted art theory to a position of superiority with respect to the production of art. It could not fail to be controversial. One contemporary polemic against the conceptualists and other alleged 'phonies' of the art world was entitled *The Painted Word* (Wolfe 1976). It began by taking to task the art critic of *The New York Times* for saying that

'given the nature of our intellectual commerce with works of art, to lack a persuasive theory is to lack something crucial – the means by which our experience of individual works is joined to our understanding of the values they signify'. (Wolfe 1976: 4)

Wolfe interpreted this as claiming that 'without a theory to go with it, I can't see a painting'. By implication, this was regarded as an affront to common sense. Neither Kant nor Hegel nor any other authority in the field of aesthetics had ever gone so far as to suggest that *theorizing* was an essential precondition of vision. And public theorizing requires words. On the other hand, as Wolfe proceeded to argue, there were indeed forms of art that required theorization if they were to be regarded as art at all. Not coincidentally, these turned out to be the dubious forms of contemporary art promoted by those who were currently influential in the New York art world.

Wolfe was well aware of the historical irony by which, after the Modernist rejection of the 'literary' character of academic art, the wheel of fortune had now come round, apparently, to this dependence on the verbal. He pointed out that as late as 1966 an exponent of Minimalist art, Frank Stella, was still saying: 'My painting is based on the fact that only what can be seen there *is* there' (Wolfe 1976: 9). So seeing was still believing. But the new reverence for theory reversed the traditional wisdom: believing was henceforth seeing. According to Wolfe's history of modern art, the roots of this revolution were to be found in the financial dependence of the artist upon the whims of fashion in *le monde*, a dependence which had brought fame and wealth to Picasso, Braque and many more. In practice, success depended on the dealer system. The dealer had become the essential intermediary who negotiated the status of the artist in the marketplace of the day. This brought about a disjunction between what artists said (and believed?) their aims to be, on the one hand, and what everyone else regarded the (fashionable) artists as doing. Very few artists, Wolfe points out, followed the lead of Gauguin and deserted the metropolis for the remote Pacific island. Most kept within walking distance of the places where, with any luck, their art could be sold. This arrangement suited all parties. The artist was free to be as iconoclastic and revolutionary as he or she might wish, provided that the resultant painting and sculpture could be marketed as expensive *chic*. (Expensive necessarily, because anything too cheap cannot be *chic*.) The reward for the patrons, in Wolfe's scenario, was the salvation of becoming 'Benefactor of the Arts' in expiation of the sin of having 'Too Much Money'.

Acceptance by the art world, according to Wolfe, is not to be confused with acceptance by the general public. Far from it. On the contrary, there would be no point in being a Benefactor of the Arts if that meant just endorsing or financing the taste of the *hoi polloi*. That would betoken an abject failure to distinguish oneself from the masses. According to Wolfe's calculation, the self-elected art world of the late twentieth century comprised no more than ten thousand individuals, concentrated in eight major cities.

Irrespective of Wolfe's arithmetic, if his perspective is roughly right that would explain the emergence of a new function for artspeak. Instead of seeking to mediate between the artist and the public, or even between the artist and the patron, artspeak was called upon to *direct* new departures in art. This was quite different from commenting retrospectively on the works of art produced, or explaining the history of the movements that had given rise to them. This new directive function was based on the recurrent marketing need to offer a new product that was constantly 'one step ahead' of anyone else's offerings. The only way this could be achieved – since there was no question of allowing time for any consensus to emerge – was by letting artspeak articulate the prospectus as well as the interpretation.

The earliest form of this phenomenon had been the artistic 'manifesto' of the first decades of the twentieth century. The first Futurist manifesto by Marinetti (1909) was followed by Boccioni's (1910), Schindler's architectural manifesto (1912), Tristan Tzara's Dada manifesto (1918), Naum Gabo's 'Realistic Manifesto' (1920) and André Breton's first surrealist manifesto (1924). There were comparable programmatic announcements in the name of Neo-Primitivism by Shevchenko (1913), of Vorticism by Wyndham Lewis (1914) and of Suprematism by Malevich (1916). In this proliferation of the genre we see evidence of a growing conviction that it was essential not just to produce poetry, paintings, buildings, music, etc. but to produce public statements explaining or proclaiming what was going on. With hindsight, it might be seen as only a matter of time before the statements would take precedence over the works of art, and only a little more time before the works of art could be dispensed with altogether. At that point, the 'dematerialization' of the art object would be complete. Barry's non-exhibition in Amsterdam reached that point. In artspeak it was marked in the same year by Sol LeWitt's famous dictum (included in a statement of the familiar 'manifesto' type, *Sentences on Conceptual Art*) that 'Ideas alone can be works of art' (Lippard 1973: 75–6).

This represents what may be called the 'strong' form of the conceptualist thesis, as distinct from the 'weak' form which merely asserts that in a work of art the idea is more important than the actual execution. The problem with 'dematerialization' when carried as far as the 'strong' thesis claimed (and Robert Barry's Amsterdam exhibition demonstrated) was – or was perceived to be – that the work of art lacked any public existence unless and until the artist's idea found expression in some shape or form. Thus the conceptualists, in spite of their own proclamations (or unless committed to some vacuous programme of Barry-type non-exhibitions), had also to tackle the problem of identifying the idea. Some – LeWitt, for example – allowed that ideas might be expressed in *any* form, including words. But this concession brought in its wake the conundrum of how to distinguish linguistic expressions of the idea from the verbal arts as traditionally recognized. LeWitt's feeble solution was: 'If words are used, and they proceed from ideas about art, then they are art and not literature' (*Sentences on Conceptual Art*, No.16). But why literature should not count as art, and why that should matter, remained far from clear. However, LeWitt seemed convinced that there was at least an important distinction between art and its verbal discussion. The concluding assertion in *Sentences on Conceptual Art* reads: 'These sentences comment on art, but are not art' (Lippard 1973: 76).

'But why not?' was the next question for conceptualists to tackle, and they proceeded to do so. The very distinction between art and verbal comment on art was called in question in the editorial to the first issue of the journal *Art-Language* in 1969. The writer raised the issue of whether the editorial itself, as an essay on conceptual art, did not qualify as a conceptual art work in its own right. What was being challenged here, clearly, was the dividing line between art and artspeak.

This unfortunately proved to be a challenge too difficult for the writer to handle. Adrift in unfamiliar intellectual waters, he first reached for an anchor in the traditional criterion of intentions.

> What has to be considered here is the intention of the conceptual artist. It is very doubtful whether an art theoretician could have advanced one of his works as a work of 'conceptual art' in (say) 1964, as the first rudiments of at least an embryonic awareness of the notion of 'conceptual art' were not evident until 1966. The intention of the 'conceptual artist' has been separated off from that of the art theoretician because of their previously different relationships and standpoints toward art, that is, the nature of their involvement in it. (Harrison and Wood 1992: 874)

In many quarters the appeal to intentions was disappointingly *déjà vu*. Whoever wrote the *Art-Language* editorial seemed never to have heard of the 'intentional fallacy' (Wimsatt 1954), and in any case gave no reason why both artistic and critical intentions should not be combined in the same work. The editorial then went on to consider the possibility of hanging the text of the essay behind glass on a gallery wall. Would it then become a work of art? The writer was unhappy with that conclusion, pointing out that even if exhibited on a gallery wall, it needed to be read, not just seen. This laboured rediscovery of the obvious seemed to settle the matter, at least for the time being.

It did not, however, convince many conceptual artists of the day, who frequently exhibited work consisting solely of texts hung for display in the manner appropriate to traditional paintings, thus by implication claiming parity of status with the latter. This invasion of the picture-space by words was accompanied by a rather desperate search for linguistic theorizing which would provide some justification or backing for 'materializing' the art work in this manner.

One of the more arresting reflections of this was Kosuth's work entitled *One and Three Chairs* (1965). The three components of this work comprise the text of a dictionary entry for the word *chair*, hanging alongside a photograph of a chair, while on the floor below stands the chair shown in the photograph (Atkins 1990: 64). The relevance of this juxtaposition is obvious to anyone acquainted with the theory of signs which goes back to Plato and Aristotle and has dominated linguistic thinking in the Western tradition ever since. It could also be read as a comment on the naivety of those conceptualists who supposed that an idea could exist in the mind of the artist in some pristine state, independently of or uncontaminated by either verbal or non-verbal forms of communication. One might even have taken Kosuth's *One and Three Chairs* as making Saussure's point that concepts do not exist until they are verbally delimited. But that is not suggested by Kosuth himself, who later commented as follows:

> Language began to be seen by me as a legitimate material to use. Part of its attraction too was that by being so contrary to the art one was seeing at that time [i.e. mid–60s] it seemed very personal to me. I felt I had arrived at it as a personal solution to personal art problems. So then I used photostats of dictionary definitions in a whole series of pieces. I used common, functional objects – such as a chair – and to the left of the object would be a full-scale photograph of it and to the right of the object would be a photostat of a definition of the object from the dictionary. Everything you saw when you looked at the object had to be the same that you saw in the photograph, so each time the work was exhibited the new installation necessitated a new photograph. I liked that the work itself was something other than simply what you saw. By changing the location, the object, the photograph and still having it remain the same work was *very* interesting. It meant you could have an art work which was that *idea* of an art work, and its formal components weren't important. I felt I had found a way to make art without formal components being confused for an expressionist composition. The expression was in the idea, not the form – the forms were only a device in the service of the idea. (Kosuth 1991: 50)

One notes the absence from these remarks of any explicit recognition by Kosuth (i) that what makes the idea 'the same work' in its various manifestations then becomes the unchanging verbal definition, or (ii) that this conception of the 'idea' resurrects a long discredited linguistic theory which treats words like *chair* as mere labels for antecedently given objects.

Although in his published writings on art Kosuth makes reference to linguists, including Saussure and Sapir, and even uses the Saussurean technical terms *langue* and *parole*, such references tend to be both fleeting and opaque. Like others associated with the Art & Language group, he seems reluctant to engage with linguistics in any serious way. One is left with the impression of vague theoretical gestures in a linguistic direction, but nothing more.

Typical is Kosuth's deployment of the notion that art forms are 'languages'. This, although insistently repeated, never advances beyond hackneyed metaphor. Commenting on Sapir's statement that 'we see and hear and otherwise experience very largely as we do because the language habits of our community predispose certain choices of interpretation', Kosuth observes:

In art the 'means of expression' is also not unlike language. Even
accepting the common view that art's history goes back hundreds of
years, it is possible to see that the 'language' of the art of the west has
been painting and sculpture for some time. Up until the very recent past
it has been assumed that if one wanted to speak as an artist he had to
speak in the 'correct' language. That's how we knew he was an artist and
what he made was art or meant to be art. Whatever was done, it had to
be done *within* that language. (Kosuth 1991: 43)

Here Kosuth seems to be applying the term *language* to art as meaning no
more than 'accepted set of conventions' and viewing the art work as an item
of 'discourse' conforming thereto. He evidently fails to see that even at this
simplistic level the analogy he wishes to draw does not hold. The point Sapir
is making has nothing to do with conventionality or 'correctness' in verbal
discourse. Sapir is talking about the way established *verbal* habits influence
perception of *non-verbal* reality. The parallel point about art would have to be
that the ways in which a society's artists habitually depict nature influence
how members of that society see natural phenomena. But even there the
art/language parallel is weak, because whereas all members of society are
habitual language-users, not all are habitual painters or sculptors.

The connexion between art and language is strained further still by
Kosuth's tendentious account of the history of modern art:

In art before the 'modern' period the language form was the carrier of
"the depiction of religious themes, portraiture of aristocrats, detailing of
architecture" and so on. The modern period brought an end to art's
invisibility and first painters, then sculptors began to focus on art's
language – not as a means, but as an end. While art was still being
conveyed by the use of the same language form (painting and sculpture)
it was vastly different from earlier 'art' because the 'art condition'
became singularly identified with the language form itself. Up until ten
years ago [= c.1960] the modern period was about really only this one
thing: the myriad uses of art's language *as* art. Focusing on art's
language was the one immediate way to make art and only art *without*
the confusion of subject matter or a new language form which might be
interesting in their own right.

In the past few years artists have realized that their traditional
language is exhausted and unreal. (Kosuth 1991: 44)

In all this Kosuth shows no inclination to address the fundamental question
of what makes language in the traditional sense a distinctive mode of human
communication and whether these distinctive properties bear any convincing

relationship to those of painting and sculpture. He also seems quite unaware that the thesis that art is a 'language' had already been critically explored with far more sophistication and in far greater detail by a number of writers, from Collingwood (*The Principles of Art*, 1938) down to Nelson Goodman (*Languages of Art*, 1968). So although *language* is a key term in Kosuth's brand of artspeak, its theoretical backing is lamentably weak. Much the same might be said of other apologists for conceptual art. They indulged in much cultural name-dropping (trendy references to Wittgenstein, Freud, *et al.*), but no conceptualist came close to offering a serious rationale for the way in which, by the late 1960s, verbalization had supplanted execution in the concerns and activities of at least one sector of the contemporary art world.

*   *   *

In retrospect, conceptual art was just another dead-end in the history of modern art. But the reasons for its failure are undoubtedly more interesting than the reasons for the failure of many similarly short-lived art movements. It was not simply that its products were often boring, both visually and in other ways, or that it lacked among its adherents any artist of stature. It failed because it set itself from the beginning a problem which it did not have the intellectual resources to solve, i.e. the relationship between art and artspeak, or, more generally, the relationship between word and idea. Its practitioners never succeeded in getting to grips with distinguishing the diverse functions that words may fulfil in human communication or the means by which those functions are fulfilled.

One of the ironies in this failure was that the conceptualists themselves were trapped in an oligarchic artspeak which reserved the term *art* primarily for their own concerns. Although claiming to be searching for a new 'language' of art, they were not particularly interested in the ways in which the divisions between the various arts, as traditionally recognized, were being eroded by experimental work in other areas. Thus we find Kosuth flatly rejecting the suggestion that his own use of verbal material had anything in common with concrete poetry, even though the similarities were obvious to less biased observers. According to Kosuth there was: 'Absolutely no relationship at all. It's simply one of things superficially resembling one another' (Kosuth 1991: 51). For Kosuth, 'the typical concrete poem makes the worst sort of superficial connections to work like mine, because it's a kind of formalism of typography – it's cute with words, but dumb about language' (Kosuth 1991: 51–2). The implicit claim that Kosuth, on the contrary, was 'smart' about language reveals both the pretentiousness and the self-deception that conceptualists concealed from themselves. For Kosuth, concrete poetry was significant merely because it represented the end of the road for traditional poetry:

In New York the last decadent stages of poetry can be seen in the move by 'Concrete' poets recently toward the use of actual objects and theatre. Can it be that they feel the unreality of their art form? (Kosuth 1991: 24)

In a dismissive footnote which reflects his underlying concern to distance conceptual art from anything that might be 'literary', Kosuth adds: 'Ironically, many of them call themselves "Conceptual Poets"'. Elsewhere he states that concrete poetry 'merely hailed the death of poetry' (Kosuth 1991: 35).

But this unconvincing attempt to uphold a traditional artspeak boundary between visual and verbal art was perhaps the last of its kind. From a later perspective it seemed obvious that concrete poetry 'can appropriately be considered a visual art, though it is also a literary one' (Bann 1996). In certain respects, therefore, conceptual art was a belated attempt to breach a barrier that concrete poetry had already breached many years earlier. The presentation of 'verbal material' as visual art was no longer new. According to one historian of the movement, conceptual art usually came in one or other of four formats: (i) *readymade*, (ii) *intervention*, (iii) *documentation*, or (iv) *words* (Godfrey 1998: 7). The last of these formats had the attraction that

A language-based art allowed communication via the postal service or even the telex system. It obviated the need for unnecessary production. When Victor Burgin called for 'an art of pure information' it was firstly out of revulsion at 'all those bent bits of metal and acres of canvas clogging up the basements of museums. A form of ecological pollution.' Secondly, Burgin was calling for an art that could communicate directly. Whereas Donald Judd might use the telex to send instructions for a sculpture's fabrication, other artists were using it to convey artworks themselves. (Godfrey 1998: 166–7)

This account of what happened, if plausible, presumably reflected the pathetic naivety of conceptual artists when bedazzled by modern technologies of communication. Its apogee is the misguided notion of an art of 'pure information'. This would hardly escape unscathed nowadays in an undergraduate classroom, let alone pass muster as a serious theoretical proposition.

Be that as it may, 'word-based art' eventually became a distinct sub-branch of the conceptualist movement. Among its better-known practitioners were Kosuth, Bruce Nauman, Robert Barry and Jenny Holzer. Not many seem to have realized an inherent problem in choosing words as the preferred mode of materialization for their ideas. Their dilemma is described by Godfrey as follows:

If one wanted to make an art of pure information, then words might initially have seemed an appropriate means, but [. . .] such a project was doomed to failure. Words cannot exist without matter: paper, ink, a computer screen, the air through which we speak. (Godfrey 1998: 351)

Those who did recognize both the problem and its insolubility, such as John Baldessari (quoted in Godfrey 1998: 351), eventually abandoned word-based art, realizing that 'it becomes all visual spectacle and the meaning is lost'.

For some conceptualists, an appeal to language was even more central in defining conceptual art. According to Mel Bochner:

A doctrinaire Conceptualist viewpoint would say that the two relevant features of the 'ideal Conceptual work' would be that it have an exact linguistic correlative, that is, it could be described and experienced in its description, and that it be infinitely repeatable. (Quoted in Smith 1994: 259)

This at least makes it clear what some conceptualists saw as one of the key properties of language; i.e. it made exact 'quotation' possible. Language could elide the difference between the original (artistic) act and its subsequent re-enactment. What conceptualists showed no indication of understanding was (i) where this idea about 'language' came from, or (ii) what was wrong with it.

Part III
ARTSPEAK AND COMMUNICATION

Linguistic preliminaries to Part III

The connexions between philosophy of art and philosophy of language have been curiously neglected throughout the Western tradition. The neglect is all the more remarkable given that the connexions are already evident in antiquity. The same thinkers who inaugurated Greek philosophy of art were those who inaugurated Greek philosophy of language. The relationship between these two enterprises is not fortuitous. Both are aspects of a more comprehensive intellectual effort to understand the role of human activities in their social setting. Once we recognize this, it seems natural to ask for some more explicit account of how Western thinking about the arts relates to Western thinking about language.

Superficially it might seem easy enough to identify a nucleus of propositions or types of statement which are – and always have been – basic to artspeak in the Western tradition. This nucleus would probably include the following:

1. 'Activity *A* is / is not an art.'
2. 'Activity *A* is / is not an art of type *T*.'
3. 'Individual *I* practises / does not practise an art of type *T*.'
4. 'Condition *C* is / is not a necessary condition for all art (of type *T*).'
5. '*W* is / is not a work of art (of type *T*).'
6. '*W* is / is not a work by individual *I*.'
7. '*W* is / is not a work which has the property *P*.'

When lexical values are supplied for the variables in the above statement-types, we might have, for example:

1. 'Poetry is an art.'
2. 'Music is one of the liberal arts.'
3. 'Michelangelo was a sculptor.'
4. 'Not all art is beautiful.'

5. '*Fidelio* is an opera.'
6. 'Shakespeare wrote *Hamlet*.'
7. 'The Eiffel Tower is a functional building.'

A fully explicit descriptive account of Western artspeak would need to examine all the values which, at different times in history and in different languages, have been assumed to hold for the lexical variables *A, C, I, T, P* and *W*. Such an account would require many volumes and many contributors, but it is not impossible in principle. It might reveal a multitude of interesting details about the development of artspeak and the case histories of particular terms. It would not, however, serve the purposes of the present inquiry for at least two reasons.

Such an investigation, one suspects, would inevitably end up presenting a highly complex picture in which a clear view of the wood was obscured by the trees. In other words, the central question of what *necessitated* the linguistic maintenance of artspeak in general over so many centuries would get hidden behind a mass of particular observations about particular artspeak usages. In the second place, assuming we had such an account available, that would not automatically answer the question: 'What do these statements mean?' And this would not be a matter of asking for other artspeak paraphrases or translations of them. It would be a matter of going into the underlying assumptions about what makes such statements meaningful at all.

This is the level at which linguistic theory becomes relevant to any enterprise of discourse analysis. But there is no neutral or impartial way to proceed here, because linguistic theory itself is riddled with controversy. That is why anyone rash enough to propose an investigation of the linguistic underpinnings of Western artspeak incurs the obligation to begin by laying a few linguistic cards of their own on the table. I here lay out mine.

Card No. 1 is my assumption that different theories of the linguistic sign will yield different analyses of artspeak (and other forms of discourse).

Card No. 2 is my assumption that words are neither labels for concepts nor substitutes for other words (as the format of traditional dictionaries seems to suggest) but integrated components of communication processes.

Card No. 3 is my assumption that the structure of a communication process cannot be decontextualized, being created by the participants themselves.

Card No. 4 is my assumption that there are no autonomous linguistic signs. What we recognize as a linguistic sign (e.g. a word) is always the product of a particular communication situation.

Card No. 5 is my assumption that the vocabulary of artspeak is subject to the same semantic indeterminacy as all other vocabulary.

Anyone acquainted with recent developments in linguistic theory will recognize these as typically 'integrationist' assumptions. Anyone not thus acquainted will need to be told that integrationism is an approach to language and communication which takes issue rather radically with some of the basic presuppositions that are accepted in orthodox linguistics (Harris 1996; Toolan 1996). There can be no question of setting out the main points of contention here, since that would require a historical detour as long as, or longer than, the rest of this book. What matters most for the comprehension of the following three chapters is the integrationist critique of a set of widely held beliefs about language which constantly crop up in different guises throughout the Western tradition.

These flawed beliefs take roughly the following form. The archetypal communication situation is taken to be one in which A has an idea and wishes to communicate that idea verbally to B. Let us suppose, for the sake of argument, that the idea in question is that water boils at a temperature of 100 degrees Celsius. A's problem is then to find a language, known also to B, in which this idea can be expressed. (Note that nothing depends on whether the boiling point of water can be shown to be 100 degrees Celsius or not. The illustration would work just as well if A wished to tell B that water boils at 150 degrees Celsius, or any other temperature for that matter.)

For A's specific purpose, many languages will not do as instruments of communication. Latin, for instance – at least, the Classical Latin of Cicero and Caesar – lacks the appropriate terminology. The Romans did not measure temperature by means of thermometers, and in any case Celsius had not been born when Caesar died. So if A wishes to communicate this idea about the boiling point of water to B, A must look for a language with more up-to-date credentials, which has the requisite verbal equipment.

Underlying this is the notion that languages are basically sets of verbal rules for expressing ideas. Ideas cannot be forced into a linguistic mould incapable of accommodating them. If a language has no numerical vocabulary for dealing with numbers higher than three, then it is futile to look there for any way of expressing the square root of forty-nine. Nor is it possible to say 'Today is Tuesday' in a language which does not have names for the days of the week. And, *mutatis mutandis*, this goes for all ideas and all languages.

So artspeak is no exception. For the example 'Water boils at a temperature of 100 degrees Celsius' we might substitute, say, 'Photography is not an art', or 'Palestrina's development of the art of polyphony was not affected by his expulsion from the papal choir.' In other words, a linguistic statement *of any kind* presupposes the existence of established procedures for expressing it, and it cannot be expressed in the absence of such procedures. Where there are no appropriate procedures, communication breaks down.

To believe this is how language works is to subscribe to something like the following proposition: linguistic communication is a matter of knowing a verbal code, by means of which one individual may transmit precise thoughts, feelings, etc. to another, on condition that the other individual likewise knows the verbal code in question. Knowledge of the code is thus essential both in order to encode the message at the outset and in order to decode it correctly at the receiving end. This summarizes a set of popular beliefs and assumptions which integrationists call (with intentional disparagement) 'the language myth' (Harris 1981). The ramifications of this myth extend deep into the foundations of Western society, since they support a whole range of claims about the rights and responsibilities of individuals *vis-à-vis* society, and of society towards its members. Integrationists have argued – persuasively, in my view – that the language myth is implicated in many diverse areas of public discourse; not only, as it obviously is, in legal discourse (Love 1998; Toolan 2001), but also in, for example, racial theory (Hutton 2001) and modern neuropsychology (Taylor 2001). Thus it comes as no surprise that it should likewise be implicated in the discourse of the arts.

For integrationists, the language myth is a myth because what it takes for granted is something which can never be verified or even made to appear plausible, except by manœuvres that are intellectually circular. (These include asking: 'How could language possibly work otherwise?') The myth assumes (i) that communication is a process of telementation, i.e transference of the message that originated in *A*'s mind to *B*'s mind, and (ii) that this telementational process is possible because *A* and *B* both have access to the same fixed code for transmitting messages. What is clear enough is the internal rationale of the myth. The 'fixed code' component underwrites the 'telementational' component. For without a fixed code it is difficult to see how telementation could work. Complementarily, there would be no point in postulating a fixed code unless communication between *A* and *B* were envisaged as a telementational process.

What I shall be arguing in the three following chapters is that Western artspeak always has been – and still is – deeply committed to this language myth. Furthermore, this commitment explains at least some of the impasses that Western art theorists have manœuvred themselves into.

For the language myth, over the course of many centuries, has been extended and applied to a variety of arts. In its most generalized form, it can be applied to music, architecture, ceramics, television and many other sets of 'artistic' practices. In this more extended role, it becomes society's basic communication myth. A preliminary description might run as follows:

Certain forms of communication involve a process of transmitting messages. Individuals are able to send and/or interpret messages whenever they have come to understand and follow the relevant procedure of transmission (public or private, voluntary or involuntary, natural or artificial). This is based on recurrent instantiation of certain invariant items.

These items are 'signs'. They are invariant items in two respects: form and meaning. Knowing the form and meaning of a sign enables one to identify and interpret the message it conveys.

In this generalized form of the myth, a 'sign' or complex of signs can take any physical form whatsoever. It may be a gesture, a building, a symphony, a ceremony, a piece of legislation. Treating *as many activities and relationships as possible* in these terms has become, cumulatively, characteristic of Western culture. To be a culturally competent member of one's society is conceived of as being familiar with all the various communicational codes that society has developed as a framework for the conduct of human affairs. Whether any individual is fully competent in this sense, at least in the communicational labyrinths of the modern world, may be open to doubt; but this nevertheless remains the ideal.

The major problem for those who believe in any version of the communication myth has always been to explain how any sign is set up in the first place. How does it come to have the determinate form and meaning required for its function *as a sign*? Where do the meanings of signs come from? What establishes that a meaning shall take this particular form, and not some other form? The problem constantly resurfaces throughout the Western tradition.

In Chapters 9 and 10 I shall discuss in some detail two types of solution that are particularly relevant to the development of artspeak. Between them they have provided the foundation for most of the artspeak in the Western tradition. One solution suggests that linguistic codes have their source in Nature and reflect the way the world is (or is conceived to be). The other solution suggests that linguistic codes are the product of human conventions, irrespective of how the world is or seems to be. (A convention, it is assumed, can be set up simply by fiat or by consensus: it does not additionally require the backing of Nature. Thus double yellow lines at the edge of the road, in certain cultures, conventionally prohibit the parking of motor vehicles; but not because Nature makes it impossible to park on surfaces thus marked.) The terms I shall adopt for these two interpretations of the linguistic code are (i) 'surrogational' for the former, and (ii) 'contractual' for the latter. The first, I shall argue, is the theory of the linguistic code which underlies traditional artspeak from Plato down to Hegel, while the second underlies much of modern artspeak in the nineteenth and twentieth centuries.

These two ways of interpreting linguistic codes are relevant here because the whole discourse of the arts, as it developed in European culture, was always intimately interwoven with the language available for discussing other everyday topics. *It had to be*, because the arts were always envisaged as playing an important part in social affairs. The necessity of artspeak was in the end the necessity for some form of discourse enabling practitioners of the arts to communicate with the general public. This ensured that it always remained open for the lay observer to express an opinion about artists, artistic practices and works of art, however much this lay opinion might be derided by experts.

The surrogational and contractual theories that I shall be discussing provide quite different validations for artspeak; but both theories underwrite the necessity of artspeak. That is, they provide a linguistic logic for artspeak, within the framework supplied by the communication myth. In this way they bring artspeak into line with other forms of discourse deemed to be necessary for running a well-organized society.

In Chapter 11 I shall go on to consider artspeak from an integrationist point of view. This more recent approach to linguistic theory probes behind the traditional doctrines of the communication myth. It attempts to show how, at any given point in history, the choice and meaning of key terms deployed in discussing the arts derives from the social and intellectual activities which those discussions serve to integrate. Artspeak thus emerges as a powerful instrument in moulding public perception of the arts, rather than a mere reflection of current views. I shall also argue that the range of possible outcomes in any debate concerning the arts tends to be restricted in advance by the form of artspeak adopted. Surrogational artspeak favours certain tactics and types of argument, whereas contractualist artspeak supports others.

Once we see the role of artspeak in this light, it opens up a new perspective on the history of the arts in Western civilization. It also raises the question of how much longer artspeak can continue to play this linguistic role in the contemporary world.

9

Surrogational artspeak

Probably language would be, within the bounds of possibility, most excellent when all its terms, or as many as possible, were based on likeness.

Socrates

Plato's version of the communication myth starts from the assumption that reality exists independently of human attempts to comprehend it or describe it (either verbally or in any other way). This leads him to the view that the best we can expect of language or other forms of communication is some not-too-misleading way of representing reality. But the approximation will almost certainly be imperfect in various respects. The beginning of wisdom, for Plato, is to try to understand the nature of these imperfections. And this is very relevant to his conception of the arts.

What Plato came up with was a surrogational theory of language and, simultaneously, surrogational theories of painting and poetry. Surrogational models of communication in general are models which explain X by saying that X is a surrogate, substitute or proxy for something else. The characteristic surrogational claim is a claim to the effect that X 'stands for' Y. When we explain the casino chips as 'standing for' real money, or the communion wine as 'standing for' the blood of Jesus Christ, or an inch on the map as 'standing for' a mile, we are engaged in surrogational discourse. The surrogationalist posits a relationship between X and Y which allows the meaning of X to be interpreted by reference to Y, where Y is already assumed to exist independently of X.

As regards language, surrogationalism manifests itself as a view about the way words relate to the non-verbal world. Here we have the city of Athens. There we have the name of that city: *Athens*. Here we have an individual who played a leading role in the politics of that city during the fifth century BC. There we have his name: *Pericles*. But this model can also be extended to the entire natural world. Here we have a certain metallic substance, heavy, dull yellow in colour, and having various other properties that can be listed. There we have its name: *gold*. Similarly for actions and processes. To *walk* is what we call a certain manner of locomotion which involves putting one foot in front of the other. To *melt* is what we call a certain process by which solids become liquids. And so on. Names can be combined (in accordance with the 'rules of grammar') into sentences: e.g. *Fish swim*. By this we understand that the creature whose name appears as the first verbal unit in the sentence (*Fish*) engages in the activity whose name likewise appears as the second verbal unit (*swim*). Whether what *Fish swim* says is true or not depends accordingly, from a surrogational point of view, on whether that combination of names corresponds to what actually happens in the non-verbal world. As Hobbes put it so succinctly in the seventeenth century:

> When two Names are joyned together into a Consequence, or Affirmation; as thus, *A man is a living creature*; or thus, *if he be a man, he is a living creature*, If the later name *Living creature*, signifie all that the former name *Man* signifieth, then the affirmation, or consequence is *true*; otherwise *false*. For *True* and *False* are attributes of Speech, not of Things. And where Speech is not, there is neither *Truth* nor *Falshood*. *Errour* there may be, as when wee expect that which shall not be; or suspect what has not been: but in neither case can a man be charged with Untruth. (Hobbes 1651: I.4)

This is a classic statement of the surrogational position – much clearer than anything we find in the linguistic theorizing of antiquity. Aristotle anticipates it, however, in his pronouncement in *Metaphysics* (1011b26) that 'to say of what is that it is, or of what is not that it is not, is true'. This already presupposes that there are two domains that have to be correlated: one verbal and one non-verbal. It also presupposes that not everything that belongs to the first domain corresponds to something actually existing in the second. Surrogationalism, in linguistics, is the theory of language that operates within these parameters of correspondence. (In philosophy, it became known as 'the correspondence theory of truth'.)

For the surrogationalist, therefore, the simplest way of explaining meaning, wherever possible, is to point to or demonstrate whatever the word or words 'stands for'. What *daffodil* means is explained by showing someone a daffodil. What *smile* means is explained by smiling. Augustine (*Confessions*: I.8) describes his own language-learning in childhood as a process of guessing what was meant by the words his elders uttered, on the basis of observing what it was they seemed to be talking about, insofar as this could be inferred from the clues provided by accompanying gesture, gaze, etc. This approach to semantics became formally recognized (in the twentieth century) as 'nomenclaturism' and the method of establishing correlations between words and objects as 'ostensive definition'. Nomenclaturism was eventually criticized and rejected both by Saussure and by Wittgenstein (Saussure 1916; Wittgenstein 1953). But it had reigned virtually unchallenged in Western thinking for the previous two millennia. It had certainly supported much of Western artspeak since the days of Plato, who was largely responsible for setting up this surrogational model in the first place. The dependence of traditional artspeak on such a model goes a long way towards explaining the limits within which questions concerning the arts have been debated, including why the mechanical or utilitarian arts were hardly deemed worthy of serious theoretical discussion *as arts* at all.

*   *   *

During the many centuries in which surrogationalism dominated discussions of language it had generated many puzzles and controversies (including the medieval schism between 'nominalists' and 'realists'). It had also bifurcated into two doctrines, which may be called for convenience 'reocentric surrogationalism' and 'psychocentric surrogationalism'. According to the latter, what a word 'stands for' is something in the mind of the speaker or hearer. According to the former, we have to look outside the mind for something in external 'reality' (whatever or wherever that might be). Locke's philosophy of language is a late-seventeenth-century example of psychocentric surrogationalism at its most intransigent. Frege's philosophy of language is a no less intransigent example of reocentric surrogationalism in the early twentieth, and is sometimes regarded as an updated version of Plato's (Harris and Taylor 1997: 126–38; 196–208).

These surrogational doctrines have obvious implications for traditional artspeak. Take, for instance, the ascription of a property to a work or works of art, as when someone says 'Capability Brown's landscapes are picturesque'. Does this merely claim something about what is going on in the mind of the claimant. Or in Capability Brown's mind? (Is the picturesque in the eye of the beholder?) Or does it state something more 'objective' than that? And, if so, what? What is the external correlate or source of the picturesque? Is there a timeless standard for assessing it? These questions do not even make sense unless we accept a surrogational assumption about the meaning of the term *picturesque*. And if it turns out that there is nothing, either in the external world or in the mind, that the word *picturesque* can be shown to 'stand for', then statements to the effect that Capability Brown's landscapes are picturesque are neither true nor false but meaningless.

*   *   *

It was Plato who first raised the problem of artspeak itself as a linguistic issue. He did this by refusing to accept that an 'art' is established as such simply on the basis of its practitioners' say-so. He demanded specific criteria for drawing a distinction between the practices which qualify as arts (*technai*) and those which do not. Thus he wrote as someone acquainted with a society in which the status of professions counted for something. He clearly did not regard it as satisfactory to let the matter be decided or fought out by the interested parties themselves. For then self-promotion, snobbery, popularity and social pressures of all kinds would be brought into play. In short, he demanded (and proposed) an independent rationale. Artspeak, for Plato, like all forms of discourse, had to be accountable to principles of some kind. By bringing attention to focus in this way on discourse about the arts, Plato's initiative marks the beginning of theoretical inquiry into the arts themselves. The two enterprises go hand-in-hand; for there can be no systematic inquiry unless there is a discourse in which to conduct it.

In retrospect it is possible to identify a number of recurrent themes which ensured the subsequent continuity of artspeak throughout the European tradition. It is no coincidence that prominent among these themes is that of 'nature'. For nature in its totality supplies the indispensable foundation for all reocentric models of language. (The word *gold* is a human invention, but gold itself is not: it is a product of nature.) All discussion of the relationship between art and nature is inevitably given a reocentric slant from the very beginning. For nature is conceived as that which exists prior to and independently of human interference, and hence prior to and independently of the development of the arts. (Gold would still occur in nature, even if no language had a word for it and no society had goldsmiths.) The products of nature, in short, are those which automatically support reocentric surrogational definitions.

It is no coincidence either, however, that there are other recurrent themes in Western artspeak (including beauty, creativity, imagination, emotion and pleasure) which seem to demand a psychocentric rather than a reocentric definition of terms. The relationship of each of these to nature raises problems. For instance, does the artistic imagination transcend nature? Or does it merely reflect and re-order what is present in nature? Why are there things in nature which we find repugnant, but which, when represented in art, give us pleasure? (A question Delacroix asked.) From such problems as these is drawn an agenda of topics which remains more or less constant over the centuries, but the focus of attention and explanation shifts in different periods from some to others.

This raises two issues for reflection. If, by the end of the eighteenth century, it seemed that discussion of the arts was reduced to recycling the same old rota of topics, albeit with varying emphases, such a state of affairs might be seen as support for the view associated with Hegel that art was approaching its end, having 'exhausted all its significant possibilities' (Inwood 1993: xxxi). On the other hand, it could also be argued that what led Hegel to this gloomy view were the limitations of a traditional artspeak which had exhausted all *its* significant possibilities. In other words, what Hegel took as the end of the road in art was no more than the obsolescence of a certain form of discourse about the arts (i.e. surrogational discourse, although Hegel did not recognize it as such or envisage any alternative).

The second issue is more difficult. Granted that the focus of debate about the arts changed over the course of the centuries, what determined those changes? The answer is not immediately obvious, but clues to it are already to be found in the list of themes given above, from which two complementary features emerge. First, the questions these topics raise do not include any which are 'internal' to the development of the arts themselves. This is all the more striking when one considers the innumerable ways in which, over a period spanning more than two millennia, the artifacts and activities involved had changed.

One might have imagined that the introduction of new materials and the discovery of new techniques would pose revolutionary questions about the relationships between art, workmanship and design. But although Alberti, for instance, distinguishes in *De re aedificatoria* between 'necessity', 'convenience' and 'pleasure' in the construction of buildings, he does not seem to notice that the flying buttress and the pointed arch, quite apart from changing the whole appearance of architecture in Europe, raised serious problems about the validity of separating these three aspects of architecture. No less fundamental questions about poetry seem to be raised by the difference between *chanson de geste* and *roman courtois*, the former being an essentially oral form and the latter an essentially written composition. (Writing taking over the functions of speech is another example of the impact of a new technology.) The invention of new musical instruments and the phasing out of old ones profoundly altered European music, the way it sounded, the way it was played and the way it was composed. But none of these innovations, although they do not pass without comment, seems to have provoked any radical questions of a theoretical nature *about art*. Even quite new art forms based on specific technological advances, such as stained glass and etching, fail to spark controversy and are rapidly taken for granted, although their execution demands artistic skills unknown in previous centuries. When an innovation does cause excitement – Renaissance perspective is a clear example – it is either because this advance provides grounds for reassessing the status of a traditional art form, or else (as in the case of opera) because it pits the devotees of one party against devotees of a rival party. The *querelle des Bouffons* in the mid-eighteenth century is a celebrated case of the latter, but it was fought out mainly along personal and quasi-political lines.

By contrast, the topics that loom large on our list all raise 'external' questions. They call for consideration of the arts in relation to matters that go far beyond the scope of the arts as such. They connect the work of artists to broader domains of human activities and values. This is why they are controversial; but the controversy comes from 'outside', not from 'inside' the arts. In this respect, the function of artspeak might appear to be to facilitate a dialogue between artists and the rest of society, by rationalizing the role of the arts. One would expect this rationalization to vary in response to prevailing intellectual, religious, economic and political conditions. A more sceptical view of the matter, however, might question the notion of 'dialogue' and suggest that we are dealing with a cultural tradition in which it is society which is accustomed to telling the artist what art is, rather than the artist telling everyone else what art is. All the topics of debate seem to be chosen as ones which cannot be settled by appealing solely to the artist's own intentions, expertise or experience; for such concepts as 'beauty', 'imagination', 'pleasure', etc. by definition involve problems which go beyond the artist's competence *qua* artist. So a tension is set up between the viewpoint of the artist and the viewpoint of society. That the arts must serve society and not society the arts is a thesis spelled out unmistakably in Plato's *Republic*.

That thesis remained the basis of all subsequent Western thinking on the subject. It lurked in the background, even when not directly addressed. It explains why, for more than two thousand years, the issue which overshadows discussion of the arts is the question of their *justification*. For in the end the artist is a member of society, and the artist's public is society itself (even if the artist's immediate clients are particular individuals or groups within society). That applied equally to all the arts, whether 'liberal', 'mechanical', 'fine', etc. In this respect, traditional artspeak might be seen as a discourse in which the key definitions provide society's terms of employment for the artist. They grant the artist a provisional working permit, but lay down the criteria by which the work will eventually be approved or disapproved.

The same social rationale explains why the utilitarian or mechanical arts commanded far less attention from Western thinkers. From a surrogational perspective these arts are far less problematic, since the claims of their practitioners lend themselves to assessment by relatively straightforward reocentric criteria. Either a remedy cures ailments or it does not. Either certain agricultural practices produce more abundant crops or they fail to. The results speak for themselves. But where arts such as poetry and painting and music are concerned, the results are often as debatable as the methods by which they were allegedly produced.

All this is perfectly comprehensible within the confines of a surrogational understanding of artspeak. It explains why the most difficult task was seen as being the justification of those arts which do not appear to minister directly to

any social necessity but appeal to abstract aims and concepts that are difficult
to pin down in surrogational terms. It is here that there is most room for disagreement and proof is hard to come by.

*   *   *

A surrogational semantics, however, is not the only available option. Surrogationalism has to be distinguished in the Western tradition from
contractualism. A contractualist semantics puts its emphasis not on the
question of correspondence between the verbal and the non-verbal, but on
agreement between speaker and hearer; or more generally, between sender
and receiver of a message. What takes priority, in the contractualist model of
the linguistic code, is whether or not there is a consensus between these
parties on how to formulate and interpret messages. Exactly how this
consensus is reached or maintained becomes a secondary issue. What matters
in communication is that such a consensus should be in operation; for
otherwise communication fails. The contractualist thus attaches great importance to conventions and the observance of conventions; for conventions,
according to this view, make language what it is. Contractualism, in Western
linguistics, was traditionally the creed of the professional grammarians, the
exponents of the *ars grammatica*. The reason is not difficult to grasp. What
counts most for pedagogic purposes is not the underlying reasons for linguistic conventions, but establishing what linguistic conventions in practice obtain
at certain times and places.

In Plato's dialogue *Cratylus* we are present at an imaginary debate about
language between an extreme contractualist (Hermogenes) and an extreme
anti-contractualist (Cratylus). Both are made to look ridiculous. But this is
because Hermogenes insists on everyone's right to lay down and insist on
their own contractual conventions, while Cratylus insists on a natural 'correctness' dictating the proper relationship between a name and what it shall
designate. Socrates has an easy time showing that neither of these extreme
positions on language is tenable. But he does not succeed in reaching any satisfactory compromise between them.

The contractualist model too raises important considerations for the
analysis of artspeak. For example, a moderate contractualist might well argue
that it does not matter how such terms as *poetry, music,* etc. are defined, or
whether satisfactory definitions can be supplied at all, provided there is no
substantive disagreement about how in practice the relevant terms are applied
to particular arts and works of art.

Plato was obviously dissatisfied with adopting a contractualist model,
whether for artspeak or for any other important mode of discourse. In
Phaedrus, Socrates maintains that there are some words about which we never

disagree, but others about which we all have our own ideas. The former class includes words for familiar everyday objects (Socrates' examples are words for 'iron' and 'silver'). The other class includes words for more abstract properties (Socrates' examples are words for 'just' and 'good'). When there is no common agreement about it, the meaning of a word is 'uncertain' or 'ambiguous' and it is in these cases that we are liable to be confused or misled. Evidently, Plato considers this latter class of cases philosophically more important than the words about which everyone agrees, since it includes the most philosophically contentious terms. (It does not seem to occur to Socrates that there might be just as much philosophical dispute about silver as about justice.)

Plato's general point here is that we would be misled if we assumed that, in respect of all words, everybody was bound by the same linguistic contract: on the contrary, the opposite is commonly the case. From this Socrates proceeds to draw the following conclusion:

> Then the man who embarks on the search for an art of speaking must first of all make a methodical classification, and find a distinguishing mark for each of the two kinds of words, those which in popular usage are bound to be ambiguous and those which are not. (*Phaedrus* 263; Hamilton 1973: 77)

Earlier in the same dialogue, Socrates has already remarked contemptuously that

> the art of speaking displayed by a man who has gone hunting after opinions instead of learning the truth will be a pretty ridiculous sort of art, in fact no art at all. (*Phaedrus* 262; Hamilton 1973: 75–6)

These two observations repay careful consideration. It is clear that the 'art of speaking' differs from one case to the other. In the earlier remark, it is a question of the art manifested by what the speaker says in the course of presenting his case (which may be no art at all); whereas in the later remark Socrates seems to have in mind some hypothetical treatise drawn up by a teacher. Since there were no dictionaries in Plato's Greece, the suggestion that a systematic indication would be needed of the two types of word (ambiguous and unambiguous) may be taken as Socrates' advice for an art of lexicography which did not yet exist.

More important still is the fact that if the distinction drawn is a quite general one, then it would presumably apply to all types of discourse. In other words, such an 'art of speaking' as Socrates appears to regard as desirable would be the foundation for all sound discussion of the other arts, and for any serious intellectual discussion at all. This seems to be confirmed by what Socrates goes on to say to Phaedrus; that when a speaker has to deal with a given subject

> it must be perfectly clear to him, without any possibility of mistake, to which class the subject of his speech belongs. (*Phaedrus* 263; Hamilton 1973: 77)

If we wish to profit from Socrates' words of wisdom, then it would seem that in discourse about the arts the first requirement is to identify the 'ambiguous' terms and set about their disambiguation. It hardly needs to be pointed out that here Plato runs the risk of jeopardizing his own position. That is to say, if the term *techne* itself is one of those terms about which we all have our own ideas, then there is no basis for differentiating between practices that are merely called arts by their practitioners and practices that are genuine arts. Plato's attempt to draw such a distinction, one might object, does not actually resolve any ambiguity, but merely insists on priority for his own view of the matter. To which Plato might well have responded that at least he had presented a case for his view, rather than upholding it merely on the ground that it was his (as Hermogenes in *Cratylus* is represented as doing). A more serious complaint is that Socrates proposes no method by which the hypo-thetical author of a treatise on the art of speaking will ever be able to distinguish between words that have a commonly accepted meaning and words that do not.

Nevertheless, the importance of Plato's move here cannot be over-estimated. It was to leave its mark on all subsequent discussion of the arts. Plato is insisting that there is a superordinate verbal art (yet to be elaborated) to which artspeak and all other forms of rational discourse are rationally sub-servient. This is the move which, in the intellectual history of Europe, fundamentally alters the relationship between the arts and what apologists may claim on their behalf. Plato makes that move in the interests of his own philosophical agenda. It is clearly designed to raise questions about the arts, but it does not aim at producing better works of art, or producing them more efficiently. There is no suggestion that Phidias would have been a better sculptor if he had taken lessons from Socrates (even though Socrates was sup-posedly the son of a stone-mason). What Plato is trying to do is not improve the Greek arts or train their apprentices. Plato is not the avatar of Ruskin. Artspeak both worries and exercises Plato because he sees that artspeak is far too important to be left in the hands of artists.

*   *   *

Plato's preferred solution, followed by other thinkers in Graeco-Roman antiquity, was to try to develop an artspeak which was surrogational (and reocentric) in its underlying assumptions. Given that there existed practices already established in society and called 'arts' by their practitioners, the theoretical questions to be addressed concerned the basis on which these practices were conducted (in particular, the basis of knowledge or skills required in each), their criteria of excellence and their social implications. This strategy of inquiry led to setting up hierarchical distinctions between the arts. But it never seems to have occurred to anyone in antiquity to question the validity of comparisons between the arts on the ground that every art is *sui generis*. Thus, if the art of war is never compared to the art of agriculture, this is because they are seen as pursuing quite diverse objectives; whereas the art of poetry is commonly compared to the art of painting, presumably on the ground that both poet and painter can share a common 'subject matter' (e.g. the battle of Thermopylae, or the view from the Acropolis). But this is another surrogational assumption, i.e. the notion of 'subject matter' as that independently given material, reference to which supplies the semantic basis for an activity or a message (be it verbal or visual).

The notion of an independently given reality as the bedrock on which relationships between the arts can be objectively established was pervasive in Graeco-Roman antiquity. The opposition 'art versus nature' was one between the realm of human activities and the pre-established order which provided both the theatre and the materials for those activities. Thus in respect of any art it seemed possible to ask – and to expect to answer – three types of question: (i) how it relates to nature, (ii) how it affects those who practise it, and (iii) how it affects other human beings. For example, Aristotle, or whoever was the author of the treatise on economics often attributed to Aristotle, claims that 'in the course of nature the art of agriculture is prior, and next come those arts which extract the products of the earth, mining and the like' (*Economics* 1343a: 25–27). The reasons then given for this priority fall into three categories: those which pertain to relations between mankind and nature, those which pertain to relations between men and other men, and those which pertain to the effects that agriculture has upon the farmer. Agriculture, we are told, is a natural pursuit, inasmuch as man derives his sustenance from the earth. It is also a just pursuit, for it does not involve taking anything from other men, as do the arts pertaining to trade or war. (Marx would doubtless object, on the ground that all depends on whether some exploit others in the process of extracting the bounty of nature from the earth.) Third, unlike the illiberal arts, agriculture is not harmful to men's bodies, but makes them strong, healthy and brave (for, since their land lies outside the city walls, they have to be prepared to defend it against invaders). The possibility that some agricultural practices might involve working in unhygienic conditions or exposure to disease does not seem to have crossed Aristotle's mind.

*　　*　　*

The doctrine of mimesis, central to both Plato's and Aristotle's treatment of the arts, was a surrogational doctrine through and through. The notion that X 'stands for' Y in virtue of being an 'imitation of' Y already presupposes that Y is given in advance of – and independently of – X. There are both logical and chronological implications in the concept of mimesis. It is intimately connected with the twin surrogational doctrine of truth. Truth as correspondence between statements and states of affairs presupposes not only a distinction between that which actually is the case and that which merely appears so, but the possibility of establishing what actually is the case independently of any description. Thus an accurate description of the famous Athenian statesman Pericles and what he achieved must tell the truth about him: it is in the person and life of Pericles that we must seek the facts which provide the criteria for determining whether what is said about him is true or otherwise. Parallel reasoning can be extended in an obvious way to a statue or a portrait of Pericles: it must (ideally) show Pericles as he actually is or was, and not otherwise. The sculptor who deliberately caricatures Pericles by exaggerating certain features, or presents him as looking more handsome than he was in real life, is like the historian who gives a biased description of his appearance. Thus even non-verbal arts can be made accountable to the same surrogational criteria as are required in language. Aristotle (*Poetics* 1448a) explicitly draws such comparisons between the work of painters (Polygnotos, Pauson, Dionysius) and the work of poets (Homer, Cleophon, Hegemon, Nicochares).

This surrogational connexion between mimesis and truth (as forms of correspondence to reality) is implicit in Plato's criticisms of poets and painters. But it is also the source of some major difficulties in Plato's position. For if we take seriously Socrates' contention (*Republic* X) that a picture of a bed is twice removed from reality, and hence a deception, it would seem that Plato is setting up surrogational criteria for truthful representation which cannot be met. The same would apply to a description of a bed, which will be defective for much the same reasons: it will inevitably focus on certain aspects of the bed and ignore others. (The mind boggles at how to achieve a fully comprehensive description of the total bed. Where would one start? At the sub-atomic level?) At this point it is open to Plato's critics to object that using artspeak to set up impossible objectives is itself a form of deception. For in judging whether a picture or a description provides an accurate representation we do not expect – and it would be absurd to expect – fidelity in every possible respect. What Plato has failed to do is give any account of the way in which, *in spite of* everyone's knowing that Pericles was not made of wood or stone, it is nevertheless possible to recognize the statue as a likeness of Pericles (and even distinguish between a good likeness and a poor likeness). This is a typically surrogational dilemma.

*   *   *

It is initially tempting to see Aristotle's various treatises on logic, politics, physics, rhetoric, etc. as the work of a philosopher keen to take up the gauntlet thrown down by Plato's arguments about the arts. Such a programme, if carried out thoroughly, would presumably require a comprehensive survey of the most important arts in Greek civilization and their claims to be based on knowledge. The programme would need, evidently, to provide in each case a detailed rationale to justify the inclusion of the art in question. But on further consideration it seems less plausible that this was Aristotle's aim. Or if it was, then it was less well executed in some instances than in others.

The *Poetics* is an interesting case in point. For it is never quite clear why poetry would have been included in such a programme at all, particularly in view of Plato's scathing strictures on the so-called mimetic arts. But perhaps, as Gilbert Murray suggests, these strictures were what motivated Aristotle, and 'his treatise on poetry was an answer to Plato's challenge' (Murray 1920: 1). On the other hand, if refutation of Plato's criticisms was even part of Aristotle's motive, it seems odd, to say the least, that these criticisms are quietly ignored. According to Murray, the *Poetics* was 'a first attempt, made by a man of outstanding genius, to build up in the region of creative art a rational order like that which he established in logic, rhetoric, ethics, politics, physics, psychology, and almost every department of knowledge that existed in his day' (Murray 1920: 18). What must be of prime interest, if this is so, is how Aristotle proposed to accomplish such an ambitious task in such a brief span, and without any detailed examination of particular poets or poetic works. So what kind of enterprise is Aristotle engaged in here?

Had Aristotle himself been a poet, he would at least have been protected from the charge of posing as an authority in a field in which he lacked any practical expertise. But as far as is known, Aristotle's own ventures into poetry were limited to writing occasional verse. Furthermore, Aristotle's seems to have been the first 'art of poetry' in Greek. Thus the *Poetics* can hardly be compared to his writings on rhetoric, where he had many precursors and the path was well trodden. That makes it all the more significant that the *Poetics* does not begin, as a reader of Plato might have expected, with an attempt to argue the case that poetry actually *is* an art. Aristotle apparently takes that for granted. This is significant on at least two counts. One is that his *Art of*

Rhetoric, although it likewise assumes *ab initio* that rhetoric is indeed an art, at least begins by offering a reason for believing it to be so. The second is that a case could easily be made out, as Aristotle must have been well aware, for saying that poetry (at least, the best poetry) is not an art at all, but the product of natural or even supernatural gifts (a possibility already adumbrated in Plato's *Ion*). One might have thought it incumbent on anyone expounding the first 'art of poetry' to address that issue at the outset.

All the more remarkable is that Aristotle accepts without comment of any kind Plato's classification of poetry as belonging to the 'mimetic' arts, and then bases his whole analysis on that single premiss. There is no attempt to proceed 'empirically', i.e. by first considering and comparing examples of poems, and then drawing general conclusions from them. The approach Aristotle adopts is the reverse of that. It has been described as one in which the first step for the investigator is to

> divide the genus into its primary species and then examine the proper-
> ties peculiar to the species, working through the nearest common
> *differentiae*. That is, he should find the definition of each species and
> deduce from the definition the essential properties of the species. These
> will necessarily be the properties of the genus, since the genus has no
> existence apart from its species. This is the procedure followed by
> Aristotle himself in his *pragmateia* of the art of poetry, allowance being
> made for the nature of the subject. Poetry as imitation is divided into its
> species, and from the definition of one of these, tragedy, it is deduced
> that this particular species or form has six essential properties or parts.
> [. . .] Tragedy is an imitation in language and in dramatic form of the
> actions of serious persons. No other species of imitation has all these
> differences. (Hutton 1982: 9–10)

This is very relevant to understanding the role of Aristotelian artspeak. The adoption of such a method, whether with poetry or any other traditional art, immediately poses a typical artspeak problem, which hinges on the fact that the art in question will already have a terminology in place. In other words, granted that tradition already supplies a certain number of established terms (e.g. *tragodia*) by which products of the art are known, or by which features of those products are commonly referred to, the analyst faces a choice. If there are no currently accepted terms which correspond to the divisions and dis-tinctions revealed by the proposed analysis, the analyst must either invent new terms, or risk burdening subsequent discussion with awkward repeti-tions and circumlocutions. (It is interesting to observe that right at the beginning of the *Poetics* Aristotle resists the temptation to invent a word. He notes (*Poetics* 1447a,b) that there is no Greek word for art which imitates in language alone; but he refrains from supplying one. He would probably have been obliged to do so if his subsequent discussion had invoked this particular concept repeatedly.) The question of what to do about already established terms is more awkward: if they happen to fit the analysis proposed, there is no problem; but it may happen that they do not.

Aristotle complains, for instance, about the terms by which poets are generally classified:

> people in general attach the word 'poet' to the name of a particular meter and speak, for example, of elegiac poets and epic poets, calling them poets, not on the basis of imitation, but indiscriminately according to the meter they use. (*Poetics* 1447b; Hutton 1982: 45)

The thrust of this particular objection to popular artspeak becomes clearer when it is realized that etymologically the Greek word *poietes* means 'maker'. Hence, for Aristotle, a designation such as 'elegy-maker' is completely misleading: it misrepresents the activity by focusing on a minor feature of it, while ignoring its major function. (It would be like calling doctors 'pill-givers'.) Such misnomers in turn, according to Aristotle, breed confusion about what poetry is.

> This is customary even when what is produced is a versified treatise on medicine or natural science. But Homer and Empedocles have nothing in common except just their meter, and it is right, therefore, to call the one a poet and the other a physical philosopher rather than a poet. (*Poetics* 1447b; Hutton 1982: 45)

This is a significant remark. It is the first explicit recognition by an important philosopher that artspeak influences the way people think about the arts. It throws more light than anything else in his introductory remarks about poetry upon Aristotle's conception of what distinguishes one art from another. It also draws our attention straight away to the fact that Aristotle's approach to artspeak is unashamedly prescriptive. Both points call for further comment.

Empedocles, we are being told, does not qualify as a poet, even though, like poets, he wrote verse; which means that, for Aristotle, versification is only a contingent feature of poetic practice and not a sufficient condition. Writing verse does not make Empedocles a poet. The fact that people call Empedocles a poet does not make him one either. For in calling him a poet they have overlooked what is for Aristotle the essential function of poetry, i.e. the mimetic function. Empedocles' verse does not fulfil that function, but a different one. (Putting on a policeman's uniform does not make you a policeman.) Hence, even though he uses the same metre as Homer, Empedocles is not producing poetry.

Here we see very clearly what distinguishes one art from another as far as Aristotle is concerned: it is the intention or purpose that informs the practice, rather than the observable products or concomitants of the practice itself. And this also explains why Aristotle shuns the 'empirical' approach to determining the basic features of an art. Anyone who naively set out to define poetry by the detection of common features would almost certainly class the works of Empedocles as poems, simply because they employ the same metre as Homer's.

For Aristotle, then, verse and poetry are two distinct things; and this already marks an important difference between Aristotelian artspeak and popular artspeak, where – Aristotle implies – the two are commonly confused. In theory, presumably, although Aristotle does not go as far as to say this, it would be possible to have two identical verse compositions, of which one was a poem while the other was not. *Mutatis mutandis*, the same would apply to the products of other arts. (Thus, for example, the same cooked dish might count as a medicament if prescribed by a doctor for health reasons, but not if proposed by an innkeeper for gastronomic reasons.)

As regards the prescriptivism of Aristotelian artspeak, what can be said without fear of contradiction is that, for Aristotle, those who call Empedocles a poet, and thus by implication regard poetry as defined by such an inessential feature as metre, are in error. Their language reveals their mistake. Likewise, anyone who applies the term *tragodia* to a work that does not conform to the (Aristotelian) criteria for tragedies is also in error. Nowhere in his *Poetics* does Aristotle entertain the possibility that *tragodia* might be an 'ambiguous' term, i.e. that different people might have differing but not unreasonable views about what makes a tragedy a tragedy. He is not interested in examining how, in practice, the term *tragodia* is actually used and what people might understand it as meaning. Instead, the basis of Aristotelian artspeak in the *Poetics* is the assumption that there is something that any true tragedy (and other poetic forms) must always be; and his objective is to make explicit what this is. In short, the semantics of Aristotle's artspeak is, like Plato's, strictly surrogational. And this is exactly as one might expect from Aristotle's general remarks on language in the introduction to *De Interpretatione*.

Sounds produced by the voice are symbols of affections of the soul, and writing is a symbol of vocal sounds. And just as letters are not the same for all men, sounds are not the same either, although the affections directly expressed by these indications are the same for everyone, as are the things of which these impressions are images. (*De Interpretatione* 16a)

The very brevity of these remarks makes them important. They presumably summarize for Aristotle truths about language which do not stand in need of any more elaborate argument. They postulate a direct conformity between the psychocentric and the reocentric features of meaning, with the latter under-writing the former. The relevance of this to the present discussion can be stated as follows. Poetry, for Aristotle, is an oral art, an art for which the medium is the human voice. (Any written texts can be dismissed from con-sideration, because writing is merely a metasign. We do not understand it unless we understand what oral reality it represents.) The sounds 'of Greek poetry are not the sounds of poetry in other languages: in that sense, poetry is a language-bound art. Nevertheless, the 'affections of the soul' expressed in speech are the same for all people. So too is the external world which gave rise to those 'affections of the soul' in the first place.

It cannot fail to strike a reader of the *Poetics* that the last two points should have found some reflection in that treatise; inasmuch as they provide the grounding for Aristotle's account of, e.g., tragedy as being something more ambitious than an account of a particular cultural institution established in Greece. And this, to be sure, is implied in Aristotle's treatment of the topic. Nowhere does Aristotle suggest that different communities may have different susceptibilities to the provocation of such emotions as awe and fear. The possibility that sacrificing your daughter to the gods might be regarded in some parts of the world as commonplace never enters his mind. Anthropo-logically, Aristotle is a naive universalist. His universal linguistics is equally naive, i.e. the notion that what differentiates languages is no more than the sounds by means of which certain language-neutral 'affections of the soul' are expressed.

But this view of language jars with Aristotle's own criticisms of the artspeak of his time. For someone who distinguishes as sharply between art and nature as Aristotle (*Physics* 192bff.) it seems curious to proceed as he does in the *Poetics*; that is to say, treating cultural concepts (e.g. poetry, tragedy) as if they were on a par with concepts of the natural world (e.g. water, fire). Aristotle does not seem to sense the incompatibility between his prescriptive artspeak and an impartial ('philosophical'?) investigation of artistic practice. He happily harnesses the former to serve the purposes of the latter. But then Aristotle, like Plato, did not live in a society that had dictionaries on hand to resolve disputes about terminology. As a proto-lexicographer, Aristotle evidently believed in 'real definitions' (Robinson 1954: 153–4). He is, in this sense, a reocentric surrogationalist.

This is very pertinent to the way in which Aristotle deploys artspeak. Anyone who believes in 'real definitions', whether in the arts or any other sphere of human inquiry, will always be tempted to deal with awkward terms either by ignoring them or else by redefining them (so that they 'fit' reality better). In the *Poetics*, as Gilbert Murray points out, there is a glaring omission. Aristotle either forgets or ignores the great debt that Greek poetry owed to religion and the sacred myths. This forgetfulness goes so far that Aristotle 'falls into using the word *muthos* practically in the sense of "plot", and writing otherwise in a way that is unsuited to the tragedy of the fifth century' (Murray 1920: 13). Which is a polite way of saying that Aristotle twisted the terms of traditional Greek artspeak to suit his own analytic purposes. Similarly, according to Murray, the controversial Aristotelian term *katharsis* (usually translated 'purification' or 'purgation') is a hangover from the ritual Dionysiac origins of tragedy, on which Aristotle has foisted his own psychological interpretation.

The conclusion to which one is led is not just that all the key terms of Aristotelian artspeak in the *Poetics* are heavily 'theory-laden'; rather, the point is that only by recognizing and unpacking this theoretical lading can we begin to understand the linguistic role of artspeak *vis-à-vis* the art(s) in question. When we do this, it emerges that the *Poetics* does not describe or report upon the agreed practice of poets in Aristotle's day. Nor, in spite of many misunderstandings to the contrary, does it attempt to teach Greek poets how to practise their art successfully. What it does is propose a theoretical perspective from which that art may be viewed. And Aristotle's manipulation of Greek artspeak in his *Poetics* is intrinsic to that purpose.

A contractualist might describe this as Aristotle's attempt to impose his own linguistic contract on the terminology in which poetry shall be discussed. But the key to the artspeak of the *Poetics* lies in seeing how it attempts to integrate two quite different enterprises: (i) establishing what poetry is, and (ii) establishing how non-poetic language relates to reality, i.e. how in general we manage to make verbal sense of the world. For Aristotle, (i) cannot be attempted independently of (ii). That is why he says (*Poetics* 1451b) that poetry is of more serious philosophical import than history. In other words, there is a simple (reocentric) explanation of what has happened when Herodotus gets his facts wrong or his dates awry. But that kind of explanation cannot be transferred without further ado to Homer, because the art of poetry is not the art of history.

The reocentricity of Aristotle's artspeak is confirmed by what he says at the beginning of his *Metaphysics* about the difference between art and experience as bases for action. His example is medicine. If medicine is an art, this is not just a matter of the doctor's accumulated experience in dealing with cases of illness. For

art arises, when from many notions gained by experience one universal judgement about similar objects is produced. For to have a judgement that when Callias was ill of this disease this did him good, and similarly

in the case of Socrates and in many individual cases, is a matter of experience; but to judge that it has done good to all persons of a certain
constitution, marked off in one class, when they were ill of this disease,
e.g. to phlegmatic or bilious people when burning with fever, – this is a
matter of art. (*Metaphysics* 981a)

In other words, the basis of art is empirical generalization. It goes without
saying, however, that the generalizations in question must be *true* generalizations. For it would be absurd to regard anyone as practising the art of
medicine who made false or random generalizations about cures and treated
patients accordingly. This would be a quack, not a physician.

The artspeak of the *Poetics* is not artspeak in the service of poetry, but
artspeak in the service of philosophy. The game being played in Aristotle's
Lyceum, as in Plato's Academy, was the subordination of one art to another.
And that entailed, metalinguistically, the subordination of one form of
artspeak to another form of artspeak. Although they may not quite have
realized what they were doing, these two masters between them made
artspeak into an art of its own.

*   *   *

The chief objection to reocentric surrogationalism where artspeak is
concerned is that so few of the more interesting artspeak claims can be given
plausible reocentric interpretations. The remainder are problematic. If the
semantic game is to be played by strictly reocentric rules, it becomes
important to establish that even the most apparently subjective of artistic
judgments actually has a non-subjective basis and reflects something 'real'.
That is what accounts for the centuries of agonizing over the concept of beauty
in the Western tradition, and efforts to ground it in something less contingent
and ephemeral than individual delectation. These efforts included, notably,
attempts to relate beauty to the universal laws of mathematics. But even
Alberti, who believed in this approach, worried that there were others who
maintained that the perception of forms varied from one individual to another
(*De Re Aedificatoria* VI.2). This is another surrogational dilemma, in that
the only alternative to reocentrism is seen as being a potentially anarchic
psychocentrism.

Thus throughout the history of theoretical debate about the arts we see the
same linguistic problem constantly reappearing. The arts which are most
difficult to 'justify', and therefore provoke most discussion, turn out to be
those in which both statements of aims and terms of critical appraisal resist
straightforward surrogational definitions. On this score arts as diverse as
history and agriculture pose no problem. The historian must get his facts right

and the farmer must produce crops. But painting and poetry are altogether more difficult to pin down by surrogational criteria. Their relation to 'reality' is more complex.

Attempts to establish a reocentric basis for even the most elusive concepts of Western artspeak became increasingly bold. They culminated in Hegel's desperate bid to identify beauty with 'the representation of the absolute', which can most charitably be seen as a latter-day attempt to secularize Plotinus's concept of beauty as emanating from the divine. This is about as far as it is possible to go, reocentrically, in the direction of distancing beauty from the vagaries of individual appreciation or the regimentation of conventions. For the reocentric surrogationalist, the biggest mistake it would be possible to make is to regard beauty as residing in conformity to conventional canons and the adjective 'beautiful' as being licensed by contractual agreement. In the end, as with Plato in the beginning, reocentric Western artspeak always tends to fall back on appeals to the superhuman and transcendental. That is its most enduring but least endearing characteristic.

10
The artspeak contract

The initial assignment of names to things, establishing a contract between concepts and sound patterns, is an act we can conceive in the imagination, but no one has ever observed it taking place.

Saussure

Since the Renaissance the concept of what an art is has shifted globally in response to a cultural revolution. The revolution in question is the revolution which brought 'science' to dominate our paradigms of knowledge. The polar opposition which today exists between 'art' and 'science' was not yet in place when Bacon wrote *The Advancement of Learning*. But it now structures the whole field of discussion concerning human activities and social responsibilities. To call something an 'art' is nowadays to imply, at the very least, that it is not to be judged by 'scientific' criteria. As a result, artspeak has moved into areas of radical disputation. It is not just that Tolstoy's question 'What is art?' can be answered in a variety of conflicting ways, but that it cannot be answered at all with any confidence. For it presupposes so many non-scientific indefinables in an area where consensus is conspicuously lacking.

That has not put a stop to attempts to provide answers. Books with titles that echo Tolstoy's continue to appear (Tilghman 1984: *But Is It Art?*; Margolis 1999: *What, After All, is a Work of Art?*). But none of them matches Tolstoy's modern masterpiece of sustained polemic. Tolstoy realized how central the question of the relationship between science and art had become, and he devoted his final chapter to addressing it. His conclusion was that the two were 'as closely bound together as the lungs and the heart.' If science takes the wrong path, he argued, so inevitably will art.

Many others construed the relationship as anything but an organic collaboration. For them, the days when art owed anything at all to science had gone for good. The liberating implications of this independence were quickly grasped by the more adventurous practitioners in the arts, who exploited it to break with the past in ways that would not have been possible in those professional activities falling under the aegis of science. The antithesis between science and art is far from being a cultural constant throughout the Western tradition. When D. H. Lawrence complained that 'knowledge' (by which he meant scientific knowledge) had 'killed the moon', and Lowes Dickinson lamented that 'when science arrives it expels literature' (Dickinson 1931: 52) both of them were striking attitudes that would have puzzled the editors of the *Encyclopédie*.

What Tolstoy doubtless overlooked was that when the scientist rules the intellectual roost, whatever resists definition and replication becomes the archetype of the unknowable. The corollary of this is a situation in which not even the champions of the arts seem to know any longer what art is – except that it is not science. Surrogationalism becomes the linguistic creed of science, while artspeak resorts to various forms of contractualism.

*   *   *

This development, however, was slow to reach completion. In the history of artspeak, the Romantic movement was a prolongation of surrogationalism rather than a revolt against it. Where it differed from what had gone before was in the Romantics' enthusiastic acceptance of the psychocentric rather than the reocentric version of the surrogational doctrine. The hallowed distinction between art and nature is maintained, but the traditional conception of mimesis is abandoned or marginalized in favour of emphasis on expression of the sensitive individual's reactions to nature. These are lauded, celebrated, glorified. (Aristotle, reocentric to the last, would have regarded that emphasis as utterly misplaced and potentially pernicious. He would probably have been right.)

Delacroix, once described as 'the quintessential artist of French Romanticism', wrote exasperatedly in his diary on 8 October 1822:

When I have painted a fine picture, I haven't expressed a thought. Or so they say. What fools people are! They deprive painting of all its advantages. The writer says nearly everything to be understood. In painting a mysterious bond is established between the soul of the sitter and that of the spectator. He sees the faces, external nature; but he thinks inwardly the true thought that is common to all people, to which some give body in writing, yet altering its fragile essence. Thus grosser spirits are more moved by writers than by musicians and painters. (Harrison, Wood and Gaiger 1998: 27)

This is one of the most interesting passages of artspeak on record in the nineteenth century, particularly so since it occurs in a personal diary and not in a public proclamation. (Delacroix was not writing for publication. A few weeks earlier he reminds himself that he is 'writing only for myself'. He adds: 'this will keep me truthful, I hope (*je serai donc vrai, je l'espère*) and it will do me good.') His remarks show how a major figure in the 'art world' of his time was still enmeshed in the net of oppositions between 'external nature' (*la nature extérieure*) and 'the true thought that is common to all people' (*la vraie pensée qui est commune à tous les hommes*). This is a traditional surrogational distinction if ever there was one (and a distinction that Aristotle would have been the first to endorse). As a painter, however, Delacroix is keen to claim that painting bypasses the verbal arts. It somehow establishes a more direct – but more mysterious – link between sender and receiver. It does not have to 'go through' words. But what exactly is this 'true thought that is common to all people'? And to which one can 'give body in writing', but also in music and painting? It makes no sense except within the confines of a surrogational view of the arts.

*   *   *

Surrogationalism in artspeak foundered not on the rocks of Romanticism but in the shallows of the doctrine of art-for-art's-sake. Taken seriously, this doctrine demands a licence for rewriting the artist's linguistic contract. Not that this was immediately appreciated at the time. Why not? Because so many of those who approved the doctrine in principle (can one say in the spirit rather than the letter?) still confused the pursuit of the arts with the pursuit of beauty in one or other of its many forms. And they continued to use the term *beauty* to cover anything that they regarded as ultimately important in critical judgment. Thus when Marinetti claims that a roaring motor-car is more beautiful than the Victory of Samothrace (Marinetti 1909) his very terms of comparison (deliberately) imply the obsolescence of a certain traditional conception of what beauty is.

But once that confusion is sorted out, i.e. once it is accepted – as it gradually was – that the autonomy of beauty is one thesis, while the autonomy of art forms is quite a different thesis, there can be no holding back from the conclusion that new forms of artspeak are required. The disengagement of a rhetoric of art from a rhetoric of beauty is the inauguration of a new playing field. The game of critical appraisal and justification can no longer be played by surrogational rules at all, because surrogational artspeak implicitly subjects all forms of art to other demands. Its categories and judgments appeal beyond the arts to some presupposed reality – physical, psychological or spiritual, whether personal or collective – and to goals which exist independently of the artistic activity itself. And this is precisely what the doctrine of art-for-art's-sake is committed to rejecting. From now on, the arts would be free to make their own rules – or no rules – as they went along, irrespective of the wishes of society or the protests of academies, and artspeak would be the instrument by which they did so.

Many were too timid to follow such a revolutionary path, or found it unnecessary to do so; but, for the more adventurous and those who had nothing to lose, this ushered in the heyday of contractualism in artspeak. It continued well into the twentieth century, when various movements and 'isms' sought to establish their own legitimacy by setting out, in proclamations and manifestos, the contractual terms of their own particular brand of artspeak. Rivals, it was understood, operated under different linguistic contracts that one was not obliged to accept, while the old guard (i.e. defenders of traditional artspeak) were rejected as trying to enforce an out-of-date contract that no longer had any legitimacy anyway. It thus became almost obligatory in the *avant-garde* to have a manifesto, not only in order to differentiate one's use of the current artspeak terminology from that of rival groups, but in order to explain why the products of one's own group or school counted as works of art at all (there being no surrogational doctrine to fall back on). Surrogational criteria were to be relegated to a quite different enterprise, known as 'science'.

Here we see the modern resolution of a professional difficulty that had plagued academic artspeak since the middle ages (when music and astronomy had both been liberal arts). Henceforward, the language of science was supposedly answerable, in the final analysis, to the facts of physical nature, whereas artspeak was not: it was free to explore every nook and cranny of the imagination and speculation. Thus the language of science would demand increasingly stringent criteria before accepting new terms into its vocabulary, and discard a term like *ether* when the existence of ether was called in question; whereas it would not have worried Boccioni in the least if someone had questioned the reality of the 'internal plastic infinite' (Boccioni 1912). To anyone who complained that this did not make sense, Boccioni would doubtless have replied with equanimity that it did not make sense in terms of traditional artspeak. But so what? Artspeak now had a new licence both to draft and to underwrite entirely new contracts for the artist.

*   *   *

In contractualism as applied to language the key question concerns the validity of the contract. At one far end of the spectrum we find the radical individualism of a Hermogenes, who proclaims everyone's inalienable right to draw up whatever contract they please (and, moreover, to alter it at will). This, for obvious reasons, strains the notion of a linguistic 'contract' to its limits (and some critics would say beyond). At the opposite end of the same spectrum we find a form of contractualism in which the individual has no option but to accept a contract already drawn up in advance and without consultation. This too, it may be argued, stretches the concept of a linguistic 'contract' beyond recognition; but it is the view associated with that powerful intellectual movement known as 'structuralism'.

Structuralism, in its original linguistic manifestation (Saussure 1916), is that extreme form of contractualism which treats the meanings of words as deriving not from any external relations which may hold between words and anything non-verbal, nor from any premeditated consensus between their users, but from the internal structural relations between the words themselves. Thus *yes* has no meaning except in opposition to *no*, or *good* except in opposition to *bad*, or *John is alive* except in opposition to *John is dead*. And these oppositions in turn contrast with others. Thus *yes* versus *no* contrasts with *perhaps*, and *perhaps* with *certainly*, and so on. Each item derives its meaning from its own position in a network of contrasts with other linguistic items. If items are added to or drop out of the network, that automatically alters the position of every other item. The network as a whole is the only autonomous structure. The items it includes have no meaning independently of the whole.

Here was a linguistic theory which not merely rejected but deracinated surrogationalism. As the price for this achievement, however, it imposed Draconian restrictions on the viability of all forms of artspeak.

In the artists' manifestos of the early twentieth century, including those of Marinetti, the Dadaists and the surrealists, the artspeak that emerges tends towards the Hermogenean end of the contractualist spectrum. There is little attempt to justify or rationalize the terms used. In the case of the Dadaists that would even have been seen as contrary to the spirit of the movement, a concession to the Establishment. Proclamation is preferred to persuasion, defiance to definitions.

Dadaism itself, paradoxical though it may seem, is an extreme form of contractualism. The paradox derives from its apparent rejection of all conventions where art and language are concerned. But if we look at the small print we find that what is actually being rejected are agreed *public* contracts of any kind. In their place is a radical individualism. When Tristan Tzara proclaims that 'everyone makes his art in his own way' and that art criticism 'only exists subjectively, for every individual' (Tzara 1918: 5) he is expressing a view with linguistic implications that Hermogenes would have approved. That, indeed, is the reason for the scorn Tzara pours on bourgeois attempts to find a meaning for the word *dada* (by appeal to supposed etymologies). For Tzara, such attempts are futile because they are attempts to allocate to the word *dada* a place in a public linguistic code. And the whole symbolic point of the word *dada* is that it has no place in such a code: it is meaningless. But that does not abrogate – on the contrary, it establishes – the right of every Dadaist to use the word in his own way, and even in contradictory ways. This is an assertion of the authority of the individual over language that Plato would have deplored. Socrates would have had a harder time arguing with Tzara than with Hermogenes.

*   *   *

'New art, new artspeak' was never a principle that any of the modern movements preached, but it was the policy they all practised. The predictable result of this Hermogenean fervour is that artspeak in the early twentieth century is more chaotic and anarchic than at any earlier period in history. Equally predictable are attempts to restore some kind of order into artspeak, while admitting that a great revolution is taking place. An early example of this reaction is Clive Bell's *Art* (1914), which introduced the doctrine of 'significant form', a doctrine so loosely formulated as to fit the work of Poussin just as comfortably as the work of Picasso.

Bell is very clear about the proper role of artspeak. The critic, he asserts, cannot *tell* me that something is a work of art: 'he must make me feel it for myself' (Bell 1914: 9). It goes without saying that the same goes for the artist: the artist's proclamation or *profession de foi* is not enough. Ideally the work should speak for itself, and it must speak by arousing what Bell calls our 'aesthetic emotion'. But if words are needed to explain the work, then they too must be directed towards arousing that aesthetic emotion. If not, they are useless. As Bell's modern editor shrewdly observes, this is 'the rhetoric of Ruskin, not Marinetti': 'Bell's message is one of continuity, not confrontation, and it was one which in 1914 the British wished to hear' (Bell 1914: xlix).

For Bell, however, the individual was still in the end the judge of both work of art and artspeak. A quite different contractualist reaction was to emerge much later in what is now known as the 'institutional theory of art'. According to this view, a work is a work of art when it is described and accepted as such by an informed consensus of opinion in the 'art world'.

> That is, there are institutions – such as museums, galleries, and journals and newspapers that publish reviews and criticism – and there are individuals who work within those institutions – curators, directors, dealers, performers, critics – who decide, by accepting objects or events for discussion and display, what is art and what is not. (Feagin 1995: 379)

This is a very reactionary form of contractualism, which puts the artspeak contract in the hands of a clique of 'experts'. It is no longer art-for-art's-sake, but art-for-institutions'-sake. The artists who gain from this are those who are approved by the relevant institutions and produce work that suits institutional requirements; and the critics who gain are those who can help to market and publicize such work. The fact that this contractualist strategy for defining 'art' produces a definition that is merely circular counts for nothing, provided the institutions are successful in selling it to the public. Here it ceases to matter how or why the public is taken in, provided they turn up in sufficient numbers to exhibitions, theatres and concert halls, or watch the relevant television programmes. Thus the arts end up as components of a modern entertainment industry catering for populations with an increasing proportion of leisure time and disposable income.

*   *   *

A structuralist approach to artspeak is considerably more demotic. It offers no role for 'experts' who have to explain to the public what the currently fashionable forms of art and artspeak 'mean'. At its most radical, the structuralist claim is that we all know what art is because the term *art* is part of our everyday language. Any mystery about it is a confusion bred by our own timidity in face of an elitist 'art world' conspiracy. There is no more reason for thinking that we do not, as enfranchised members of our linguistic community, understand the word *art* (and its associated terms) as for thinking that we do not understand the word *blue* (and the rest of our colour vocabulary).

According to at least one philosopher, anyone not mystified in this way would be perfectly capable of picking out the works of art in a warehouse full of a random collection of items of all kinds. 'We are able to separate those objects which are works of art from those which are not, because we know English' (Kennick 1958: 321). This form of structuralism, however, is evidently too radical for some philosophers. One of Kennick's critics objects that being a native speaker of English no more equips you to identify works of art than to identify insects. What you need in the case of insects is not just a knowledge of English but a knowledge of entomology (Tilghman 1984: 49). This objection seems to imply that in the case of art there is some body of specialist knowledge which stands in relation to artspeak as entomology stands in relation to everyday talk about insects. The objection, however, is a surrogational objection. It makes no inroads into a structuralist defence which will counter by pointing out that the entomologist is using a different language from the man-in-the-street, but a language nevertheless. Furthermore, it would be naive to suppose that the distinction between insects and non-insects is on a par with the distinction between works which are works of art and works which are not. (Although that, again, is an assimilation that a reocentric surrogationalist might swallow.)

One legacy of structuralism was the New Critical insistence on analysing a poem 'in its own terms' (i.e. as an internally ordered autonomous structure) and without reference to alleged authorial intentions or historical context. The combination of structuralism with the doctrine of art-for-art's-sake could even lead to a position that undermined artspeak itself, inasmuch as critical discourse was seen as potentially misleading or even futile. Thus what starts with T. S. Eliot's insistence on the 'autotelic' nature of poetry leads gradually towards Cleanth Brooks's tautological conclusion that 'the poem says what the poem says' (Brooks 1968: 60). This is a typically structuralist thesis: language is here presented as making it impossible to express what the poem expresses other than through the words of the poem. The work does not 'stand for' anything else: it simply *is*. Thus 'the poem itself is the *only* medium that communicates the particular "what" that is communicated.'

Another structuralist legacy was the Russian formalist notion of 'poetic function', which implies a 'focus on the message for its own sake' and 'projects the principle of equivalence from the axis of selection into the axis of combination' (Jakobson 1960). Poetics, according to Jakobson, 'deals primarily with the question, *What makes a verbal message a work of art?*' Its main subject is 'the *differentia specifica* of verbal art in relation to other arts'. It is thus 'entitled to the leading place in literary studies'. It 'deals with problems of verbal structure, just as the analysis of painting is concerned with pictorial structure'. However, for Jakobson *qua* linguist, linguistics is 'the global science of verbal structure'. Poetics, accordingly, 'may be regarded as an integral part of linguistics'. Here the cat is let out of the bag. This is not artspeak in the service of art, but artspeak in the service of *ars grammatica*. Another takeover bid, but considerably cruder than Plato's.

Structuralism has clear implications for non-verbal arts too. Its most obvious application is in relation to abstract painting, where shapes and colours make no pretension to 'representing' objects in the external world. They relate to one another solely as constituent elements of an autonomous composition. Historically, it can hardly be regarded as a coincidence that the year in which Worringer published his landmark treatise *Abstraktion und Einfühlung* (1908) was the year in which Saussure was giving the second of his three courses of lectures on the foundations of linguistics in Geneva. Worringer wrote:

> Our investigations proceed from the presupposition that the work of art, as an autonomous organism, stands beside nature on equal terms, and, in its deepest and innermost essence, devoid of any connection with it [. . .]. (Worringer 1908: 68)

This, in its own way, is a rejection of surrogational semantics no less emphatic than Saussure's.

*   *   *

The most challenging of the structuralist legacies in artspeak did not emerge until after the Second World War. It involved querying the credentials of what had formerly passed for 'history of art'. Awkward linguistic questions began to be raised, somewhat belatedly, about 'Classical art'; questions which threatened the whole notion of a Western artistic tradition. Since the eighteenth century at least, when the history of art had been set up as an academic discipline, it had been generally assumed that there were no chronological (or geographical) limits to what counted as a work of art. Greek vases were in that respect on all fours with Italian maiolica and Wedgwood, while the Elgin marbles could be compared with the relief carvings of Gothic churches. Ruskin had happily bumbled on about 'Fine Art' as 'it was two thousand years ago, in the days of Phidias' (Ruskin 1859: 296). But did Phidias and his contemporaries have Ruskin's conception of 'Fine Art'? Structuralism made this a difficult position to maintain. By the mid-twentieth century it was commonplace to question whether the Greeks had any notion at all which corresponded to the modern term *art*. And it was Greek artspeak that was taken as providing the *prima facie* evidence for doubting it.

The linguistic crux of the matter hinged on interlingual comparison of vocabularies. Professor Sir John Boardman in his book *Greek Art* says: 'Greek had no separate word for Art in our sense; only Craft (*techne*)' (Boardman 1996: 16). Eric Havelock states categorically that 'neither "art" nor "artist", *as we use the words*, is translatable into archaic or high-classical Greek' (Havelock 1963: 33). According to Iris Murdoch, 'the Greeks in general lacked our reverential conception of "fine art", for which there is no separate term in Greek, the word *techne* covering art, craft, and skill' (Murdoch 1977: 1). Alison Burford in *Craftsmen in Greek and Roman Society* declares that the modern distinction between arts and crafts was unknown in antiquity, 'the most obvious indication of this conceptual difference being given by the language' (Burford 1972: 14). In this all four echo R. G. Collingwood, who claims in *The Principles of Art* that in Greek and Roman civilization no consistent distinction was drawn between what we would now call 'art' and what we would call 'technique'. Collingwood writes:

> *Ars* in ancient Latin, like *techne* in Greek [. . .] means a craft or specialized form of skill, like carpentry or smithying or surgery. The Greeks and Romans had no conception of what we call art as something different from craft; what we call art they regarded merely as a group of crafts, such as the craft of poetry [. . .], which they conceived, sometimes no doubt with misgivings, as in principle just like carpentry and the rest, and differing from any one of these only in the sort of way in which any one of them differs from any other. (Collingwood 1938: 5)

Although Collingwood had probably never read Saussure, his claim is one that many structuralists would have endorsed. For it is based on a Saussurean thesis: the incommensurability of lexical systems across languages. According to Collingwood:

> If people have no word for a certain kind of thing, it is because they are not aware of it as a distinct kind. Admiring as we do the art of the ancient Greeks, we naturally suppose that they admired it in the same kind of spirit as ourselves. But we admire it as a kind of art, where the word 'art' carries with it all the subtle and elaborate implications of the modern European aesthetic consciousness. We can be perfectly certain that the Greeks did not admire it in any such way. (Collingwood 1938: 6)

Collingwood went on to make the point that it would be naive to assume that we can circumvent this difficulty by going directly to Plato and other Greek sources for uncontaminated information about the Greek view of art. For *the way we read Plato* may be coloured in various subtle and not-so-subtle ways by our assumption that he too is talking about 'art' when in fact he is not. If Collingwood is right, then surrogational art historians, wittingly or unwittingly, are engaged in a historical deception. Either they are confusing history with mere antecedence, which would be like insisting on including an account of the horse-drawn carriage as part of the history of the motor car. Or else they are crudely retrojecting a modern conceptual framework into a culture where it had no place. Either way, there are problems here which the historian of art cannot afford to ignore. Nor are such problems confined to the arts; for, if the linguistic argument is accepted, similar problems must arise in interpreting all aspects of ancient Greek civilization, from painting to politics.

* * *

The structuralist predicament in artspeak is not confined to discussing the art of the past, but extends to artspeak as applied to contemporary non-Western cultures. Anthropologists who write about 'art' in Australian aboriginal communities are clearly aware of it. In *Dreamings. The Art of Aboriginal Australia* (ed. P. Sutton, 1988), a scholarly work written to accompany the first major exhibition of its kind ever seen in the U.S.A., we find an Introduction which includes a remarkable attempt to prove that aboriginal products *can* properly be called 'art' in English and exhibited as such. The authors begin by stating what they take to be the main objection to their thesis:

On Defining Art

The very application of the term *art* to things made by Aboriginal people has been interpreted by some critics as an act of cultural colonialism. They say that art is a concept alien to Aboriginal culture. The evidence cited for this assertion is that the usual definition of art depends on its applicability to things found in institutions such as art museums, or to things defined as such by art curators and the art market. These critics contend that Aboriginal languages have no word for art, while many other languages do. (Sutton and Anderson 1988: 3)

But this objection, according to Sutton and Anderson, is not as telling as it might seem: we need to compare the aboriginal situation with what happens in the case of European languages:

> Speakers of European languages, for example, may share essential meanings for the various terms translatable into English as *art*, but they seldom agree entirely on the range of things to which such terms should be applied. One person's art may be another person's junk or kitsch. Speakers of Aboriginal languages are in this sense very similar. Each of the various languages has a term that essentially means sign, design, pattern, or meaningful mark. It is used to describe paintings and other designed things made by people, but it may also describe the patterns of honeycombs, spiders' webs, the wave-marked sand of the beach, varie-gated butterfly wings, and a host of other manifestations of similar formal properties. These usually include a combination of repetition, variations, symmetry and asymmetry; and, like the designs of human artifacts, they are seen as ultimately derived from the Dreaming, the power-filled ground of existence. (Sutton and Anderson 1988: 3)

Thus far, Sutton and Anderson appear to be conceding their opponents' main point; namely, that there is no indigenous term exclusively reserved in aboriginal languages for what Europeans would call 'art'. But they then proceed to argue, ingeniously, that this does not mean that aboriginal peoples do know know what art is: the explanation is simply that aborigines have a different conception of how nature relates to the human world.

There are areas of overlap between these Aboriginal terms and European terms such as *art*, *l'art*, and *Kunst*. While the latter are not normally used of things created by nature, they are used of things created by sentient, intelligent beings. Dreamings are just such beings, and they create the patterns in the world that manifest their presence as signs. In North East Arnhem Land traditions, the wax hexagons of a beehive are *miny'tji*, or designs, just as the diamond shapes in a painting of Wild Honey Dreaming are *miny'tji*, and they manifest the same spiritual and intelligently ordering essence [. . .]. But one Aboriginal group does not usually have exactly the same Dreamings as another, nor the same range of physical environments. The specific items encompassed by the Yolngu word *miny'tji* in tropical North East Arnhem Land and by the Warlpiri word *kuruwarri* in the desert at Yuendumu, in spite of the semantic closeness of the two terms, are bound to be different. What is shared, however, is a common conception of intentionally meaningful forms, or signs.

None of these signs, in the Aboriginal cultures of the precolonial past, were part of an art market in a commercial sense, but they were currency in a competitive political economy. Rights in them could be traded, bequeathed, and, at times, even stolen for their high value. Human artifacts were also subject to similar transactions. (Sutton and Anderson 1988: 3–4)

In short, what Western observers take for an aboriginal failure to grasp what art is is actually a Western failure to grasp the aboriginal belief that behind the designs and patterns in nature there lies a creative, sign-making intelligence. The conclusion the authors draw from this is then stated as follows:

As long as we restrict our sense of the English term *art* to that elementary level at which it connotes visible and intentional signs made by intelligent beings, we are not stretching a point when we say that Aboriginal paintings, carvings, and other works are art, not "by metamorphosis" and not merely because they now are in the global art market, but because they share with similar artifacts the act of representation and a particular potential for meaning. (Sutton and Anderson 1988: 4)

As far as artspeak is concerned, this is an interesting case, because here the authors are trying to conduct two artspeak dialogues at the same time. The results are both confused and confusing. On the one hand, they wish to be seen as championing aboriginal culture by deploying European artspeak in much the same way as they would if describing European artifacts. On the other hand, they are clearly concerned to defend the exhibition against the criticisms of rival anthropologists and other sceptics who question whether what is on show is art at all. So this is not a disinterested examination of the current application of the term *art*: professional reputations are at stake here.

In the opening paragraph cited above, the authors launch into an attack on the 'institutional' theory of art. The point of this is presumably to discount in advance any importance attached to the fact that Western institutions on the whole classify artifacts of this kind as ethnological material rather than as art objects. They immediately make the assumption that the only serious ground that institutions have for adopting this policy rests on a flawed linguistic argument. The linguistic argument in question turns out to be the 'structuralist' case, as advanced by Collingwood and others (although this is not explicitly referred to).

Why do Sutton and Anderson construe their most important task as being to counter the claim that aboriginal languages have no word for 'art'? It is difficult to see how this would be relevant, unless they themselves, in common with their critics, tacitly supposed that a practice requires some form of artspeak if it is to count as art at all. What they try to show is that *although* aboriginal languages have no word for 'art' as such, nevertheless they do have words that come close to it by referring to what Bell might have called 'significant forms', whether man-made or natural. That, they assume, establishes that these aboriginal words show an overlap of meaning with European terms like *art* and *Kunst*.

This is plainly a retreat to surrogational semantics. Comparing vocabulary across languages – a structuralist would argue – makes little sense in the first place, unless a common psychocentric or reocentric basis can be assumed. Whether there *is* such a basis in this case is precisely the issue in contention. So pointing out that there are aboriginal words applied to a range of things which share the common property of being created by sentient, intelligent beings is a move that begs two questions at once. One is whether the inhabitants of Dreamland actually are sentient, intelligent beings. The other is whether, even if they were, that would suffice to make their products art. Much of what sentient and presumably intelligent inhabitants of Western countries create is destined never to end up exhibited as 'art' in museums or galleries of any kind; and no one supposes otherwise. So as a move against the policies of unenlightened Western institutions, this seems particularly ill-judged. It is no use arguing that as long as we restrict our use of the English term *art* to an elementary level, then it is justifiable to call certain products of aboriginal culture 'art', because that reinforces your adversary's contention that it is not 'really' art, i.e. in the full sense of that term.

Sutton and Anderson do not seem to realize that they are deploying a linguistic strategy which in the end undermines their own position rather than supporting it. Their argument can all too easily be stood on its head. If the lexical resources of European languages matched exactly those of aboriginal languages, then one would presumably conclude that Europeans had no conception of art either. Or, more exactly, if that were the case then the question would not arise. And that is the crux of the matter. The whole question is totally Eurocentric, because the artspeak involved is itself Eurocentric. If European languages had no such term as 'art', there would be nothing to debate.

The irony is that the authors of the Introduction to the *Dreamings* volume are trying hard to be politically correct. They want to admit aboriginal culture to the privileged club of cultures that can boast a long artistic tradition. But their argument defeats its own purpose. Confronted by opponents who maintain that aboriginal languages have no word for 'art', they accept that claim as coherent and relevant – i.e. concede that aboriginal artists operate under the terms of a different linguistic contract – and then argue that having no single word for 'art' is compensated for by the presence in the vocabulary of rather different words. This is trying to have your contractual cake and eat it. All it shows is the authors' failure to understand the rationale of the very artspeak they themselves are using. It is by their insistence on describing a certain range of aboriginal cultural products in terms of 'art' that they subordinate this particular facet of aboriginal culture to values imposed from outside by white Australians.

*   *   *

The same problem is dealt with differently in Appiah's defence of the 1996 Guggenheim exhibition of 'African art'. He readily concedes that there is 'no old word in most of the thousand or so languages still spoken in Africa that adequately translates the word "art".' But he maintains that

> there is, after all, no word in seventeenth-century English (or, no doubt, in seventeenth-century Cantonese or Sanskrit) that carries exactly that burden of meaning, either. (Appiah 1997)

Thus far, his argument might seem to be taking the familiar structuralist line. But he goes on:

> What, after all, does it matter that this pair of concepts – *Africa, art* – was not used by those who made these objects? They are still African; they are still works of art. [. . .]
>   In presenting these objects as art objects, the curators of the exhibition invited us to look at them in a certain way, to evaluate them in the manner we call "aesthetic." This means that we were invited to look at their form, their craftsmanship, the ideas they evoke, to attend to them in the way we have learned to attend in art museums. (Appiah 1997)

Thus Appiah, unlike Sutton and Anderson, resolves the issue by rushing to embrace the 'institutional' theory of art and being prepared to live with the consequences. But saying 'All this may not have been art as far as the makers were concerned; but so what? It's our exhibition, not theirs' is not a reply likely to satisfy anyone who believes that art is made by its makers, not by casual spectators; or that understanding the makers' artistic purposes and problems is an essential part of appreciating any work of art.

According to Appiah:

The ways we think of "art" now in the West (and the many places in the world where people have taken up this Western idea) began to take something like their modern shape in the European Enlightenment. (Appiah 1997)

Furthermore:

Since the nineteenth century especially, we have made an important distinction between the fine and the decorative arts, and we have come increasingly to think of fine art as "art for art's sake". We have come, that is, increasingly to see art as something we must assess by criteria that are intrinsic to the arts, by what we call aesthetic standards. We know art can serve a political or a moral or even a commercial purpose: but to see something *as* art is to evaluate it in ways that go beyond asking whether it serves these "extrinsic" purposes. Many of the objects shown at the Guggenheim, on the other hand, had primary functions that were, by our standards, non-aesthetic, and would have been assessed, first and foremost, by their ability to achieve those functions. (Appiah 1997)

This is an example of modern contractualism trapped into a *non sequitur* of its own contriving. It does not follow that because the practical function of many artifacts can be assessed quite independently of their artistic merits, if any, the criteria of art somehow belong to a dimension of their own which has nothing to do with function. The *non sequitur* exposes the fallacy at the centre of the art-for-art's-sake doctrine. To suppose that the ideal work of art would have no purpose whatsoever (other than to be a work of art) secures the autonomy of art at the cost of vacuity. Art cannot be identified by subtraction: when we take away everything that might be considered as serving an 'extrinsic' purpose we are left not with pure unadulterated art but with pure unadulterated nothing. What is particularly bizarre is the attempt to invoke such an ideal in the service of an institutional theory of art. For one thing that is obvious about putting together prestigious exhibitions of exotic artifacts and calling them 'art' is that it is done for very specific 'extrinsic' purposes (financial and professional).

*   *   *

In his book *African Art*, Frank Willett discusses attempts made in recent times by Western scholars to investigate what criteria of approval or disapproval are employed in African societies in the assessment of good or bad sculpture, and to determine to what extent these coincide or fail to coincide with the judgments of Western observers. The picture that emerges is somewhat confused, in part because of the faulty logic apparently underlying some of this research. For example, it does not prove very much to establish that there is a broad consensus in judgments as to whether carving A is better than carving B, and that in turn better than carving C. Rank ordering tells us little, because it is possible for two people to agree 100% about a rank ordering, but for quite different reasons. As one might expect, there are wide differences between societies where being a wood-carver is a specialized profession and societies where almost anyone can carve. Among the Tiv, for example, according to one anthropologist, 'almost every man is a critic. Because there are no specialists in taste, and only a few in the manufacture of art, every man is free to know what he likes and to make it if he can.'

If this description is accurate, then the Tiv exemplify a state of society unknown in the Western tradition, i.e. a society before that division of labour which seems to have given rise to the cultivation of specialist skills in Graeco-Roman antiquity. Knowing what you like, as apparently the Tiv do, is a long way from appreciating something as art. And here we come up against a problem concerning the reasons given for preferences. For instance, it seems that in evaluating Yoruba sculpture importance is attached, among other things, to a quality called *didon*, which is translated as 'luminosity' (Willett 1993: 213). This apparently refers to the shine of the surface. But here straight away are two difficulties. First, does this Yoruba word, when applied to carvings, actually mean what a Western observer would mean by calling it 'shiny'? Secondly, whatever this quality is, how do we discover that it actually is relevant to the work *as art*, and not simply relevant to its function, or its value, or some other aspect of the reasons for making such artifacts? For it seems clear that in some cases what an object looks like is quite irrelevant to its cultural value in African society. Willett gives the following example:

> although the masks used along the Upper Cavally River in the Ivory Coast by the Dan, Ngere [. . .] and Wobe vary in their ranking and function, this differentiation is not related to their appearance. For them the mask is a channel of communication with the high god Zlan, but the real intermediaries are the spirits of the ancestors who are invoked through the mask. The power of the mask to influence the ancestors depends on the social prestige of the owner, since a man can only reach prominence with their help, and his very success shows that the ancestors favour him. An inherited mask retains its power over the

ancestors and the more prestigious its owner was in this life, the more powerful he will be as an ancestor. Similarly, old masks which span several generations are considered especially powerful. The prestige of a mask is thus an acquired characteristic which cannot be deduced from its appearance [. . .]. (Willett 1993: 180)

Here is another example from Willett concerning the irrelevance of an object's appearance:

Among the BaLega [. . .] Biebuyck found that all the traditional sculptures used by the *Bwami* society in their rituals were judged to be 'good' by which was meant that they fulfilled their functions. 'Criticism of the physical appearance [sc. of the sculpture] is inconceivable.' As a result, celluloid dolls obtained by trade enjoy equal regard with the traditional sculptures in ivory and wood. (Willett 1993: 215–16)

These examples seem to support Appiah's contention that – in many cases, at least – the Western collector's classification of tribal cult objects as 'art' places these objects in a perspective which is far removed from that of their original makers and users.

*   *   *

Since the days when Roger Fry admired the cave walls of Lascaux and Altamira, much earlier work of a comparable kind has been discovered, prompting a new wave of enthusiastic artspeak from archeologists and prehistorians. The Cosquer cave near Marseilles was discovered in 1991, having been protected from human intrusion for thousands of years by the rise in the level of the Mediterranean, which concealed the entrance at the end of the last ice age (Clottes and Courtin 1996). The Chauvet cave in the Ardèche was unknown until 1994 (Chauvet, Deschamps and Hillaire 1996). The earliest application of pigment from either site so far dated (at the Chauvet cave) gives a radio-carbon reading which puts it at about 31,000 years ago.

Discoveries of this nature exert considerable pressure on those whose job it is to interpret it all. The two recently explored sites are, and always were, deep underground. What is to be seen can only – and could only – be seen by artificial illumination of some kind. This already poses an interesting conundrum, unless we are prepared to believe that our ancestors could see in the dark. Why conceal what speaks to the eye in places where it will – for most of the time – be invisible? But this is only one facet of a broader question which takes priority over everything else: what did all the marks and configurations left in these caves mean to those who made them?

One has to say 'marks', 'configurations' and 'mean' because those are terms as neutral as the English language allows us if we do not wish to prejudge the status and function of this early human handiwork. For what has been brought to light tells us less about the Cro-Magnon mind than about the conceptual difficulties which hamper modern efforts to understand it. What is already clear is that the preferred intellectual framework for the experts' interpretation of the caves is still that of Fry's generation, with its problematic concept of aesthetic endeavour. The subtitle of Chauvet, Deschamps and Hillaire 1996 announces 'the discovery of the world's oldest paintings'. Both in this account and in Clottes and Courtin 1996 there is repeated reference to those responsible for the work in the caves as 'artists'. We read of 'panels' and 'frescoes' and even of 'artistic licence'. Descriptions of what is visible make free use of evaluative terms that might not be out of place in criticizing exhibits in a modern gallery. So before anyone can say 'Jack Paleo-Robinson', these unprecedented finds are already inscribed in an academic discourse about 'the history of art'.

That was perhaps inevitable, and there may be a case to be made out for it; but it is not made out very well – if at all – by prehistorians. Rather, they take it for granted. The caves are treated as studios. Schools, traditions and conventions are detected. Details of execution are rationalized on this basis. Thus a double or triple outline is read as the cave artist's attempt to portray a herd, while extra limbs are seen as a rendering of movement.

Here there is no question of asking the makers for explanations, as anthropologists can do in the case of contemporary primitive societies. Nor is there much point in speculating about whether the language of our ancestors already had a word for 'art'. So everything rests on what can be seen. It is not in dispute that what the caves offer to a modern eye can often be seen as 'representations' of recognizable animals: horses, bison, deer, etc. But if we now go on to ask why that makes it all right to call it 'prehistoric art' (in the absence of any further information about the makers or the making of it), we uncover a presupposition of roughly the following form. Art *reveals itself*, because it is universal: representing the fauna and flora of the natural world is one of the archetypal functions of the artist. So whenever we come across what looks to us fairly obviously – or even rather remotely – like a picture of a horse, bison, deer, etc. we must be dealing with some kind of artistic undertaking.

This basic assumption leads immediately to others. What *kind* of art is this, deliberately hidden away from the external world, in spaces not evidently used for domestic habitation? The experts have a pigeonhole answer ready for that too: it must be some kind of religious art. That is to say, the pictures must be related to magical practices or superstitions, the exact nature of which is unknown. (The shaman is often conjured up at this point.) So the initial supposition about art joins forces with an assumption about the rudimentary beliefs of our ancestors: together they lead directly to a theory about the function of the site. Clottes and Courtin repeatedly refer to the Cosquer cave as a 'sanctuary', although there is no evidence that it was, once we set aside the question-begging assumption that it is full of ancient works of art.

The point is not whether the hypothesis is tenable, or plausible, but what is revealed about its underpinnings. The question of whether the hunters of long ago were ever on the wavelength of what the twentieth century called 'art' is simply bypassed. They *must* have been artists, whether they knew it or not. Only on that basis can we do the decent thing and fit them in belatedly to our modern schemata of human history. Thus, just as in anthropology, 'art' functions as a supercategory which justifies classifying remote societies as 'primitive'.

A revealing example concerns the interpretation of the enigmatic 'finger tracings' that abound at Cosquer. These are assumed by Clottes and Courtin to have nothing to do with the 'art work', which belongs to a subsequent period in the use of the cave (several thousand years later), and is often superimposed on the finger tracings. The explanation proposed is that these earlier marks were made by people who felt a need to establish 'taking possession' of the cave. ('It's ours: so let's scratch it all over!') But the underlying reasoning goes something like this. These marks are not art because they have, say the authors quite firmly, no 'aesthetic value'. The implication is that they must be traces of less exalted pursuits.

An even more interesting case is that of the human 'hand' forms present at both sites. These fall, as it were, on the presupposed borderline between art and non-art. Some, at Chauvet, seem to have been made by pressing a hand dipped in pigment against a surface ('prints'). Others look like the result of spraying pigment around the outline left by a hand ('stencils'). With one possible exception, only hand stencils occur at Cosquer, and belong to the early phase of activity in the cave, long before the animal figures appear: they cannot be considered, Clottes and Courtin tell us, '"art" in the strict sense'. (What the strict sense is they do not say, but for 'strict' we can presumably read 'modern'.)

Often the prehistoric 'hand' seems to have fingers missing. Clottes and Courtin reject the usual hypotheses of deliberate mutilation, frostbite and disease. They opt for another theory: the deformed hands are coded gestures. (The maker bent down certain fingers in order to produce a silhouette of a certain shape.) So this is not quite art, but symbolic communication of some kind nevertheless. The authors add immediately that we shall never be able to crack the prehistoric hand 'code'. However, they conclude that at Cosquer a different code must have been in use than at Gargas, because the statistics of missing fingers per hand are different in the two cases. How that follows it is difficult to see, unless we knew something about the semantics of the codes, which Clottes and Courtin say is impossible. But then how can we be sure we are dealing with messages in a gesture code in the first place? What is clear, though, is that the hypothesis once again fits the history-of-art framework: one can now trace a chronological progression from primitive visual signs to full-blown depiction. Marks not otherwise identifiable go into the ragbag categories of 'signs' and 'indeterminate lines', and are interpreted wherever possible as modifications of or comments on 'hands' or 'pictures'.

The pictures, moreover, are taken to be pictures in the modern sense. They are classified by subject matter, according to what they are taken to depict. Clottes leaves no doubt about this when, in his epilogue to the Chauvet book, he asserts confidently: 'These are not stereotyped images that were transcribed to convey the concept "lion" or "rhinoceros", but living animals faithfully reproduced' (Chauvet, Deschamps and Hillaire 1996: 114). Nor does he hesitate to speak of the artist's 'quest for perspective'. What purpose a quest for perspective would serve in this context, unless we are already dealing with a frustrated Uccello living many millennia in advance of his time, it is hard to fathom. And how we can with any assurance attribute to this prehistoric Uccello the artistic aim of 'faithful reproduction' is even more questionable.

The structure of the explanation, in short, is determined less by archaeological facts than by certain preconceptions about cultural evolution. The explanatory exercise is one in damage limitation, which attempts to reconcile modern ignorance with modern self-esteem. This is why the concept of 'art' plays such a crucial role. We can accept the idea that, because of the passage of time, some of the meanings in prehistoric art now escape us. This can be admitted because it is no more problematic than the discovery of an undeciphered script: we can convince ourselves we are looking at texts in a lost language of art, to which we merely lack the key. What is unacceptable is the far more disturbing idea that this is not a lost language of art at all, but a quite different form of activity. For then we lose our grip on the primitive 'text' altogether.

The design of the two books reinforces the message. We are invited to see for ourselves – with the help of an artist: and here the artist is a photographer. Both works contain detailed photographic records of the cave interiors; at once brilliantly informative and brilliantly deceptive. The camera cannot lie, yet in this case it is lying all the time. For what there is to be seen was never seen thus by the human beings who made these caves what they were. What appears on the walls and ceilings was never viewed in the hard, frozen, unblinking glare that modern photography demands, but only in the flickering, restless light of a flame. That difference cannot be dismissed as irrelevant to understanding what it is we are looking at. It affects the whole visual experience. Furthermore, by imposing its standard rectangle on a carefully selected visual field, the camera is capable of making almost anything look pictorial to the modern eye. And this bears directly on how we 'see' the evidence.

Which brings us back to the old puzzle. Why consign your best pictures to the pitch-dark of a cave? The puzzle arises precisely because rock art is assumed to deliver a visual message. There are two possible approaches to the problem, depending on whether we accept this premiss or not. If we do, it must be relevant that the site chosen totally reverses the night–day conditions of vision for human beings. For purely physiological reasons, *Homo sapiens* is not as well adapted as many creatures to living in the dark. The compensation for this is that only in complete darkness can we have complete control of the light source and hence control of the visual space available at any one time. (This is the biomechanical foundation of the modern cinema. But the modern cinema typically uses it as no more than a technical device to 'present again' narrative scenes originally enacted elsewhere.) In the dark, a light source can be moved. Different areas can be brought alive in sequence. Objects of various kinds can be used to project shadows. It becomes possible to create a world of figures and patterns which, unlike the painting or the static photograph, is a world never still. Even fixed surfaces can be made to 'move' visually, especially if covered with grooves with a depth of two or three millimetres, as 'finger tracings' have. The cave thus provides an optical arena of which the shape and contents can be altered at will and in ways the tyranny of daylight does not permit. That deliberate reversal itself emerges as the most probable basic source of signification, and makes it even less likely that what the cave 'pictures' mean depends on how skilfully they recapture in line and colour the visual details of scenes and figures from the daylight world.

The alternative approach involves questioning whether what appears in the caves was meant to be seen at all. (There might have been light in the dark only to enable the makers to do their work.) One possibility is that the motive was indeed to hide something, with whatever that concealment implies at the level of social rationale (persecuted sects? secret societies?). The other possibility discounts concealment as a motive: which, if correct, would suggest that the marks and configurations are where they are basically because that is where they needed to be. Their *visual* character then becomes secondary. Their primary source of signification would derive from their location, how they were placed in that location, when, by whom and why. In that case, the 'artistic' capabilities of the agents involved again become an irrelevance. We are back in a different era of semiosis, where the notion of mimetic representation as an artistic objective is itself an anachronism. Since we do not know what artspeak contract, if any, is reflected in the prehistoric painting of these caves, it is quite gratuitous to assume that it must somehow have corresponded fairly well to our own. Well enough, at least, to warrant deploying modern artspeak in their description.

'Scepticism is always healthy,' writes Paul Bahn in his introduction to Chauvet, Deschamps and Hillaire. But the scepticism prehistorians welcome concerns the authenticity of new finds rather than the validity of old ways of describing them. In the heroic age of prehistorical studies, the prehistory of Breuil's generation, the artspeak idiom served an essential chronological purpose. 'Styles' were the principal evidence for dating. With the advent of less subjective methods of dating this form of discourse sounds increasingly archaic. The artspeak of prehistory may now have become a hindrance rather than a help to understanding the past.

*   *   *

In all these cases we see contractualism struggling with linguistic problems of its own making. They cannot be resolved except by reverting to a surrogationalism that has already been rejected. So there is nowhere left to go. Not, at least, within the intellectual confines imposed on artspeak by the language myth.

11

The Devil's question

Everybody is an artist.
Josef Beuys

Every utterance and every gesture that each one of us makes is a work of art.
Collingwood

The artspeak stalemate outlined in the preceding two chapters involves a stand-off between surrogationalism on the one hand and contractualism (including its structuralist versions) on the other. The stalemate might appear to be irresoluble. At one extreme we find an unconvincing attempt to base artistic judgments on objective and presumably universal criteria: at the other extreme we have what amounts to artistic Humpty-Dumptyism. (Humpty Dumpty made a personal appearance on the art scene a few years ago in the form of Robert Rauschenberg, who replied to an invitation to undertake a portrait of Iris Clert with the memorable telegram: 'This is a portrait of Iris Clert if I say so.') Somewhere in between Plato and Humpty Dumpty, in a dubious compromise position, hover 'experts' whose role is to mediate between artist and public for the alleged benefit of society (but also to the immediate advantage of the institutions and markets they serve). These experts tend more and more nowadays to opt for some version of contractualist artspeak, and the reason for this is hardly open to doubt: it enables them to champion whichever *avant-garde* trends they fancy, or which become commercially viable. But the impasse between surrogational and contractualist artspeak remains. It *is* irresoluble in its own terms. Does that mean it cannot be bypassed?

The theoretical basis for a radical alternative to both views of artspeak has become available in recent years with the emergence of integrationism as philosophy of language. The integrationist critique of orthodox linguistics (Harris 1998) rejects both surrogationalism and contractualism as being committed to a long-standing myth about how language works. The myth in question is based on two assumptions, both problematic. One is the psychological assumption that words enable thoughts or ideas to be transmitted from one person's mind to another's. The other is the sociological assumption that languages (English, French, etc.) are fixed codes, put in place by society in order to enable this transmission to take place.

In challenging both assumptions simultaneously, integrationists have proposed a quite different account of human communication. For the integrationist, communication is not a matter of transmitting an encoded 'message' from 'sender' to 'receiver'. Instead, communication is seen as a complex of processes which allow human beings to integrate the many and varied activities which go to make up their individual and social lives. That integration is the foundation of both. Accordingly, words are not to be seen as 'standing for' something else, as the surrogationalist assumes. Nor are they to be seen as the terms of a contract, as the contractualist supposes. Words, for the integrationist, are signs devised to facilitate the integration of whatever activities human beings engage in.

Homo sapiens, for the integrationist, is first and foremost *homo communicator*. Communicational skills are integrational skills and come into play across the whole range of activities traditionally called 'arts'. Thus the integrationist point of view is one from which the painting of a picture or the building of a bridge are just as much communicational enterprises as the performance of a symphony or the writing of a novel. Whether words actually feature in the end-product of such an enterprise is of less importance than the fact that they will have been implicated in some way or other at all stages of its development.

From this perspective the relationship between communication and the arts might be summed up as follows: *the arts are forms of communication and all forms of communication are arts*. This does not involve supposing that each community will share with every other a common communicational profile or programme. Nor does it mean that every art has its counterpart from one community to the next. The extent to which and the precise ways in which communication develops will depend – and always have depended historically – on the various macrosocial and circumstantial factors obtaining in particular cases. But once communication is seen not as a matter of sending messages to and fro but of integrating human activities, it follows that where there is no communication, questions of artistic value cannot arise. For values – whether they be artistic, moral, economic, or of any other kind – are products of, and in turn guides to, the way human beings integrate their activities and, by so doing, interact with one another. These various patterns of integration, considered at the macrosocial level, are what society calls 'trade', 'law', 'politics', 'education' and – in the case which concerns us here – 'art'.

The integrationist view of communication thus opens up a range of questions about artspeak that cannot be tackled from within the intellectual confines of either surrogationalism or contractualism. It also provides theoretical support for such apparently iconoclastic pronouncements as Josef Beuys's 'Everybody is an artist' and R. G. Collingwood's claim in *The Principles of Art* that: 'Every utterance and every gesture that each one of us makes is a work of art.' From an integrational perspective, such statements are far from being as perverse or unfounded as they must have seemed to many.

*   *   *

The concept of communication in the arts is often associated with Tolstoy, who fulminated against what he saw as the degenerate and dehumanizing art of his day. Was Tolstoy an integrationist *avant la lettre*? Some of his claims certainly have an integrationist ring to them. He says, for example, that 'art is one of the means of intercourse between man and man' (Tolstoy 1898: 56). He goes further than that. He describes art as 'one of the indispensable means of communication without which mankind could not exist' (Tolstoy 1898: 61). He points out, very perceptively, that linguistic standards are like aesthetic standards in that they commonly have a social class basis: they are regarded as depending on 'the judgments of the finest-nurtured' or 'the authority of the people who are considered educated' (Tolstoy 1898: 131). (He could have added that the whole of the Western *ars grammatica*, from Dionysius Thrax down to the *Oxford English Dictionary*, took this for granted.) Tolstoy also insists that we must not be misled by those limited applications of the term *art* in which it is reserved for particularly notable or praiseworthy works, thus encouraging us to overlook the fact that art in its humbler manifestations is part of everyday existence.

> As speech does not act on us only in sermons, orations, or books, but in all those remarks by which we exchange thoughts and experiences with one another, so also art in the wide sense of the word permeates our whole life, but it is only to some of its manifestations that we apply the term in the limited sense of the word. (Tolstoy 1898: 60)

In all these insights Tolstoy ranks for an integrationist as one of the great theorists of art in the Western tradition. His personal prejudices (he thought ballet, 'in which half-naked women make voluptuous movements, twisting themselves into various sensual wreathings', was 'simply a lewd performance') do not detract from this achievement. Nevertheless, from an integrational point of view, he falls at the crucial hurdle when called upon to explain where and how artspeak fits into the overall cultural scheme.

Although he (rightly) complains that what happened in Europe was that the term *art* was successively redefined in order to fit those cultural products that pleased an elite (a typically surrogational move), he thinks that the remedy is first to set out the correct definition of *art*, and then find which cultural products fit it.

> Instead of giving a definition of true art and then deciding what is and what is not good art by judging whether a work conforms or does not conform to this definition, a certain class of works which for some reason pleases a certain circle of people is accepted as being art, and a definition of art is then devised to cover all these productions. (Tolstoy 1898: 51)

The critical arrow hits the mark; but Tolstoy's alternative, unfortunately, is no more than surrogationalism stood on its head. From an integrationist point of view, it is indeed simplistic to assume that artspeak is merely epiphenomenal on the arts. But no less simplistic is the assumption that the relationship is the other way round, i.e. that the arts can be *defined by* some form of artspeak which itself stands outside them all. If the integrationist is right, something much more complex is going on, and in understanding what that is we cannot abstract from the integrational role that artspeak plays *vis-à-vis* the particular activities involved. The failure of Western theorizing has always been that, in thrall to the language myth, it offered nothing but a choice between inadequate alternatives as ways of interpreting that role.

A further difference between the integrationist's position and Tolstoy's is that Tolstoy supposes that whereas speech communicates ideas, art communicates emotions. The two transmissions are analogous: it is *what is transmitted* that distinguishes the two cases.

> Speech transmitting the thoughts and experiences of men serves as a means of union among them, and art serves a similar purpose. The peculiarity of this latter means of intercourse, distinguishing it from intercourse by means of words, consists in this, that whereas by words a man transmits his thoughts to another, by art he transmits his feelings. (Tolstoy 1898: 57)

This reveals Tolstoy's own commitment to the language myth, and specifically to the telementational fallacy. How it would be possible to transmit thoughts without at the same time transmitting feelings, or vice versa, Tolstoy never explains, nor even regards as calling for explanation.

*   *   *

The distinctive character of integrationism as a theory is its insistence that communication, whether verbal or non-verbal, has to be understood in any given instance by reference to the particular activities involved in those particular circumstances. The integration of these activities is itself the source of meaning. Meaning does not come from somewhere 'outside' them. The activities in question vary from situation to situation and from occasion to occasion. A symphony varies from one performance to the next. A poem is never the same for two readers. Two buildings cannot occupy the same site: each is unique. A residential building is a different structure for each of its occupants, and different again for passers-by who only view it from outside.

The integration of human activities can take effect at various levels, depending on whether the relationships involved are between one individual and another, or between one group and another, or even between one nation and another. The consequences can be minuscule or massive. But this does not affect the principle that no act of communication can be decontextualized.

For the integrationist, it is illusory to imagine that there is any overriding system or set of rules in place which can guarantee how any work of art or act of communication will be interpreted, or how any communication situation will develop. Such interpretations and developments depend on circumstances and individuals. There is no superordinate *logos* which dictates meanings in human affairs. Whatever traditions or expectations or disputes may develop, communication is in the end the product of individuals acting as free agents. The arts are areas of activity in which that freedom is maximal, despite the constraints which society may, for various reasons, try to impose upon it, despite the demands of patrons upon the artists whom they employ, and despite the attempts which groups within the arts may make to control the activities of their own members. The inevitable conflict between freedom and constraint is constantly reflected in artspeak, which acts as a two-edged weapon. It can as easily serve to reinforce regimentation and conformity as to champion innovation or iconoclasm. It can as easily be used against the artist as for the artist.

As a communicational enterprise, no work of art carries a permanent signification around with it. Nor do the terms of artspeak, including the term *art* itself. All works of art and all artspeak are constantly subject to an ongoing process of contextualization and recontextualization.

In rejecting the notion that art and artspeak can be considered in isolation from the human activities which they integrate, integrationism rejects not only the contractualist assumption that the term *art* can be pinned down by means of intralinguistic verbal definitions, but also the surrogational assumption that the word *art* is just a cover term for certain approved ranges of products and skills. For the integrationist, these two misconceptions are head and tail of the same coin. Both are products of flawed theorizing not about art so much as about the way language performs its integrational function in human activities.

Recognizing those misconceptions is only the starting point. Much more important is the next step: recognizing that *language, as one of humanity's basic communicational resources, is also one of humanity's basic forms of artistic activity.* This recognition needs to be distinguished carefully from the prejudice underlying much Western artspeak, which either claims or assumes a privileged position for the verbal arts. The grammarian and the poet long benefited from this privilege, willingly accorded to them in an educational system based on literacy. But here the integrationist is talking about something more fundamental. There is an asymmetrical relationship obtaining between language and other forms of communication. All other forms of communication are accessible to language; but not vice versa. That is to say, other forms of communication deploy methods, materials and procedures that are open to description, discussion and evaluation. So does language itself, as Western culture recognized in its institution of the traditional *ars grammatica*, limited though its scope was. But this was already an acknowledgment that language as an art can be turned back upon itself, in a sense that neither music nor painting can. We can perform a piece of music or copy a painting, but neither music nor painting achieves reflexivity. Every Alfred Brendel can play his own interpretation of Beethoven's sonata. But the keyboard does not allow him to *explain* that interpretation, only to present it. For explanation he must have recourse to words (which then contextualize his playing in a way that would have been impossible without them). Similarly, a painter can copy the *Mona Lisa*; but the copy can only suggest a comment, which words would be needed to confirm. The notion of a self-explanatory work of art is the ultimate illusion generated by the Western communication myth.

Once the importance of this point is grasped, it puts the whole question of artspeak in a different light. If language itself is an art form, artspeak involves using one form of art as the basis for analysing others. One might accordingly expect to find that how other arts are represented in artspeak will reflect at one remove how language itself is seen as functioning. Thus all arts in the end come to be viewed through the artistic grid imposed by language. Is that what we find happening in the Western tradition? The integrationist will argue that that is exactly what does happen, right from the time when Plato first addresses the key questions 'What is the function of art?' and 'What is the function of language?'. Thus the arts are compared and evaluated on the basis of an implicit comparison with language. The individuality of the various arts is assessed in accordance with predominant beliefs about how language achieves its own ends.

For the integrationist, the act of speech is already an artifact, implicitly designed to integrate other activities. Without that integrational function, constructing sentences makes no more sense than designing keys for a door with no locks. But in language, as in all other art forms, design cannot be decontextualized – even hypothetically – without running the risk of incoherence. Thus an integrationist would argue against Plato that in the mimetic arts we cannot cash such vague notions as 'likeness', 'verisimilitude' or 'accuracy of representation' without, either implicitly or explicitly, contextualizing them by reference to the integration of particular activities *in which it matters* how far and for what purpose similarities count. The fallacy of the surrogational concept of mimesis, from an integrational point of view, is that it fosters the idea that absolute and independent criteria of similarity are available, to which our judgments are ultimately answerable. Nor, an integrationist would add, are there any other context-free criteria in any art form. There is no such thing as an ideal knife: everything depends on what there is to be cut. There is no such thing as an ideal narrative: everything depends on what there is to be told, by whom and to whom.

Likewise, an integrationist would take issue with the contractualist assumption that the terminology of artspeak is validated solely by a linguistic covenant, implicit or explicit, which set up the terminology in the first place. For even linguistic contracts – if there are any (Saussure pointed out that we never see them being drawn up) – cannot plausibly be conceived as floating free in a communicational vacuum, independently of whatever activities they serve to integrate. A contract serves a practical purpose: its obligations on the parties involved are not unmotivated. Thus while an integrationist might agree with a structuralist's contention that the meaning of the word *sublime* as used in the eighteenth century by Burke cannot be equated with the meaning of *sublime* as used in the twentieth century by postmodern critics, it would not be for the structuralist's reasons, i.e. that the contractual structure of the language has altered since Burke's day, and *sublime* is now defined by a range of lexical contrasts which did not exist in the eighteenth century.

The integrationist view of artspeak is thus radically different from that of both surrogational and contractualist approaches. If the integrationist is right about communication in general, this means that neither arts nor artspeak can be understood without reference to the communication situations which constitute their cultural matrix. Since that principle applies to all forms of discourse, discourse about the arts does not by any means constitute a special case.

What an integrationist perspective throws into relief is what is special about the way this discourse in Western civilization has come to be organized; that is, by reference to a supercategory, i.e. 'art(s)', which both subsumes and interrelates a wide diversity of otherwise quite independent practices which seem to have little in common. It is difficult to see, for example, how a training in music would qualify anyone as an architect, or a training in architecture qualify anyone as a musician. Nor does an appreciation of music necessarily go hand in hand with an appreciation of architecture; or vice versa. Yet at all periods in the Western tradition both music and architecture have counted as arts. Why?

It is not at all hard to imagine another civilization which had developed much the same forms of painting, poetry, music, etc. as our own, but felt no need whatsoever to subsume all these under a single supercategory. Or, to put the point another way, without some form of artspeak we might argue about the merits or defects of the same comedies, motets or glass vases; but we would not be arguing about their status or their properties *as art*, nor about the corresponding creative activities *as arts*. It is in this sense that the availability of artspeak is a necessity. Once we see this, we see also that the key question, both linguistically and historically, is: 'Where does this supercategory come from?' And this is a question to which neither surrogational nor contractualist theories of artspeak yield an answer.

The integrationist answer runs as follows: the supercategory is a metalinguistic construct which arises from the attempt, at different times and places and for different reasons, to integrate different – and superficially incompatible – forms of discourse. This integration is required in order to justify activities and claims which would otherwise lack a convincing rationale. The macrosocial function of the supercategory is to hold all this together, both conceptually and rhetorically, i.e. to make it possible to transfer criteria and arguments across the boundaries separating one form of activity from another. If it could not facilitate such assimilations and comparisons, the supercategory would have no *raison d'être*. The questions 'Is this activity an art?' and 'Is this a work of art?' would be simply unaskable.

*   *   *

What, then, are these integrational enterprises which the supercategory subserves? The various answers, according to the integrationist, become apparent when we consider the various cases. Let us begin by taking three modern examples.

1. It is true that Communist governments for a certain time will use, as a means of monumental propaganda, figurative monuments in the style of Greek and Italian classicism, but this is only because these governments are forced to use them in the same way as they are compelled to use specialists of the pre-revolutionary school. Figurative monuments (Greek and Italian) are at variance with contemporary reality in two respects. They cultivate individual heroism and conflict with history: torsos and heads of heroes (and gods) do not correspond to the modern

interpretation of history. Their forms are too private for places where there are ten versts of proletarians in rows. At best they express the character, feelings and thoughts of the hero, but who expresses the tension of the emotions and the thoughts of the collective thousand? A type? But a type concretizes, limits and levels the mass. The mass is richer, more alive, more complicated and more organic. (Punin 1920: 312)

2. Artists who speak and work from explicitly feminist perspectives – Mary Kelly and Barbara Kruger, for example – have been labeled post-feminist by feminist art historians and critics in an attempt to distinguish their work from earlier, supposedly essentialist feminist art practices. But, I am arguing, the end result of the application of this term, with all of the historical implications of its 'post' prefix, is to promote anti-feminist ends. Although far more subtle and certainly more thoughtful than the popular media's blatant attempts to dismiss feminism *in toto*, discourses of postmodernism tend to address the relationship between feminism and postmodernism through modernist and ultimately masculinist models of interpretation – models that work to empower the postmodern critic through 'aesthetic terrorism,' hierarchizing art practices on the basis of avant-gardist categories of value and excluding work not deemed to be 'radical' or anti-modern enough. The incorporation of one particular kind of feminism into a broadly conceived, even universalizing, project of postmodernist cultural critique tends to entail the suppression of other kinds of feminist practices and theories. It encourages the collapse of the specific claims of feminism into postmodernism, allowing the postmodern theorist to claim postmodernism as an antimasculinist (if not explicitly feminist) alternative to an authoritative and phallocentric modernism. The strategic appropriation of feminism both radicalizes postmodernism and simultaneously facilitates the silencing of the confrontational voices of feminism – the end result being the replacement of feminism by a less threatening, postfeminism of (non)difference. (Jones 1993: 388)

3. I believe the evidence shows that in the past twenty-one months the arts are well set to be better governed and better managed than ever before. With the increase in the length of life that we are promised, and the increase in leisure, they need to be. They are vital capital for our future. At last the arts in Great Britain are poised to build on the superb platform of opportunity constructed by Jennie Lee in the 1960s, when boldness was our friend and we saw the arts as a Promised Land. In that seminal decade, the arts bloodlessly and seamlessly embraced liberty and equality, quality and fraternity – very heaven. Now it has come

again. Without question, there is much to do, but much has already begun.

[. . .] I believe that the Government has made an impressive beginning, the more impressive because it has worked within budgetary constraints and against a *Bleak House* inheritance, which of course notched up achievements, but also left neglect, bungle and cynicism – a tradition that Conservative councils like Westminster carry on regardless, trampling over the arts with loutish indifference. (Lord Bragg, Speech in the House of Lords, 1999; Wallinger and Warnock 2000: 34)

The above may be regarded as spectacularly crude examples, but from an integrational point of view they are none the less typical. For we stand no chance of understanding what is going on in these kinds of rhetoric until we grasp the following fact: the supercategory of 'art(s)' is being enlisted in order to integrate the activities of those who present themselves as artists or art-lovers into a wider political agenda. In the three examples the politics is different in each case. Furthermore, the rhetoric of the first example is starkly surrogationist, while the rhetoric of the second is subtly contractualist, and the rhetoric of the third tries to combine both. But that does not affect the point at issue: in all three cases the writers are playing political football with the supercategory in order to advance a partisan agenda of their own. The function and value of the supercategory as far as they are concerned is precisely that it allows such a game to be played.

If I am right, similar recruitments of interests and attitudes can be observed throughout the history of Western artspeak. In antiquity the supercategory provided a basis for articulating the claims of many different professions having specialized skills. It served to integrate those claims within the framework of a political discourse about the responsibilities of the citizen towards the state and fellow-citizens. For the medieval universities, the supercategory was essential because it made it possible to integrate certain branches of study with the learning of the past, via the preservation of key texts. It thus served to justify and perpetuate a curriculum, and hence ultimately to validate the existence of the universities themselves. For the medieval church the integrational function of the supercategory was to provide the crucial link between worldly ecclesiastical patronage of certain arts and the spiritual values professed by Christianity. For the ambitious painters, sculptors and architects of Renaissance Italy, the primary function of the supercategory was to facilitate their own advancement in Renaissance society. It fulfilled this function by establishing their twin right to intellectual respect and more lucrative commissions. (Leonardo hit the nail on the head when he related the low status of the art of painting to the failure of painters to produce treatises which 'display her accomplishment in words':

Paragone 12; Richter 1949: 31–2.) For the *ancien régime* of eighteenth-century France, it was the supercategory that underwrote the canons of aristocratic taste, thus justifying the *de facto* position of the aristocracy as privileged leaders of the nation and their role as patrons of the arts.

And so on. The list of examples could be extended, and each example could be discussed in great detail; but what has been said suffices to make the general point clear. The supercategory arose and survived because, over the centuries, it supported – or could be adapted to support – so many sectional interests in a culture to which *continuity* (or at least the appearance of continuity) was extremely important. Without it there would have been no clear link at a certain level between the civilizations and values of Greece and Rome and those of medieval and post-Renaissance Europe. (It was not the only such link, but without it the nations of modern Europe would have had to sacrifice much of their self-flattering image as cultural heirs of the Classical past.)

Seeing the preservation of the supercategory as the primary integrational function of artspeak begins to explain why, when a strong sense of historical continuity fades and is no longer imperative, the relative unity of Western artspeak begins to fragment. And why, once that process of fragmentation had begun (in the early decades of the twentieth century), all the king's horses and all the king's men would struggle in vain to put artspeak together again.

*   *   *

An integrational perspective explains too why some arts always feature in the discourse of Western artspeak much less prominently than others: these are the arts that never required an elaborate social rationale to justify their existence. They cater for basic and constant consumer needs which hardly vary from generation to generation. These are the arts relegated to the humble ranks of the 'utilitarian' or 'mechanical'. The more useful they are, the less they have any need to shelter under the umbrella of a supercategory, or lay claim to virtues they do not possess. At the other end of the scale come those specialized artistic endeavours which lack any obvious usefulness or other social value, such as displaying dead animals in tanks of formaldehyde in public museums (for artistic purposes, it should be noted, rather than to satisfy scientific curiosity). If there were no supercategory to shelter under, such enterprises, answering to no social demand whatever, would have no cultural location at all. So there is, it would seem, a trade-off in terms of necessity between art and artspeak. The more necessary the art form, the less it needs artspeak: the more gratuitous or controversial the art form, the greater that necessity.

To this generalization language itself might seem at first sight to offer a counterexample. But more careful consideration suggests otherwise.

Language as an art form never needed linguistics: grammar as artspeak (*ars grammatica*) arose as a justification for the linguistic preferences of a social elite and to supply pedagogic instruction. It was never necessary to underwrite the verbal transactions of the market place or the family circle.

At the end of the spectrum where the necessity of artspeak is greatest, a curious transformation occurs. It ceases to matter exactly what the relation is between the discourse and the corresponding art. For the focus has shifted entirely to *interpretation*. And this shift too is something that neither surrogational nor contractualist theories can account for. When such a transformation occurs, there are fewer and fewer substantive issues to be resolved about the practices and works subsumed under the supercategory of 'art(s)'. It all becomes a game of words.

The beauty of this game is that it enables the arts to achieve self-levitation by tugging at their own linguistic bootlaces. Almost any item or event can be redescribed in such a way as to validate the artistic criteria required. Thus the schoolboys who reportedly ate what appeared to be sweets left on a shelf in Birmingham's Museum and Art Gallery (*The Times*, 23 December 2000), and thus unwittingly destroyed a work of art by Graham Fagen, are ridiculed for making a basic category mistake. They seemingly failed to distinguish between the sweets as comestibles and the sweets as art. But anyone uncorrupted by artspeak can see that the boot is on the other foot. The category mistake is in reverse. The schoolboys were right: the sweets were sweets.

The game of words – and the integrational function of artspeak – is revealed most clearly when new practices appear. They are either assimilated to already recognized arts, or else relegated to some alien domain. This assimilation/rejection takes place in the first instance at the linguistic level, i.e. by applying or withholding appropriate artspeak descriptions and criteria. In some cases, a long debate may ensue. (The most accessible recent example is the invention of photography.) In such cases, artspeak provides an interesting example of how, in literate societies, language can be used not only to mould public perceptions of certain practices and skills but to encourage extensions of those practices and skills along lines which will in turn validate the language used to describe them.

From an integrationist point of view it would be naive to suppose that there is any professional practice involving skills of some kind which could *not*, given the appropriate conditions, be accepted as an art form. Whether it is or not depends in many cases on the professional interests involved. Thus, for example, it would serve no purpose today to start claiming that snooker was an art. Those who play snooker at a professional or quasi-professional level are much better off by promoting it as a sport, since this involves competitions, league tables, sponsorship and all the competitive rigmarole that goes with it. But one could imagine a quite different social scenario for snooker –

and a quite different snookerspeak – in which it was counted as an art (doubtless a 'performance' art), but with exactly the same skills of cue and ball as are required in the present-day game.

The difference between arts and sports is a difference of social standing. There have been few intelligent commentators who, like Neville Cardus, were highly articulate in idioms as diverse as the language of cricket and the language of music. It is interesting that Cardus made a point of relating the two activities and denying the cultural superiority of either. That conclusion is exactly what an integrationist would claim, although on different theoretical grounds. From an integrationist perspective, Bradman was no less an artist than Beethoven. To say this is not to flatter the cricketer by hyperbole, nor to denigrate the musician accordingly, but to recognize cultural prejudices for what they are. It is ironical that enthusiastic sports writers who described Bradman as an 'artist' of the cricket field thought they were employing a metaphor. But that itself is an eloquent comment on the role of artspeak in shaping cultural attitudes. It confirms, for an integrationist, the notion that artspeak is a language-game in competition with other language-games being played in contemporary cultural arenas.

Diderot glimpsed much of this – but did not follow it up – in his remarks under the rubric '*De la langue des arts*'. These are included, almost as an aside, in his ground-breaking essay on '*Art*' in the *Encyclopédie*. In spite of their casual presentation, his observations constitute the first serious attempt in post-Renaissance Europe to address the question of artspeak. Diderot evidently saw the artspeak of his day as an obstacle – rather than an aid – to understanding the arts. But his critique is based, as one might expect at that time, on a thoroughly surrogational approach to language. The burden of his complaint is that in order to set up a rational language for the arts we would need to abolish synonyms and recognize that the same tools and the same processes are used in a variety of arts, even though they are called by different names. He even proposes a *grammaire des Arts* (i.e. a grammar of Artspeak) in which the first step would be to establish a common measure for comparative and quantitative terms (*grand, gros, moyen, mince, épais*, etc.). He thinks that this could be done by identifying *une mesure constante dans la nature* and requiring artists to make their vocabulary conform to it. This is patently a surrogational demand: words should conform to an independent standard set by – or at least selected from – those available in nature. Only thus will an ideal one–one correspondence be established. And only then will it be possible to tackle the problem of those more elusive concepts, such as *grace* in painting, *nœud* in haberdashery, and so on. Diderot is evidently still thinking in terms of Aristotelian definitions (based on *genus* and *differentiae*) and much influenced by what Locke says about the desirability of definitions. But although it is easy to ridicule Diderot's conception of an ideal artspeak as naive, he must be given credit for facing up to the problem in his own way.

Today the problem is ignored, and the game of words becomes a game of verbal double-bluff. To take a simple but not atypical example, what are we to make of an artspeak text such as the following?

> Rietveld's designs, and in particular the 'Red/Blue' chair are strong influences on Kerr's work. He maintains that the Red/Blue chair was not a chair, but a sculpture masquerading as a chair. In the present work he has produced a piece which he confirms is a 'sculpture' but in which he has consciously blurred the boundaries between sculpture and furniture by placing the instantly recognisable mass-market cushions upon it. The result is sculpture masquerading as chair masquerading as sculpture, and challenges the viewer's need to cling to familiar formulae for distinguishing 'art' from 'furniture' as well as 'traditional' from 'modern'. It echoes Donald Judd's remark that 'A work of art exists in itself. A chair exists as a chair itself but the idea of a chair is not a chair.'

An integrationist would say that in order to understand what is going on in this tortuous piece of gobbledegook we need to consider the circumstances in which the text is presented, by whom, and for whom it is intended. When we do this, things begin to fall into place. The text occurs in a glossy catalogue produced by a London auction house, immediately under a half-page colour photograph of what looks like a rather uninteresting wooden armchair, which would barely merit a second glance in a department-store window. And we then realize that this is artspeak sales talk, designed to integrate (i) the presence of the object in the auctioneer's showroom with (ii) its eventual purchase for a handsome price by a collector. Given this integrational function, we begin to see why the object is described as it is. It has to be presented not just as a chair (for then it would be worth relatively little) but as a work of art; in particular as a piece of sculpture, for sculpture is notoriously expensive. In order to make this plausible, the first point the text makes is a reference to the work of a highly esteemed pioneer of twentieth-century furniture design (i.e. Rietveld), whose work is much collected. This sets the level at which the prospective purchaser is encouraged to be thinking about the purchase. We then have an interpretation offered by the designer of this particular chair concerning Rietveld's 'Red/Blue' chair; an interpretation to the effect that it was not actually a chair at all but a sculpture. This introduces a similar claim about the chair for sale: that it is not a chair but a sculpture. At this point the reader looks at the photograph and is struck by the fact that this particular piece of sculpture nevertheless looks oddly like a chair. The puzzle is then solved by the explanation that the designer has actually opted for deliberately making the sculpture *look like* a chair. But then, the purchaser

wonders, doesn't that in effect *make it* a chair? Ah, no! Not at all. To suppose
that would be to confuse a chair with the *idea* of a chair, a confusion oppor-
tunely elucidated by quoting the sapient observation of a famous art theorist,
Mr Judd. Reassured, the client is expected to conclude that the estimated price
of the work is not so unreasonable as it first seemed. How often, after all, does
one have the opportunity of buying a chair that is not a chair?

Another example of a very similar game of double-bluff, but played out for
bigger stakes, may be cited from Sir Nicholas Serota's Richard Dimbleby
Memorial Lecture entitled 'Who's afraid of modern art?' (Serota 2000). Here
Serota enjoined his audience to take seriously Michael Craig-Martin's work
entitled *An Oak Tree*. The work in question Serota described as 'a glass of tap
water placed on a glass bathroom shelf' and drew attention to the accompanying notice with which the artist had 'explained' it.

> 'It's not a symbol. I have changed the physical substance of the glass of
> water into that of an oak tree . . . . I didn't change its appearance . . . . The
> actual oak tree is physically present, but in the form of a glass of water.'

Diderot must have been laughing in his grave. He would have laughed
even more when Serota provided his own gloss on Craig-Martin's notice:

> We may not 'like' Craig-Martin's work, but it certainly reminds us that
> appreciation of all art, including painting, involves an act of faith com-
> parable to the belief that, through transubstantiation, the bread and wine
> of holy communion become the body and blood of Christ. (Serota 2000)

Presumably this is not much help to those unfamiliar with the Christian
doctrine of transubstantiation. Nor to those who, although familiar with it,
regard it as pure superstition. In short, here we have a verbal explanation of
dubious relevance (the appeal to a Christian sacrament) – and the concomitant
suggestion that appreciating the art of Michael Craig-Martin is akin to a
religious experience – brought in to rescue a prior verbal explanation which
made no sense at all. There was no oak tree 'physically present' in the glass of
water, and no one in their right mind supposed for a moment that there was.
Only words put that notion up for consideration. But not very convincingly.
That is implicitly conceded in Serota's feeble explanation. Another case of
artspeak coming to its own rescue. The suggestion is that its very value
somehow lies in being a form of verbal hypnosis. At best this is artspeak as
mantra. ('Oak tree', 'Oak tree', 'Oak tree' . . . .) Presumably the same glass of
tap water would have done under any other verbal label the artist had chosen.
(? 'Lime tree', 'Lime tree', 'Lime tree' . . . .) If not, there is a lot of explaining to
be done about the non-arbitrariness of the sign. But that requires another –
and rather different – act of faith.

Even less convincing is Serota's claim that *all* art demands some such surrender. This is implausible. No one supposes, or ever has supposed, that a statue of Pericles is Pericles. Pericles is *not* 'physically present' in his statue. Here we neither believe in nor need any doctrine of transubstantiation. On the contrary, that would be not an act of faith in art, but a stupid misunderstanding. As Socrates pointed out long before the development of biological cloning, there is an important difference between creating a likeness of a person and creating another person in that image. It does not matter whether the creator is a Phidias or a Shakespeare. Unless we grasp at least the distinction between cloning and portrayal, there is no room for most of what the Western tradition counts as art. One might have hoped that the director of the Tate Gallery at the beginning of the twenty-first century would have grasped it too and explained it to his vast (i.e. television) audience.

For the integrationist, the interesting question is why he chose not to. We can presumably discount any hypotheses that would attribute this to lack of acquaintance with the Western tradition, lack of acquaintance with other forms of art, lack of rhetorical skill, or even lack of intelligence. So did Sir Nicholas think it much too subtle for the *hoi polloi* to understand? Does the Nanny State require a Nanny Tate? More plausible explanations become apparent when this example is placed in the context of the occasion. Having just raised and spent an unprecedented amount of money on setting up 'Tate Modern', the director was seizing the public opportunity of vindicating not only his artistic policy and his artistic judgment, his interest in certain London artists, but even his appointment and his salary (referred to explicitly in the opening paragraph of his lecture). His plea for a necessary act of faith in all art becomes a metaphor for an act of faith in Sir Nicholas Serota (and, by extension, all other custodians of such institutions in the Western art world).

What is laudable about this, it could be argued, is the recognition that some such public apologia for the funds involved is called for. What is deplorable, in this particular case, is falling back on a contractualist artspeak which has already overdrawn its linguistic account. No one can any longer take seriously the notion that an *avant-garde*, selected and supported financially by elite institutions, really *knows* what art is, or what the arts are. Artists themselves had long since sold the pass when they championed, in their own interests, the doctrine of art-for-art's-sake.

Serota, however, does not aim at yet another vindication of art-for-art's-sake – far from it: here Serotaspeak is artspeak in the service of an institutional theory of art (and, by implication, in defence of the institutions and their directors). The question is not whether anyone *wants* these institutions. They already exist, whether one wants them or not. The reasoning is: Art institutions exist; therefore art exists; therefore what the institutions present *is* art. What matters is money and public credibility. For if public confidence collapsed, the funding might/would collapse too. So the problem for today's Serotas is how to integrate (i) the financing of their institutions with (ii) the limited selection of not particularly attractive art actually on display and (iii) public reaction to it. Here the function of artspeak is to deliver an apologia which secures that connexion.

Serota seems to have taken on board Tolstoy's observation that 'no matter what insanities appear in art, when once they find acceptance among the upper classes of our society a theory is quickly invented to explain and sanction them' (Tolstoy 1898: 51–2). The only update that Tolstoy's comment seems to call for is that nowadays not even the acceptance of the upper classes is required, but merely the active support of a few extremely wealthy individuals whose exploits in advertising, commerce and other fields have left them with surplus income that they are willing to spend on becoming known and feted as megapatrons of the arts. These are, in present-day society, the millionaires who can afford to signal their financial status by spending many thousands of pounds on selected contemporary trivia. By so doing they can demonstrate their superiority over a preceding generation of rich people who spent fortunes competing with one another in acquiring art which they personally *liked*. As Serota sees and admits, it is difficult to *like* a glass of tap water on a bathroom shelf (even though one might appreciate its utility when brushing one's teeth, or its value as a potential overnight repository for dentures). Some other intellectual pretext must be drummed up.

It is the next move which reveals the ultimate ingenuity in this particular artspeak game. One selects a rationale which both anticipates and pre-empts the criticism that the rationale makes no sense. How can this be done? Just watch the platform for a polished lesson in verbal legerdemain. The fact that the work as verbally contextualized by the artist makes no sense is highlighted by Serota as its *artistic* merit. The thesis, in short, is that modern art is good for you precisely because it challenges your common sense. And the more it upsets common sense and outrages everyday expectations (particularly expectations *about art*) the better it is. You are not expected to *like* it: that might actually prevent it from doing you good.

*   *   *

At this point someone may well ask: 'Why wheel on the heavy artillery of linguistics merely in order to demolish the pretentiousness of certain contemporary artists and critics? Is not their pretentiousness already evident?' The answer is: 'Yes, it is.' We do not need theories of artspeak to expose either pretentiousness or obscurantism. But (the many) critics of contemporary artspeak who confine their criticism to such accusations are, from an integrationist perspective, missing the point. In themselves, such vices as obscurantism and pretentiousness are defects attributable to individual writers. Much more interesting is any case where such features become characteristic of a whole mode of discourse.

But I am not wishing to claim that integrationists are the first to notice this more widespread phenomenon either. As one recent observer puts it:

> The language used by some critics in certain sectors of the arts is in serious disrepair. Countless artists speak about their own works in ways that are anything but illuminating, and often in ways that would, if taken at face value, actually demean their work. Often the words of artists and critics possess merely a contingent connection to the art they describe: the work and the words do not organically connect, and one is left wondering if the words might not have been attached with equal plausibility to any of a hundred other works. (Hagberg 1995: 116)

Artspeak, in at least some of its more recent manifestations, seems to many people to be in exactly such a state of 'disrepair'. But it is one thing to note the phenomenon: quite another to propose a diagnosis of the ailment. Here we need explanations which link current trends to the history of the discourse itself. Are there forms of discourse which eventually exhaust their own possibilities of justification and explanation?

Western artspeak is arguably just such a case. (Godspeak – the language of traditional Western religion – would be another.) What we are witnessing in artspeak is a terminal phase in which the supercategory, which formerly held it all together, is now unable to sustain the integrational burden imposed upon it. There is no longer any communicational coherence in the diverse propositions it sponsors.

*   *   *

When the Devil in Kipling's poem 'The Conundrum of the Workshops' (1890) raised the question of whether Adam's first rude sketch was 'Art', Picasso was still a schoolboy and Art Nouveau was the latest thing. The readers for whom Kipling wrote could still remember the famous libel suit, twelve years earlier, in which Whistler had sued Ruskin for describing his work as 'flinging a pot of paint in the public's face' and been awarded damages of one farthing. The year after Kipling's poem appeared, the same public was entertained by *Patience*, Gilbert and Sullivan's satiric operetta mocking Rossetti, Swinburne and the 'greenery yallery' art admired by patrons of the Grosvenor Gallery. It was a public accustomed to contradictory judgments concerning art, having been told by William Morris that 'nothing can be a work of art which is not useful' and by Oscar Wilde that 'all art is quite useless'.

Nowadays the contradictions have multiplied. We have seen sober institutions of the London art establishment engage in such perplexing enterprises as defending plagiarism, exhibiting pornography and mounting exhibitions deliberately designed to offend members of the public who come to see them. The universities too are implicated. A revealing example is the minor scandal involving thirteen third-year art students at Leeds University, who in 1998 decided to dupe their examiners. They were awarded a grant of a thousand pounds to undertake an artistic expedition to Spain, on the basis of which they would mount an exhibition (ironically entitled *Going Places*). The students duly went off. On their return they invited tutors to a degree show in which the audience was first shown into a room containing a bowl of sangria, with flamenco music playing in the background. There followed a bus trip to Leeds airport, where the students emerged, looking tanned, from the arrivals lounge. They had photographs apparently showing them on the beach at the Costa del Sol. All this was an elaborate hoax. The students had not been further abroad than Scarborough, and had acquired their tans on sunbeds. The airport officials had been duped into allowing them to use airport facilities to stage their 'homecoming'.

So far, so good. We apparently have no more than a student prank. Until their tutors begin to come out with artspeak explanations of the exercise. Reporting this under the caption *Talented artists or just con artists?* the *Times Higher Education Supplement* (29 May 1998) quoted the head of the fine art department at Leeds University as claiming: 'This is performance art in the best possible tradition. It is an attempt to out-sensationalise sensation. The students have taken on board difficult questions about what is truth in art.'

The episode was widely reported in the British press, largely thanks to the efforts at self-publicity by the students themselves. Condemnations for deception and waste of public money were only to be expected. Of more significance, to anyone interested in the history of artspeak, were the justifications offered. One commentator defended the hoax by comparing it favourably to the current vogue in art galleries for displaying dissected animals (presumably a disparaging reference to the work of Damien Hirst). Another defended it as 'a very good joke' in which the students had managed to 'challenge our perception of art'.

No one commented on the fact that the resultant art 'exhibition' was totally devoid of visual, intellectual or any other kind of excellence, and would have been, regardless of whether the students had been to Spain or not. In other words, the internal logic of commentary assumed that the sole claim to any status of the episode as a work of art resided in the deception of those claiming to judge it as art. The possibility that it might have been a comment by the students on the poverty of their own art education seems to have been lost on most, in particular on the head of their own department. Unless, of course, his own artspeak justification of what his students had done is construed as support for that view, rather than as pathetic inability to concede that his own students had done anything wrong, or even stupid. But at this point the contradictions and ambiguities in the discourse become self-stultifying. 'Art is a con' is not a message that needs such tortuous, boring and unimaginative exposition. This is artspeak pressing the self-destruct button.

As, thanks to artspeak, more and more contradictions shelter under the traditional supercategory, the question 'Is it art?' is increasingly felt to be trivial, rather than important. In Kipling's poem it is already presented as the Devil's question, a question maliciously designed to provoke a worry that something may *not* be what it seems to be. It is one of those suspicious questions like 'Is it legal?' or 'Is it genuine?', the very asking of which indicates scepticism or requests reassurance. But whereas for Kipling's generation the question 'Is it art?', even on the printed page, doubtless seemed to suggest the rising intonation of doubt, today it suggests the quite different flat intonation associated with questions that are not even rhetorical but just futile.

There is no way such questions can be reinvigorated or artificially resuscitated. They have come to the end of their useful life. Their fate is inevitable, given the history of the discourse from which they arose in the first place. The end of their story is reminiscent of what happens at the death of a star. Rapid expansion of the core concept is followed by explosion and implosion. The supercategory becomes a supernova. Brilliance is succeeded by collapse.

The integrationist explanation of the collapse of the supercategory is quite simple: artspeak attempted to integrate too much. When the range of art forms purports to extend from Homer and Rembrandt on one side to such enterprises as bandaging public buildings or rearranging rubbish tips on the other, the end is in sight.

The resultant implosion, one suspects, is the process taking place at the present time. There is less and less temptation to believe that every new fad taken up by galleries, museums and critics is actually a new form of art, whose potential existence was previously unsuspected. There is less and less temptation to believe that those schools claiming to 'teach' the arts have anything serious to teach. There is even less temptation (if that were possible) to think that the answers to questions about the arts reside in a certain body of knowledge, either practical or theoretical, which some possess and others lack. That seems increasingly like treating 'Is it art?' on a par with 'Is it sodium chloride?' And one thing we are now confident of (or think we are) is that these two questions are of irreconcilably different orders. We are confident that the hallmark of cultural questions is that they do not presuppose ready-made definitions of their key terms but, on the contrary, query such definitions and the values that underlie them.

But this in turn does not mean that cultural questions have a timeless lifespan. There is no eternal conundrum of the workshops with a perpetually elusive answer, as perhaps Kipling already saw. An artspeak that no longer ministers to cultural necessities but only to the narcissism of its own perpetuation is already living on borrowed time. The longer it borrows, the more of a cultural antiquity it will become.

Even more boring than yesterday's sensation is sensation contrived for its own sake. That is why those areas of the arts where sensation is the only novelty left are already in danger of devaluing their own products. As Stephen Farthing observes, 'Today the standard response is disinterest'. He notes that on 24 October 1999, when the Turner Prize winner was announced, there was a significantly mixed reaction on the part of the London press. The *News of the World* did not even mention the event or the exhibit, Tracey Emin's *My Bed*, which was on show at the Tate.

> The serious press, however, could still not contain their mixture of scorn and admiration for the Turner Prize's front-running nominee, and ran reviews that could have appeared in the news sections.
>
> A large unmade bed surrounded by the detritus of one of the artist's lost weekends (or perhaps it is just an average weekend) was pictured in the newspapers. Dirty sheets, vodka bottles, soiled knickers and used condoms frame the bed in the expectation of accumulating meaning [. . .]. Art critics framed her object with an array of words. 'Her strewn things sum up the look of the time we live in,' said Matthew Collings in the *Independent on Sunday*. On the other side of the bed, so to speak, John McEwen in the *Sunday Telegraph* reminded us that this wasn't simply art and that the emotions the artist had set before us were real. But then he asked, 'Her sob story may be sad, but what makes her think it will interest the rest of us?' (Farthing 2000: 53–4)

The answer must be that she thinks, or hopes, it will interest us *as art*. In other words, given that there is nothing particularly remarkable about Tracey Emin's soiled underwear and used condoms, their claim on public attention must hinge on the scandal attached to exhibiting them at the Tate. For this the co-operation of the critics is required. Only the 'quality' papers oblige. The *News of the World*, which yawns and declines to mention the event, preferring to entertain its readers with 'the demise of a couple of Casanovas, one cad, one bounder and the hair colour of Michael Jackson's son' (Farthing 2000: 53) is just not playing the game. Its silence heralds the demise of artspeak, a demise hastened by self-inflicted injuries over many decades.

Artspeak will doubtless be replaced in due course by a different form of discourse. One can already see indications that artspeak is likely to be taken over and absorbed into an increasingly dominant mediaspeak, which is oriented to a quite different cultural supercategory. Artists are required to become media 'personalities'. Art 'shows' are judged by attendance figures. The merger between art and showbiz is symbolized by the choice of Madonna to present the award at the 2001 Turner Prize ceremony. There is not much more public mileage to be got out of the claim that what justifies the extravagances of an *avant-garde* is its boldness in questioning accepted assumptions about art. For there are no more accepted assumptions about art. The public is already bored with the Devil's question. Artspeak is now terminally slotted in to a media framework which allows it a meagre ration of upmarket television programmes, pays the salaries of a few 'arts correspondents' in national newspapers, a few curators of galleries, and a few teachers in art schools. Just as institutionalized 'art' has become a small part of a huge entertainment industry, so artspeak has become an esoteric dialect of journalese (both popular and academic). No longer a necessity except for those professionals who still live by it, artspeak expires not with a bang but a whimper. The whimper feeds in to the uproar of a society which seems, to adapt Postman's formulation (Postman 1986), intent on 'amusing itself to death'.

Postscript

So what have we learnt from this romp through the archives of Western artspeak? We have learnt that it was all based on a myth about language. And the arts themselves, as creations of artspeak, have the same mythological basis. But that may change. Myths are not reflections of sempiternal realities, but products of particular cultures. The demythologization of language, if we are willing to embark upon it, entails automatically the demythologization of the arts. For language is itself an art form, as well as being much more.

There are probably few people who would see, without prompting, any connexion between the question 'What is art?' and the question 'What is language?' Or, if they did, they would see it as relating specifically to poetry or other verbal art forms. The obscurity of that connexion between language and non-verbal arts bears testimony to the authority that the language myth still exercises over our cultural perceptions.

Failure to see that connexion means that many people who engage in comment and discussion about the arts, and even undertake to educate others about such matters, are missing something important. And this in turn means that a great deal of what passes for sound thinking or even erudition, where the arts are concerned, is biased and superficial.

Who bears the collective responsiblity for this sad state of affairs? Primarily those who deny that such a state of affairs exists: in other words those experts on the arts whose expertise is predicated on the assumption that Western artspeak, which they have inherited and now practise professionally, is in good order.

Perhaps their problem is a lack of historical perspective, even though some of them claim to be historians. The secular artspeak of antiquity, which tried to rationalize the arts by reference to a hierarchy of social values, was fine as far as it went. But it was then overlaid by mysticism from two sources. Neoplatonism sought the origin of artistic inspiration in the divine. Then Christianity conveniently appropriated selected arts for the service of God, thus justifying the penchant of many prelates for rivalling kings and princes in their display of pomp and wealth. The medieval universities confused the issue by their influential restriction of the arts to certain privileged subjects of the standard university curriculum. But it was the efforts of German philosophers in the eighteenth and nineteenth centuries whose love of idealizations is chiefly to blame for opening Western artspeak to the infiltration of high-sounding nonsense. The consummation or *coup de grâce* was delivered by those artists who opted out of social responsibility and social institutions altogether, declaring the arts to be an autonomous province of human endeavour, answerable only to its own laws (which the autonomists either dictated in their own favour or else left shrouded in impenetrable obscurity).

Small wonder that the term *art* ended up, as it has done today, as one of those 'mythological words [that have] come to replace thought' (Saul 1992: 47). It is admirably qualified for such a role.

This role is profoundly underestimated, both by experts on the arts and by experts on society. Many of them cannot see how language is not merely useful but also *necessary* in order to integrate the activities involved. Theorizing about the arts still shows unmistakable signs of intellectual immaturity. Not only is there no general consensus about which among the many human pursuits count as arts. There is no consensus either as to what the function of any given art is. Consequently, discussion of the arts floats in a curious intellectual limbo. No one seems quite sure about whose job it is to explain what the arts are, or what form such an explanation would take. Increasingly, the public role of critics is reduced to recommending (or condemning) certain entertainments currently on offer, but without any commitment to a set of principles or standards underwriting their judgment.

That, it will be said, is only to be expected in a time of pervasive uncertainty about civilized values. Anyone who believes that the arts, politics, religion and economics can be divorced must be living in cloud-cuckoo land. They have never, at any time in Western history, been separated or separable. This, at least, is one lesson that a retrospective study of artspeak can teach us.

Unfortunately, that conclusion makes it all too easy to blame the current impasse on a motley variety of social factors and institutional forces. It is less usual to seek the roots of the malaise, as I have tried to do here, in a deeply flawed view of language. The self-propagating seeds of that view are the very terms in which the arts are nowadays discussed. If the present book serves to direct attention to that source of the problem, it will have served its purpose.

If the diagnosis is correct, one question remains. What can be done about it? For an integrationist, the solution is not to call on all interested parties and people of good will to sit round a table and hammer out a few definitions of 'art', 'beauty', 'meaning', and the like. On the contrary, apart from doing more harm than good, that would imply a complete misunderstanding of the message. The *necessity* of artspeak reflects needs that cannot be catered for by committees or lexicographers or common sense. To grasp that is – perhaps – the beginning of an answer.

So let us go over some basic points.

1. Artspeak is not, and never has been, something that is *under control* (except for limited periods under totalitarian regimes, whether of the political or the educational or the religious kind, and only then in certain limited arenas of discussion). It is not like the public discourse of weights and measures, or the discourse of the natural sciences in general. It is open-ended in a sense and to a degree that these latter are not.
2. We cannot understand theories of the arts without understanding the theories of language that support them. Or, to put the point more trenchantly, artspeak is an integral and integrating part of art.
3. Artspeak is now, whether we like it or not, irreversibly opposed to sciencespeak. Given that opposition, in sciencespeak what allegedly matters is the thing spoken of. In artspeak, on the other hand, what matters is what we say about it. In other words, where the arts are concerned, there are not two separate questions, one being 'What is art?' and the other 'How shall we discuss it?'. These are *one and the same question*.
4. Suppose we were living in a society which would like to have an artspeak not in servitude to the demands of vested interests and the self-promotion of experts. What must the citizens of such a society do? They must take up the responsibility of questioning, at every possible opportunity, the terms in which artistic judgments are delivered. In just the same way as they should, and must, question the language of society's politicians, its doctors and its scientists if they wish it to remain a free and a healthy society. The condition of liberty is still, as Curran rightly identified it, eternal vigilance. There are no short cuts to doing this. But the opportunity to do it is presented daily by every product – programme, interview, article, book, essay or review – that the modern media juggernaut delivers. Including this one.

References

Alberti, L. B. (1966), *On Painting*, trans. J. R. Spencer, 2nd ed., New Haven, Yale University Press.

Appiah, K. A. (1997), 'The arts of Africa', *New York Review of Books* XLIV.7: 46–51.

Arendt, H. (ed.) (1969), *Walter Benjamin, Illuminations*, New York, Schocken.

Arnheim, R. (1966), *Toward a Psychology of Art*, Berkeley, University of California Press.

Atkins, R. (1990), *Artspeak*, New York, Abbeville.

Atkins, R. (1993), *Artspoke*, New York, Abbeville.

Augustine, *Confessions*, trans. W. Watts, 2 vols, London, Heinemann, 1912.

Bacon, F. (1605), *The Advancement of Learning*, ed. G. W. Kitchin, London, Dent, 1973.

Bann, S. (1996), 'Concrete poetry', *The Dictionary of Art* (ed. J. Turner), London, Macmillan, vol. 7, pp. 698–9.

Barker, A. (1984), *Greek Musical Writings: Volume I. The Musician and His Art*, Cambridge, Cambridge University Press.

Barr, A. (1934), 'Foreword' to the catalogue for the exhibition 'Machine Art' at the Museum of Modern Art, New York, March 6 to April 30, 1934.

Baxandall, M. (1991), 'The language of art criticism'. In S. Kemal and I. Gaskell (eds), *The Language of Art History*, Cambridge, Cambridge University Press, pp. 67–75.

Bell, C. (1914), *Art*, ed. J. B. Bullen, Oxford, Oxford University Press, 1987.

Benton, T., Benton, C. and Sharp, D. (eds) (1975), *Form and Function: A Source Book for the History of Architecture and Design 1890–1939*, London, Crosby Lockwood Staples/Open University Press.

Bernadac, M.-L. and Michael, A. (eds) (1998), *P. Picasso, propos sur l'art*, Paris, Gallimard.

Blunt, A. (1940), *Artistic Theory in Italy 1450–1600*, Oxford, Clarendon.

Boardman, J. (1996), *Greek Art*, 4th ed., London, Thames & Hudson.

Boccioni, U. (1912), 'Technical manifesto of futurist sculpture', trans. R. Chase. In J. C. Taylor, *Futurism*, New York, Museum of Modern Art, 1961, pp. 129–32.

Breton, A. (1924), *Manifeste du surréalisme*. Reprinted in A. Breton, *Manifestes du surréalisme*, Paris, Gallimard, 1973.

Breunig, L. C. and Chevalier, J.-Cl. (eds) (1980), *Guillaume Apollinaire, les peintres cubistes*, 2nd ed., Paris, Hermann.

Briggs, A. (ed.) (1962), *William Morris, Selected Writings and Designs*, Harmondsworth, Penguin.

Brooks, C. (1968), *The Well Wrought Urn: Studies in the Structure of Poetry*, rev. ed., London, Dobson.

Bull, G. (1965), *Vasari: Lives of the Artists*. Harmondsworth, Penguin.

Burford, A. (1972), *Craftsmen in Greek and Roman Society*, London, Thames & Hudson.

Burke, E. (1759), *A Philosophical Enquiry into the Origin of Our Ideas of the Sublime and Beautiful*, 2nd ed., ed. J. T. Boulton, London, Routledge & Kegan Paul, 1958.

Butcher, S. H. (1951), *Aristotle's Theory of Poetry and Fine Art*, 4th ed., New York, Dover.

Carrier, D. (1987), *Artwriting*, Amherst, University of Massachusetts Press.

Cennini, C. (1933), *Il Libro dell'arte*, trans. D. V. Thompson, Jr., New Haven, Yale University Press.

Chauvet, J.-M., Deschamps, E. B. and Hillaire, C. (1996), *Chauvet Cave: The Discovery of the World's Oldest Paintings*, trans. P. G. Bahn, London, Thames & Hudson.

Cheney, S. and Cheney, M. (1936), *Art and the Machine*, New York, Whittlesey House.

Chipp, H. B. (ed.) (1968), *Theories of Modern Art*, Berkeley, University of California Press.

Clarke, G. and Crossley, P. (eds) (2000), *Architecture and Language. Constructing Identity in European Architecture, c.1000–c.1650*, Cambridge, Cambridge University Press.

Clottes, J. and Courtin, J. (1996), *The Cave Beneath the Sea: Paleolithic Images at Cosquer*, trans. M. Garner, New York, Abrams.

Collingwood, R. G. (1938), *The Principles of Art*. Oxford, Clarendon.

Conybeare, F. C. (1910), 'Iconoclasts', *Encyclopædia Britannica*, 11th ed., vol. 14, pp. 272–5.

Coomaraswamy, A. K. (1956), *Christian and Oriental Philosophy of Art*, New York, Dover. Originally published under the title *Why Exhibit Works of Art?* (1943).

Cornford, F. M. (1941), *The Republic of Plato*, Oxford, Clarendon.

Cumming, E. and Kaplan, W. (1991), *The Arts and Crafts Movement*, London, Thames & Hudson.

Dabrowski, M. (1995), *Kandinsky: Compositions*, New York, Museum of Modern Art.

Dalhaus, C. (1989), *The Idea of Absolute Music*, trans. R. Lustig, Chicago, University of Chicago Press.

Dickinson, G. L. (1931), *Plato and His Dialogues*. London. Reprinted West Drayton, Penguin, 1947. Page references to the reprint.

Diderot, D. and d'Alembert, J. le R. (eds) (1751), *Encyclopédie, ou dictionnaire raisonné des sciences, des arts et des métiers*, Paris, Briasson *et al.*

Disraeli, B. (1845), *Sybil*, London, Nelson.

Dixon, R. (1995), *The Baumgarten Corruption: From Sense to Nonsense in Art and Philosophy*, London, Pluto.

Domecq, J.-P. (1999), *Artistes sans art?*, rev. ed., Paris, Esprit.

Fagg, W. and Plass, M. (1964), *African Sculpture*, London, Dutton.

Farthing, S. (2000), *An Intelligent Person's Guide to Modern Art*, London, Duckworth.

Feagin, S. L. (1995), 'Institutional theory of art'. In R. Audi (ed.), *The Cambridge Dictionary of Philosophy*, Cambridge, Cambridge University Press, pp. 378–9.

Finlay, H. (1963), 'Letter to Pierre Garnier'. In *Image: Kinetic Art: Concrete Poetry*, London, Kingsland Prospect Press, 1965, pp. 9–10.

Fischer, E. (1963), *The Necessity of Art: A Marxist Approach*, trans. A. Bostock, Harmondsworth, Penguin. The German original, *Von der Notwendigkeit der Kunst*, was published in 1959 (Dresden, Verlag der Kunst).

Fowler, H. N. (ed. & trans.) (1926), *Plato: Cratylus*, London, Heinemann.

Frizot, M. and Ducros, F. (eds) (1987), *Du bon usage de la photographie*, Paris, Centre National de la Photographie.

Fry, R. (1920), *Vision and Design*, Harmondsworth, Penguin.

Fry, R. (1928), 'Words wanted in connexion with art'. In *SPE Tract XXXI*, Oxford, Clarendon. Reprinted in C. Reed (ed.), *A Roger Fry Reader*, Chicago, University of Chicago Press, 1996, pp. 424–6.

Gardner, H. (1980), *Artful Scribbles: The Significance of Children's Drawings*, London, Norman.

Garnier, P. (1965), Extracts from 'Manifesto for a new poetry, visual and phonic', trans. S. Bann. In *Image: Kinetic Art: Concrete Poetry*, London, Kingsland Prospect Press, p. 11.

Gernsheim, H. (1988), *The Rise of Photography 1850–1880: The Age of Collodion*, 3rd ed., London, Thames & Hudson.

Godfrey, T. (1998), *Conceptual Art*, London, Phaidon.

Gombrich, E. (1966), 'Freud's aesthetics', *Encounter* 26: 30–40.

Goodman, N. (1968), *Languages of Art: An Approach to a Theory of Symbols*, Indianapolis, Bobbs-Merrill.

Griffiths, P. (1983), 'Indeterminate music'. In D. Arnold (ed.), *The New Oxford Companion to Music*, Oxford, Oxford University Press, vol. 1, p. 904.

Grivot, D. (1976), *La Sculpture du XIIe siècle de la cathédrale d'Autun*, Colmar-Ingersheim, Éditions SAEP.

Hagberg, G. L. (1995), *Art as Language: Wittgenstein, Meaning and Aesthetic Theory*, Ithaca, N.Y., Cornell University Press.

Hamilton, W. (1973), *Plato: Phaedrus and Letters VII and VIII*, London, Penguin.

Harris, R. (1981), *The Language Myth*, London, Duckworth.

Harris, R. (1996), *Signs, Language and Communication*, London, Routledge.

Harris, R. (1998), *Introduction to Integrational Linguistics*, Oxford, Pergamon.

Harris, R. (2000), *Rethinking Writing*, London, Athlone.

Harris, R. and Taylor, T. J. (1997), *Landmarks in Linguistic Thought: The Western Tradition from Socrates to Saussure*, 2nd ed., London, Routledge.

Harrison, C. and Wood, P. (eds) (1992), *Art in Theory 1900–1990*, Oxford, Blackwell.

Harrison, C., Wood, P. and Gaiger, J. (eds) (1998), *Art in Theory 1815–1900: An Anthology of Changing Ideas*, Oxford, Blackwell.

Hauser, A. (1962), *The Social History of Art*, vol. 1, London, Routledge & Kegan Paul.

Hausman, C. R. (1991), 'Figurative language in art history'. In S. Kemal and I. Gaskell (eds), *The Language of Art History*, Cambridge, Cambridge University Press, pp. 101–28.

Havelock, E. A. (1963), *Preface to Plato*, Cambridge, Mass., Harvard University Press.

Hegel, G. W. F. (1835), *Introductory Lectures on Aesthetics*, trans. B. Bosanquet, ed. M. Inwood, London, Penguin, 1993.

Hess, H. (1975), *Pictures as Arguments*, London, Chatto & Windus/Sussex University Press.

Hobbes, T. (1651), *Leviathan*, ed. C. B. Macpherson, Harmondsworth, Penguin, 1968.

Holt, E. G. (ed.) (1957), *A Documentary History of Art*, 2nd ed., Garden City, N.Y., Doubleday.

Hutton, C. (2001), 'The language myth and the race myth: evil twins of modern identity politics'. In R. Harris (ed.), *The Language Myth in Western Culture*, London, Curzon, pp. 118–38.

Hutton, J. (1982), *Aristotle's Poetics*, New York, Norton.

Inwood, M. (1993), Commentary on Hegel, *Introductory Lectures on Aesthetics*, London, Penguin.

Jakobson, R. O. (1960), 'Closing statement: linguistics and poetics'. In T. A. Sebeok (ed.), *Style in Language*, Cambridge, Mass., Massachusetts Institute of Technology, pp. 350–77.

Janaway, C. (1995), *Images of Excellence: Plato's Critique of the Arts*, Oxford, Clarendon.

Jones, A. (1993), 'Postfeminism, feminist pleasures, and embodied theories of art'. Reprinted in D. Preziosi (ed.), *The Art of Art History: A Critical Anthology*, Oxford, Oxford University Press, 1998, pp. 383–95.

Kandinsky, W. (1911), *Concerning the Spiritual in Art*, trans. M. T. H. Sadler, New York, Dover, 1977.

Kant, I. (1787), *Critique of Pure Reason*, 2nd ed., trans. J. M. D. Meiklejohn, London, Dent, 1934.

Kant, I. (1790), *Critique of Judgment*, trans. W. S. Pluhar, Indianapolis, Hackett, 1987.

Kaufmann, W. (ed. & trans.) (1954), *The Portable Nietzsche*, New York, Viking.

Kennedy, G. (1963), *The Art of Persuasion in Greece*, Princeton, Princeton University Press.

Kennick, W. E. (1958), 'Does traditional aesthetics rest on a mistake?', *Mind*, 67.

Klingender, F. D. (1943), *Marxism and Modern Art*, London, Lawrence & Wishart.

Klingender, F. D. (1968), *Art and the Industrial Revolution*, rev. ed., Frogmore, Paladin.

Konody, P. G. (1929), 'Art', *Encyclopædia Britannica*, 14th ed., vol. 2, pp. 440–2.

Kostelanetz, R. (1996), *John Cage (Ex)plain(ed)*, New York, Schirmer.

Kosuth, J. (1991), *Art after Philosophy and After: Collected Writings, 1966–1990*, ed. G. Guercio, Cambridge, Mass., MIT Press.

Kubovy, M. (1986), *The Psychology of Perspective and Renaissance Art*, Cambridge, Cambridge University Press.

Lallot, J. (1989), *La Grammaire de Denys le Thrace*, Paris, Éditions du C.N.R.S.

Léger, F. (1923), 'L'esthétique de la machine, l'objet fabriqué et l'artiste'. In S. Forestier (ed.), *Fernand Léger, fonctions de la peinture*, Paris, Gallimard, 1997, pp. 87–102.

Lessing, G. E. (1766), *Laokoon*, trans. E. C. Beasley, rev. ed., London, Bell, 1914.

Lippard, L. R. (ed.) (1973), *Six Years*, New York, Praeger.

Love, N. (1998), 'The fixed-code theory'. In R. Harris and G. Wolf (eds), *Integrational Linguistics: A First Reader*, Oxford, Pergamon, pp. 49–67.

Lucie-Smith, E. (1966), 'Concrete poetry', *Encounter*, 26: 43–5.

McClure, R. (1982), 'Mallarmé'. In J. Wintle (ed.), *Makers of Nineteenth Century Culture 1800–1914*, London, Routledge & Kegan Paul, pp. 389–92.

McLeish, K. (ed.) (1985), *The Penguin Companion to the Arts in the Twentieth Century*, Harmondsworth, Penguin.

Maillou, R. de (1895), 'The decorative arts and the machine', *Revue des Arts Décoratifs*, 15: 225–67. The English translation quoted is from Benton, Benton and Sharp 1975, pp. 4–6.

Margolis, J. (1999), *What, after All, Is a Work of Art?*, University Park, PA, Pennsylvania State University Press.

Marinetti, F. T. (1909), 'Foundation and manifesto of futurism', trans. R. W. Flint. Reprinted in Harrison and Wood 1992, pp. 145–9.

Mitchell, W. J. T. (1986), *Iconology: Image, Text, Ideology*, Chicago, University of Chicago Press.

Moholy-Nagy, L. (1922), 'Constructivism and the proletariat'. The English translation quoted is from Benton, Benton and Sharp, 1975, pp. 95–6.

Monk, S. H. (1935), *The Sublime*, Ann Arbor, University of Michigan Press.

Murdoch, I. (1977), *The Fire and the Sun: Why Plato Banished the Artists*, Oxford, Oxford University Press.

Murray, G. (1920), Preface to *Aristotle on the Art of Poetry*, trans. I. Bywater, Oxford, Clarendon, 1920.

Murray, P. and Murray, L. (1991), *The Penguin Dictionary of Art and Artists*, 6th rev. ed., London, Penguin.

Muthesius, H. (1904–5), *Das Englische Haus*, Berlin, Wasmuth. The English translation quoted is from Benton, Benton and Sharp 1975, pp. 34–5.

Osborne, H. (ed.) (1970), *The Oxford Companion to Art*, Oxford, Clarendon.

Panofsky, E. (1951), *Gothic Architecture and Scholasticism*, New York, Meridian.

Panofsky, E. (1979), *Abbot Suger*, 2nd ed., Princeton, Princeton University Press.

Pater, W. (1877), 'The school of Giorgione'. In W. Pater, *The Renaissance: Studies in Art and Poetry*, ed. A. Phillips, Oxford, Oxford University Press, 1986, pp. 83–98.

Plotinus, *Enneads*. Quotations are from the MacKenna translation, London, Penguin, 1991.

Pollitt, J. J. (1974), *The Ancient View of Greek Art: Criticism, History and Terminology*, New Haven, Yale University Press.

Pollitt, J. J. (1990), *The Art of Ancient Greece: Sources and Documents*, Cambridge, Cambridge University Press.

Postman, N. (1986), *Amusing Ourselves to Death*, London, Heinemann.

Priestley, J. (1762), *A Course of Lectures on the Theory of Language and Universal Grammar*, Warrington, Eyres.

Punin, N. (1920), 'The monument to the Third International', trans. C. Lodder. Reprinted in Harrison and Wood, 1992, pp. 311–15.

Read, H. (1949), *The Meaning of Art*. Harmondsworth, Penguin.

Richard, A. (1971), 'Introduction' to *La musique lettriste*. Special issue of *La revue musicale*, nos. 282–3: 7–26.

Richter, I. A. (ed. & trans.) (1949), *Leonardo da Vinci, Paragone*, London, Oxford University Press.

Roberts, W. R. (ed. & trans.) (1907), *Longinus on the Sublime*, 2nd ed., Cambridge, Cambridge University Press.

Robinson, R. (1954), *Definition*, Oxford, Clarendon.

Rogers, P. (ed.) (1992), *Sir Joshua Reynolds, Discourses*, London, Penguin.

Ruskin, J. (1859), *The Two Paths*. Reprinted in E. T. Cook and A. Wedderburn (eds), *The Works of John Ruskin*, London, Allen, 1903–12, vol. XVI.

Ruskin, J. (1869), *The Queen of the Air*. Reprinted in E. T. Cook and A. Wedderburn (eds), *The Works of John Ruskin*, London, Allen, 1903–12, vol. XIX.

Saul, J. R. (1992), *Voltaire's Bastards: The Dictatorship of Reason in the West*, London, Sinclair-Stevenson.

Saussure, F. de (1916), *Cours de linguistique générale*, ed. Ch. Bally and A. Sechehaye, Paris, Payot.

Sayers, A. (1994), *Aboriginal Artists of the Nineteenth Century*, Melbourne, Oxford University Press.

Schiller, F. (1795), *On the Aesthetic Education of Man*, trans. R. Snell, London, Routledge & Kegan Paul, 1954.

Scholes, P. (1983), 'Colour and music'. In D. Arnold (ed.), *The New Oxford Companion to Music*, Oxford, Oxford University Press, vol. 1, pp. 424–32.

Schopenhauer, A. (1844), *The World as Will and Idea*, 2nd ed., trans. R. B. Haldane and J. Kemp, London, Routledge & Kegan Paul, 1883.

Scobie, S. (1997), *Earthquakes and Explosions: Language and Painting from Cubism to Concrete Poetry*, Toronto, University of Toronto Press.

Serota, N. (2000), 'Who's Afraid of Modern Art?', Richard Dimbleby Memorial Lecture, London, BBC.

Smith, R. (1994), 'Conceptual art'. In N. Stangos (ed.), *Concepts of Modern Art*, 3rd ed., London, Thames & Hudson, pp. 256–70.

Steadman, P. (1965), 'Colour music and the art of lumia'. In *Image: Kinetic Art: Concrete Poetry*, London, Kingsland Prospect Press, pp. 17–22.

Stout, D. (1960), 'Aesthetics in "primitive societies"'. Reprinted in C. F. Jopling (ed.), *Art and Aesthetics in Primitive Societies*, New York, Dutton, 1971, pp. 30–4.

Struik, D. J. (1948), *A Concise History of Mathematics*, New York, Dover.

Sutton, P. and Anderson, C. (1988), 'Introduction' to *Dreamings: The Art of Aboriginal Australia*, ed. P. Sutton, Ringwood, Viking, pp. 1–12.

Taylor, T. J. (2001), 'Folk psychology and the language myth: what would the integrationist say?'. In R. Harris (ed.), *The Language Myth in Western Culture*, London, Curzon, pp. 100–17.

Tilghman, B. R. (1984), *But Is It Art?*, Oxford, Blackwell.

Tolstoy, L. N. (1898), *What Is Art?*, trans. A. Maude, ed. W. G. Jones, London, Bristol Classical Press, 1994.

Toolan, M. (1996), *Total Speech: An Integrational Linguistic Approach to Language*, Durham, N.C., Duke University Press.

Toolan, M. (2001), 'The language myth and the law'. In R. Harris (ed.), *The Language Myth in Western Culture*, London, Curzon, pp. 159–82.

Tylor, E. B. (1881), *Anthropology: An Introduction to the Study of Man and Civilization*. Reprinted with an introduction by A. C. Haddon, 2 vols, London, Watts, 1930.

Tzara, T. (1918), *Dada Manifesto*, trans. B. Wright. In B. Wright, *Seven Dada Manifestos and Lampisteries*, London, Calder, 1977.

Tzara, T. (1921), *Dada Manifesto on Feeble Love and Bitter Love*, trans. B. Wright. In B. Wright, *Seven Dada Manifestos and Lampisteries*, London, Calder, 1977.

van de Velde, H. (1901), 'The role of the engineer in modern architecture', *Die Renaissance im modernen Kunstgewerbe*, Berlin, Cassirer. The English translation quoted is from Benton, Benton and Sharp, 1975, pp. 32–3.

van Doesburg, T. (1922), 'The will to style', *De Stijl* 5:ii.23–32, 5.iii.33–41. The English translation quoted is from Benton, Benton and Sharp, 1975, pp. 92–4.

Wallinger, M. and Warnock, M. (eds) (2000), *Art for All?*, London, Peer.

Welling, W. (1978), *Photography in America: The Formative Years 1839–1900*, New York, Crowell.

Wellington, H. (ed.) and Norton, L. (trans.) (1951), *The Journal of Eugene Delacroix*, London, Phaidon.

White, J. (1956), *Perspective in Ancient Drawing and Painting*, London, Society for the Promotion of Hellenic Studies.

Willett, F. (1993), *African Art*, rev. ed., London, Thames & Hudson.

Wilson, E. O. (1998), *Consilience: The Unity of Knowledge*. London, Little, Brown.

Wilson, T. (trans.) (1972), *Jean Duvignaud, the Sociology of Art*, London, Paladin.

Wimsatt, W. K., Jr. (1954), *The Verbal Icon: Studies in the Meaning of Poetry*, Lexington, University of Kentucky Press.

Wind, E. (1985), *Art and Anarchy*, 3rd ed., London, Duckworth.

Winterson, J. (2001), 'The eye of the beholder', *Times 2*, 30 May 2001, p. 10.

Wittgenstein, L. (1953), *Philosophical Investigations*, trans. G. E. M. Anscombe, Oxford, Blackwell.

Wolfe, T. (1976), *The Painted Word*, New York, Bantam.

Wollheim, R. (1996), 'Art', *The Dictionary of Art* (ed. J. Turner), London, Macmillan, vol. 2, pp. 505–6.

Worringer, W. (1908), *Abstraktion und Einfühlung*, trans. M. Bullock. Extract reprinted in Harrison and Wood, 1992, pp. 68–72.

Zola, E. (1866),'Les réalistes du salon'. In J.-P. Leduc-Adine (ed.), *Émile Zola, Écrits sur l'art*, Paris, Gallimard, 1991, pp. 120–5.

Index